HOW TO KILL A WITCH

A GUIDE FOR THE PATRIARCHY

CLAIRE MITCHELL KC
ZOE VENDITOZZI

monoray

First published in Great Britain in 2025 by Monoray, an imprint of
Octopus Publishing Group Ltd
Carmelite House
50 Victoria Embankment
London EC4Y 0DZ
www.octopusbooks.co.uk

An Hachette UK Company
www.hachette.co.uk

The authorized representative in the EEA is Hachette Ireland, 8 Castlecourt Centre, Dublin 15, D15 XTP3, Ireland (email: info@hbgi.ie)

First published in paperback in 2026

ISBN: 978-1-80096-190-6
eISBN: 978-1-80096-191-3

A CIP catalogue record for this book is available from the British Library.

Typeset in 12/16pt Garamond Premier Pro by Six Red Marbles UK, Thetford, Norfolk

Printed and bound in Great Britain

7 9 10 8

This FSC® label means that materials used for the product have been responsibly sourced.

Praise for *How to Kill a Witch*

The Sunday Times Bestseller
WINNER of the 2025 Goodreads Choice Awards
Blackwell's Scottish Book of the Year

'Fascinating and illuminating, this book tempers the justifiable rage with sharp and funny pinpricks to the pompous.'
–Val McDermid, author of *Past Lying*

'As well as a highly entertaining read, *How to Kill a Witch* is a tour de force of research, understanding and compassion. What the world needs is more quarrelsome dames – and Claire Mitchell and Zoe Venditozzi are two of the best.'
–Professor Sue Black, author of *All That Remains*

'A dignified, defiant memorial to thousands of ordinary women branded as witches and, all too often, put to death. Told with imagination and empathy, the stories in this book expose the tragedy of their lives, as well as the subordination, paranoia and cruelty responsible. Serious and angry, but so completely accessible, *How to Kill a Witch* is a work of real historical investigation and a fierce warning for our times.'
–Malcolm Gaskill, author of *The Ruin of All Witches*

'As a woman who has been called a witch from as early as age ten, you could say I've been waiting my whole life for this book. How did they get away with the wholesale slaughter of women simply for being opinionated, intuitive, creative or intelligent? At a time when women's rights are once again being threatened across the globe, this book could not be a more timely read if it tried.'
–Shirley Manson, Garbage

'The Witches of Scotland . . . profile persecuted women from the burning times. Their tales are woven by archivists, historians and writers – and by Venditozzi and Mitchell themselves, two of Scotland's most vivid storytellers.'
–The Times

'In this fascinating, angering and deeply sad book Claire Mitchell KC and Zoe Venditozzi set out to tell the story of the thousands of poor and uneducated women who were victims of a satanic panic in Scotland during the 16th and 17th centuries. Every village in Scotland has a memorial to the men who were killed in two world wars. Why not something similar to the thousands of women who lost their lives due to this gross miscarriage of justice?'
–The Mail on Sunday

'A unique, angry, surprisingly funny tour of what Scottish witch trial history means today.'
–Marion Gibson, author of *Witchcraft: A History in 13 Trials*

'Utterly absorbing and drags you in immediately.'
–Jenny Colgan, author of *The Bookshop on the Corner*

'The most important book I'll read this year. A manifesto, a call to arms, a historical heist and a paragon of storytelling, *How to Kill a Witch* prods some of the most topical issues of the moment and provides a wealth of insights, stitching the past and present together like some gorgeous tartan. Zoe and Claire are a dynamic duo of quarrelsome dames, and their take on witches is the very best. Brilliant, witty, searing, and necessary, this is a book to share and treasure.'
–Cj Cooke, author of *The Lighthouse Witches*

'Terrifying, fascinating and important'
–Sara Sheridan, author of *Where are the Women* and *The Fair Botanists*

'This book pulls off the difficult feat of being simultaneously entertaining, unsettling and enraging. A brilliant account of what happened during Scotland's witch "panics", and why it still matters today.'
–Mairi Kidd, author of *Scottish Fairy Tales, Myths and Legends*

'The authors' campaigning and creative approach to exploring the stories of women caught in the maelstrom of witchcraft accusations and patriarchal suspicion makes for an engaging read about a tragic subject.'
–Owen Davies, author of *Grimoires*

'Fascinating, fact-filled, funny, feminist and furious'
–The Scotsman

'The writers navigate the story of this horrific time in a way that is eloquent and full of wit but never exploitative or irreverent. Using the stories of real people accused of witchcraft, Mitchell and Venditozzi give these women a voice and explore the real reasons for these terrible injustices.'
– The Scots Magazine

'Quite possibly the most horrific portrayal of one of our darkest periods in history. This book, whilst an addictive read, also warns us of the dangers of powerful men (mostly) who used scapegoating and mass hysteria to target and murder women (mostly). The writers hand us a nightmarish blueprint of what could easily happen today, if we chose to ignore our past.'
–Aamer Anwar, human rights lawyer

ABOUT THE AUTHORS

Leading human rights lawyer Claire Mitchell, KC, and writer, Zoe Venditozzi formed the Witches of Scotland campaign with the aim of shining a light on the historic injustice of the Witch Trials. As a result, on International Women's Day, 2022, the First Minister of Scotland, at issued a formal state apology – the first time in 300 years there had been any formal recognition of those who were most wrongly accused.

Through their tireless campaigning, regular public appearances, and highly entertaining podcast, also called *The Witches of Scotland*, this pair of 'quarrelsome dames' are currently working to build a lasting memorial to the murdered women, and campaign to draw attention to the continued persecution of women as witches around the world today.

In 2022, Claire and Zoe were made Doctors of Laws by the University of Dundee in 2022 in recognition of their work. Claire lives between Edinburgh and London and Zoe lives in Fife.

This book is dedicated to the people, mostly women, who were accused, tortured and executed as witches, and those who still face those unfounded accusations today.

CONTENTS

AUTHORS' NOTE

This book is a combination of research, conversation, obsession and a little speculation. When it comes to the persecution of women as witches, historical detail is on occasion lacking. In our book, Zoe has written several pieces that are fictional extemporizations, based on what we know, in order to highlight the human stories and underscore the impact of historical events on individuals. These sections are marked in *italics*.

We've used a smattering of Scots, one of the three official languages of Scotland, throughout the book, where its vocabulary feels most apt. For non-Scottish readers, there's a Glossary of Scots Words included on page 265.

‘IN MEMORIAM’

They tried tae tak yer spirit, hen,
Destroy that which they couldnae control.
So ye spak and the world didnae listen, hen,
Smoort the smeddum that burned in yer soul.
Noo yer’re deid but never gone, hen,
There’s thaim that still cairry yer name.
There’s thaim that mind criminals, bidin in courts
Heids hingin heavy wae shame.

Auld Nick didnae ken ye fae Eve, hen,
Ye hae but yer ain een tae see.
The wrang wasnae yours,
The guilt wis misplaced,
Yer innocence plain as can be.

But they taen muckle mair than a life, hen,
A caunle snuffed oot in its prime.
A state sanctioned murder ae innocent fowks,
Punishment lackin a crime.
Yer soul’s noo at peace wae the earth, hen,
Sleep and be wan wae the sky.
We’ll aye scrieve yer name in books they cannae burn,
Write a legacy never tae die.

But we willnae just beg ae yer pardon, hen,
Those days have lang ceased tae exist.
We noo demand justice fur aw those lit you –
Lang gone, but eternally missed.

Len Pennie

Scots-language poem commissioned by the Witches of Scotland

INTRODUCTION

Allow us to introduce ourselves.

We are Claire Mitchell, a lawyer with an interest in public inquiries, human rights and crime (and a 'KC', that is King's Counsel, a senior advocate), and Zoe Venditozzi, a novelist and a creative writing/additional support needs teacher. Everybody knows us as the Witches of Scotland, although that is actually the name of the campaign that we launched. Having said that, we are very happy to be known as 'quarrelsome dames', and yes, we do live in Scotland.

This is how it all started . . .

In 2019, in the course of her work as a KC, Claire was researching the crime of violating a sepulchre, commonly known as 'body snatching' – a crime made famous by the 19th-century craze for robbing graves in order to sell the corpses to anatomists. Claire was looking into the 2004 case of two teenagers who broke into an ornate stone mausoleum in Greyfriars Kirkyard (churchyard) in Edinburgh. The boys forced open a coffin, stole a skull and played football with it until they were caught in the act by a tour guide. It was thought that the head belonged to none other than one of Edinburgh's most famous historical figures – Sir George 'Bloody' Mackenzie, who had earned his nickname for imprisoning over a thousand Protestant Covenanters in a field next to the graveyard where he was ultimately buried.† As former Lord Advocate, he was the head of the

† These Covenanters were a group of rebellious Presbyterians who were locked in an ideological (and often literal) battle with the church and state in the 17th century. On 22 June 1679, a large uprising was defeated by state forces at the Battle of Bothwell Brig and up to 1,200 prisoners were taken to Edinburgh and held in the field. They were denied basic amenities; many were executed and hundreds more starved to death at the hands of their

prosecution system in Scotland for more or less two decades until his death in 1691.

Ultimately the teen grave robbers were not jailed, but Claire's research on Mackenzie led her down an interesting rabbit hole. She discovered that during his career he was involved in numerous witch trials, including that of a woman called Maevia whom he actually defended in 1661. He was reported to have said, 'I am not of their opinion, who deny that there are Witches, though I think them not numerous.'

And this was where Claire got sidetracked and pulled into the world of witch trials. It was clear that Mackenzie was making an interesting distinction. He didn't entirely take the sceptic's position that witches did not exist, but he did seem to be arguing that accusations were too numerous for them all to be correct. This theory is borne out by the fact that during his time as Lord Advocate he endeavoured to cut down on the number of cases brought to trial. A sensible middle ground position at a time of very heightened sensibilities – as we shall see.

Even at this early stage in Claire's reading, though, the human stories exerted a pull across the centuries. As she researched Mackenzie's cases, Claire came across one poor woman who, during the course of her interrogation, asked her persecutors if it was possible to be a witch 'and not know it'. The desperate situation this woman surely found herself in affected Claire deeply.

At around the same time, Claire read Sara Sheridan's book *Where Are the Women?* In this book, Sheridan reimagines Scotland as a place where all the streets are named after women and there are museums and grand buildings dedicated to the great women of Scotland. This complete reversal of how Scotland was actually constructed brought into sharp focus how much of our civic lives are centred

---

captors. Mackenzie's cruel treatment of them resulted in the legend of his fearsome ghost, a poltergeist, who it is said still haunts the graveyard today. People would look through the doors of the mausoleum and chant the old rhyme: 'Bluidy Mackenzie, come oot if ye daur, lift the sneck and draw the bar.'

around men's achievements, and how neglected Scotland's women are in terms of being a visible part of the geography of our nation.

So it was with this in mind that one day, when she was walking her dogs, Redford and Crombie, in Edinburgh's Princes Street Gardens, Claire found herself beside a life-sized statue of Wojtek, a Polish bear who became an unofficial mascot for the Allies during the Second World War. Standing there she realized that there was not one statue of a named woman in Scotland's capital city's main green space. There were plenty of statues of men – artists, authors, soldiers – and even, in this case, a bear. But not a single woman.

And looking above Wojtek's head she saw the esplanade of Edinburgh Castle, scene of hundreds of executions of innocent women – for it was mostly women – convicted of witchcraft. These few hundred were only a small number of the many thousands of those accused of witchcraft in Scotland between the early 16th and mid-18th centuries – somewhere between 3,000–5,000 people in total. She thought to herself, not only are we not properly recording the brilliant achievements of women in our society in the history books or celebrating their success in public spaces, but we also are not recording when terrible acts have been perpetrated against them. In fact, on the esplanade at the spot of the executions there was a plaque that merely reinforced their – entirely incorrect – status as witches.

There and then, as she stood beside Wojtek, Claire resolved to do something about this. What better way for a human rights lawyer to highlight the inequality of memorializing Scottish women's achievements and redress a gross miscarriage of justice than by drawing attention to the Scottish witch trials and seeking an apology for the accused and a pardon for those convicted, and by creating a lasting memorial?

At that moment, the Witches of Scotland campaign was born.

A short while before Claire's revelation in Princes Street Gardens, the two of us had met at a mutual friend's wedding, where we bonded over our love of true crime podcasts. Discovering that we both had a ridiculously detailed knowledge of real-life murders, we came up with a theory about why women in particular love true crime. In our view, it was down to a combination of the pragmatism of learning how not to get abducted and murdered (always useful), coupled with an element of bearing witness to all the women who were not so lucky. All the while thinking, there but for the grace of God . . .

Toasting Mel and Drew, the happy couple that day, Zoe mentioned she would like to start a podcast, but couldn't think of an angle. A few weeks later, Claire got in touch with a simple idea, though one that turned out to be surprisingly effective. We would create a podcast that would promote the nascent Witches of Scotland campaign.

From the first podcast, recorded on an iPhone propped up on Zoe's washing machine in her basement, the Witches of Scotland campaign and podcast became a worldwide phenomenon.

And then something momentous happened.

On International Women's Day in 2022, the First Minister of Scotland, at the request of the Witches of Scotland campaign, issued a formal state apology to all those accused of witchcraft in Scotland – the first time in 300 years there had been any official recognition of those who were wrongly accused.

It has been an extraordinary journey. The campaign has sparked a worldwide cultural conversation about women's history and women's place in the modern world. Today, the campaign works towards its remaining aims of creating a national memorial and a legislative pardon, and is actively working with a number of Witches of Scotland-inspired groups throughout the country to bring these aims to fruition.

How to Kill a Witch is a book that details, step by step, the stages undertaken to identify, try and ultimately kill a woman as a witch. It is a book that we have researched by studying original documents and gathering advice and encouragement from some of the best historians and experts in the field. In the course of writing the book we have followed in the footsteps of those who lived hundreds of years ago, visiting graves, attending memorials and meeting with experts in history, art, music, writing. Each of these experts has generously given of their own time to help educate us, and our supporters, about the history of witch trials in Scotland and around the world. To each and every one of them we are very grateful. What we learned shocked us, even steeped as we are in the campaign. The truth about the Scottish witch trials is bloody and horrific: we hope that the resulting book is one that underlines the incredible lengths that people – mostly men – went to in order to silence women.

How to Kill a Witch also goes beyond what we learned about historical witchcraft trials here and abroad, and draws out what we see as the modern-day relevance – that when the going gets tough in any society, it is the vulnerable that are accused of causing the damage, as an easy target to avoid dealing with the greater problems of inequality.

You will soon appreciate that the book is not an academic tome – it is the experience of two women learning about their history and casting a fresh light on their present. In fact, there is some fictional writing in the book in the italicized sections, which we hope helps put the reader in the headspace of the persecuted – or indeed the persecu*tor*. Something a real historian would never do! As any listener of the podcast will know, we approach our task with reverence to those who were accused of witchcraft, and irreverence to everything else.

In fact, we even initially started to write the book in a way that was a sort of tongue-in-cheek manual for potential patriarchal persecutors out there, so that they would know just how to kill a witch if they came across one. While the 'manual' idea was dropped as we became more and more involved (and outraged) with what we found, we still found that starting point incredibly useful. Breaking the persecution of women as witches down into its individual stages made us look at the whole process forensically (in the case of the chapter about burning witches, we mean that absolutely literally). From identifying a witch, interrogating her and putting her to trial, to killing her, burying her and losing her in history – you will be surprised how much there is to find out about the subject.

We also examine how other countries such as the USA dealt with their witch problem – using the case study of the most famous witch panic of all, the Salem witch trials – and finally question whether women should still be wary today. We'll tell you about the continued use of violence against women; the rise of women identifying as witches, particularly online; and the increasing number of modern-day witchcraft accusations worldwide.

A word on historical detail (or the lack of it). Shortly after the infamously bloody witch trials of the early 1690s in Salem, USA, it was accepted that there had been a most grievous miscarriage of justice. The dreadful history was commemorated in legal writings and in family campaigns to exonerate the accused, which served to keep the story of the terrible wrongs perpetrated against their kin alive. As a result, the names of those involved and their stories were carefully recorded and subsequently studied by academics, historians and lawyers.

The circumstances could not have been more different in Scotland. Poor record-keeping of witchcraft accusations and trials leaves us bereft of much of the detail we would want to know. Sometimes we only know that trials took place because citizen historians have checked parish financial records, which merely recorded the cost of incarceration of the suspects, or of hiring a 'witch pricker' (of which, more later) or executioner.

The details of the accused and convicted in Scotland were not given the attention of academics and historians at the time. There was no contemporaneous recognition of the fact that thousands of people had been wrongly accused and convicted of witchcraft. Indeed, until International Women's Day 2022, at the behest of the Witches of Scotland campaign, there was no public recognition or apology for the wrongs done at all. With the notable exception of the lawyer and historian Robert Pitcairn who wrote about the trials a century after they finished,[†] the legal system itself all but ignored this brutal history. While many stories were passed down by word of mouth by those who couldn't read or write – no doubt containing a mix of gossip and truths – there were very few

† We will look at Pitcairn's work in Chapter 9.

contemporaneous *written* works, save for the two we discuss in this book, a pamphlet titled *Newes from Scotland* and a textbook on witch-hunting written by none other than King James VI of Scotland himself,[†] called *Daemonologie* (see Chapters 3 and 4).

'Why record the history of these terrible witches?', the thinking went. Better to convict these women, strangle them and scatter their very ashes to destroy any record of their being. The view of the state was simple: the witches were dead and justice had been done. There was no appetite for those victorious in their dealings with the Devil to immortalize the details of his handmaidens. Why record what you want to forget?

While modern academics and historians find what scarce detail they can, lack of records means that witchcraft trial records are aggravatingly incomplete. The best records to date can be found in the Survey of Scottish Witchcraft, an online database of all the known historical information about the trials. We highly recommend this resource, although the researchers note in their introduction that a good deal of evidence is still missing. That said, they have used their great skill to piece together what is available. In the meantime, we have given you what we can find; incomplete and sometimes vague as it is at times, this is the reality of working on the history of the Scottish witch trials.

However, by pulling together what scant information there is, by speaking to as many experts as possible, and by feasting on every detail that we *can* get our hands on, we hope we have done justice to these women's stories. *How to Kill a Witch* is certainly not a conventional or straightforward narrative and, like its authors, it rushes hither and thither as we plunge deeper and deeper down the rabbit hole of witch persecution. You will find in these pages stories, discoveries, world-renowned expertise, shameful facts and even parts of *Daemonologie*. You will find a sentencing statement for a witch trial, full details of what it takes to dispose of a human body using fire, and pen portraits of just a few of those many thousands of people accused of witchcraft.

† As of 1603, he became James I of England and Ireland on the death of his cousin Queen Elizabeth I. Throughout the book we'll just refer to him as James VI.

It is our sincere hope that this eclectic, patchwork book that started out as a guide for the patriarchy[†] will in fact provide every woman and marginalized group with the tools to understand how such accusations arise, and how to guard against it happening again.

Will there come a time when yet again women are accused of witchcraft? As with our theory about the popularity of true crime, we invite women to use the book as a pragmatic learning tool. To learn about and bear witness to all the women who were, and are, not so lucky, while at the same time challenging the damaging patriarchal norms of the society in which we still live.

In sharing what we've learned, we hope to create a worldwide regiment of quarrelsome dames who want an equal place in the world – in life, in public spaces, online.

We are nothing if not ambitious.

Claire Mitchell KC and Zoe Venditozzi

† We want to be emphatically clear. A patriarchal society is one where men as a group dominate the whole group. When we criticize the patriarchy, that does not 'equate' to criticism of men. Women can be in favour of the patriarchy; men can be against it. Yes, for the most part, patriarchal norms are endorsed by those who have most to gain, and many a time that is a man, but that doesn't make it always so. To end the patriarchy, we need both men and women in society to address it.

PART ONE:
THE LAW OF THE LAND

ELSPETH REOCH

A CUNNING WOMAN ACCUSED OF WITCHCRAFT IN ORKNEY

I met the two strangers on the shoreline when I was just a tender girl of 12 years. Both were tall, strong, good-looking men. One in black, one in green tartan. They were speaking away to themselves but when they saw me, they stopped and stared. I stood, just a wee lass, watchful and entranced by the pair. The man in green beckoned me over. I don't remember exactly what they said firstly, but the one in green, I cannot tell you his name, asked me if I would like to scry the future, and if I did, he would tell me how to do it. The face of the one in black was like thunder, but the man in green just nodded his head at him and told me to boil an egg, collect the water that covered its surface, and wash my face with it.

They were so serious that I knew they were not mocking me.

Would that I had ignored them, but I did as he instructed. And my life changed for the worse, though it took me time to realize that. It was like a veil had been dropped from the world and I could now see who was with child, who was sickening, even those who would pass in the coming days. They taught me a cantrip with flowers, too, and I moved around the land, helping people and managing to scratch a living.

I saw them now and then, the man in black more than the other. I never knew when they would arrive, but it was usually at night, always when I was alone. Within a year I was with child, a boy – I will not give his name – and that was when I first began to have the spells of quiet. When the quiet comes down, I can't make myself speak no matter how much I try. It's as if a big, cold hand has been clapped over my mouth and not a sound I can make.

This angers my brother no end, but no matter how firm he is with me, no discipline can heal me. I was able to keep visiting folk and, through actions, I could still help them, and my voice would come and go.

Over the years, the men would appear from time to time. Once, I saw neither for months and I thought my strange times might end but back they came. But then I was with child again and became quiet for a long time, only able to find my voice when my younger boy was beginning to crawl.

This has been a hard and lonely life, just me and my brother and the wee laddies for the last few years, but people have mostly shown me kindness and I enjoy helping those that ail.

Never have I done any of the evils you accuse me of. Never have I hurt anyone.

Sometimes I try to help but people don't get better. Sometimes their time on earth must come to an end. Of course, it sorrows us to lose those we love, but we must believe that beauty awaits us on the other side of this life. This pain I am suffering now can be borne for the love I have been so lucky to have had bestowed upon me by my wee bairns gives me strength. I am pained that I will not see them grown into fine young men.

I had thought that the men would come and visit me in my hour of need, but there has been no sign of them. I am alone and I fear that nobody will come to my aid.

1

HOW TO BELIEVE IN MAGIC

When Elspeth Reoch was accused of being a witch in 1616, she confessed that she had been given the power of second sight by two men who had come from the fairy world, whom she had first met at the age of 12.

Born in Caithness in the Scottish Highlands, Elspeth had been staying with an aunt on an island in Lochaber. The fairy men – one dressed in black, the other in green – had approached her by the loch and told her she was pretty. The one in green told her he could show her how to know anything she wanted. He instructed her to boil an egg every Sunday for three weeks, to collect the condensation in her hands and rub it into her eyes. She did so and developed the power of second sight, after which she earned a small income wandering around her local area, advising folk, discerning pregnancies and performing healing rituals with herbs.

However, Elspeth's relationship with the man in black, who had come to act as her spirit guide, soon started to sour. Not only were they having sex, but he was also controlling and abusive towards her. He told her that in return for the gifts he'd given her, he would take away her power of speech, whereupon she became largely non-verbal. Elspeth was only 14 when, unmarried, she had her first child, and later she had another by a different man. Elspeth's brother, angry that she refused or was unable to speak, beat her with a bridle, tied a bowstring around her head to torture her, then dragged her to church and prayed for her. Unsurprisingly, these tactics failed to cure her.[†]

---

† Call us suspicious, but the stories she told and her subsequent refusal to speak sound very much like the processing of trauma.

Accused of witchcraft in March 1616, Elspeth was brought to trial in Kirkwall in Orkney, where she confessed that she had met with the Devil several times, in his guise as a fairy. She was also accused of deception by feigning muteness. Found guilty, she was sentenced to death by strangulation and her body burned that afternoon.

Fairies? Witches? The Devil? This tale may seem nonsensical to modern ears. But in order to understand the period between the 16th and 18th centuries in Scotland we must embrace a fundamental truth of that epoch: magic was real.

This belief was entirely mainstream. More than mainstream; it was entirely accepted as fact. The sale of magical services was commonplace, and purveyors could be sued if the magic didn't work. Both good and bad magic were believed to exist, and it was an incontrovertible fact that the Devil was real. He could take human form, have 'carnal connections' with his choice of women, and throw wild parties complete with bountiful buffets, drink and debauchery. He could infiltrate your mind with intrusive thoughts, take over your body to do his evil business and change into whatever animal he pleased. He could use his magic to trick and deceive, to prey on the godly and ungodly alike. Most importantly for us, he could promise foolish women their heart's desire only to lure them to his dominion as witches.

Sometimes such beliefs are written off as the stupidity or ignorance of our forebears. It was nothing of the sort. In an uncertain world, they were a way of making sense of unpredictable events and offering an illusion of control. Folks have been turning to magic and rituals to influence their fate since the dawn of time, and they still do. Clever, modern sophisticates may scoff at these ideas,[†] but

† Claire doesn't. She has a spooky heritage. Her Irish granny Rose told her all about the fairies and Otherworld. She took her to the Poisoned Glen at Dunlewey, Donegal and showed her fairy rings, magic circles of pebbles. She was also known for 'reading the cups', a type of fortune telling. Claire remembers her granny solemnly turning the cup upside down on the saucer, turning it anti-clockwise three times and then turning it rightways up to do her

Woodcut showing witches offering gifts to the Devil, from *The History of Witches and Wizards: Giving a true account of all their tryals in England, Scotland, Swedeland, France, and New England; with their confession and condemnation*, 1720

they still linger on in our culture, superstitious remnants of the prevailing belief system of the early modern period in Scotland (1450–1750).

Do you avoid walking under ladders? How would you feel if you broke a mirror? What about putting new shoes on a table? People today consult spiritualists to hear from loved ones long dead, consult the tarot to find their future, pray to specific saints to solve a particular problem, read the runes, consult the tea leaves, phone a psychic for love advice, pray, manifest, join cults. This list is far from exhaustive. Ever check your phone's weather app to plan the weekend? In the 20th century, science-fiction author Arthur C Clarke wrote that 'any sufficiently advanced technology is indistinguishable from magic'. In many ways, the only difference between us and our forebears is that now, our technology has (almost) caught up. Our human desire to know what's around the corner – that has not changed.

Until the Enlightenment – which took place throughout Europe in the late 17th and 18th centuries – there was a widespread belief that the supernatural world was interwoven with the natural, material world and that the powers of the supernatural could both help and hinder the lives of humans. It was common for people to combine Christian beliefs and behaviours with magical practices to manage everyday life and its travails. From the mid-18th century onwards, religious reformers and newly 'enlightened' thinkers sought to dissuade ordinary folk of their reliance on magic. They were successful to some extent. But the beliefs did not truly go away, and remained particularly common in countries that had a strong tradition of acceptance of the 'Otherworld'.†

Celtic mythology tells us that the Otherworld was a place where spirits, demons, fairies, ghosts and sprites lived. It was a real place but not one known to be frequented by ordinary mortals. Some folk believed fairies had their own world, too: Fairyland, a place between heaven and hell, possibly a reflection of

---

reading. Claire remembers peering in at the tea leaves, expecting them to dance before her eyes, revealing the future. They never did.

† Ireland, we are looking at you. Despite the pattern of witch trials sweeping across Europe in this period, Ireland remained mostly unaffected, ironically perhaps due to its very strength of belief in magic. People were simply not spooked by the idea of devils and demons.

the fact that fairies could do good deeds as well as bad. These fairies were not of the Tinkerbell genre. They came in the same sizes and shapes as ordinary humans, sometimes having relationships with them, sexual and otherwise. Some people believed fairies were your dead ancestors who for some reason didn't make it to either heaven or hell. For many, though, fairies were tangible, real creatures, despite sometimes being insubstantial and see-through in their bodily form. They were once considered independent beings but, as the Reformation spread throughout 16th-century Europe, the prevailing Scottish Protestant understanding was that as fairies could not be angels, then surely, they must be of the Devil.

So it was that the Christian theology of God, fallen angels and the Day of Judgement was woven through with the stories of the Otherworld; for many people the Christian belief system merely slotted on top the existing supernatural beliefs. In this and in all other aspects of the interaction between the magic world and the mundane world, there were no clear lines of distinction. Kings, queens, the state, the church, academics, philosophers, civil society, intellectuals, writers, artists, the woman in the street – they all believed in magic, and its power to do good and bad. We'll say it again: magic was everywhere.

So who was it that conjured up the magic?

Welcome to the (Other)world of service magicians: charmers, cunning folk and witches. 'Service magician' is a catch-all term for a person who traded in practical magic and the name reveals the ordinary way in which people would pay for a piece of magic to be conducted on their behalf. Charmers, chairmers, or even sometimes charmerers, as the name suggests, were those who sold charms; they were literally folk who 'enchanted'. Their work was done with spells, the spoken word and magical recipes. 'Cunning folk', on the other hand, were people who used ritual or ceremonial magic, for example summoning spirits or performing magical ceremonies. What these two types of magicians have in common is that their magical powers did not emanate from the Devil. In contrast, the power of the third type of practitioner – the witch – was notably different. A witch's magic came to be defined[†] as being wholly dependent on his or her master, the Devil.

This critical distinction allowed charmers and cunning folk to continue to peddle their wares without harassment. While doubtless the church would have preferred there to be no service magicians at all, they were nevertheless tolerated as they served a useful role in society, providing magical solutions to practical problems, in love, in luck and in life. A poor crop could mean destitution and starvation for you and your family; a cow failing to produce milk could lead to homelessness; illness could mean imminent death. In such desperate times is it any wonder people tried every solution available?

The work of cunning folk or charmers was rarely full time. The roles were a way for people to make a bit of extra money on top of their main day job. So you might consult a farmer who sold husbandry potions, or someone more educated such as a priest[‡] or physician who had attended university.

Hold on now! How could a priest, a man of the cloth, have a spooky side hustle as a cunning person? Well, who better to go to for help than an educated man who has God on his side? It's counterintuitive to us today that priests used magic but, if you think about it, they were already dealing with the supernatural every day.

What if all your linen is lost? A priest might be able to summon an angel or a demon or possibly some divination with a Bible – as long, of course, as the highheidyins did not get to hear about it. That might seem a little bit over the top – troubling an angel to find your lost laundry. But in 16th-century Scotland, this was absolutely acceptable. The service magician was someone you could go to for everyday help, however mundane your problem.

But if you can believe in good magic, then it follows you must believe in bad magic. If there is an omnipotent God, able to intervene in the lives of folk at

---

† It didn't start that way, but we'll tell you more later.

‡ We're talking about pre-Reformation Catholic priests here. After the Scottish Reformation of 1560, the Catholic Church was outlawed in Scotland. As we shall see in the next chapter, Protestant ministers tended to take a dimmer view of cunning folk and charmers altogether, though they were just about tolerated as long as the Devil was not involved.

will, there must also be his fallen angel Lucifer Morningstar, the Devil – and his handmaid witches who are ready to cause you harm at a moment's notice. Service magic only becomes a problem when things go south – to hell.

The belief in magic, then, real as it was, did not cause the bloody horror of the witchcraft trials. The causes of those? Oh, they were very much man-made.

Let us explain . . .

THE VILLAGE CHARMER

We've always been a very important part of the village, you know. Oh, yes, I learned from my mother, who learned from her mother, who learned from her mother.

There are few of us around the burgh, and we all do different things, different charms. Now you'll go to Charlie Clark if it's something to do with the big livestock: lame horses, cows not milking, that sort of thing. It's Jonnet Murray for women's doings: babies, love, all those wifie concerns.

Me, I'm the one you go to if you've lost something, or you've got problems with your skin or your stomach. As you'd expect, I'm fair busy. The lost items involve a charm. No, I'm not telling you what that is. You need to pay like anyone else. Have you lost something? No, well keep me in mind for when you do. Sometimes things disappear and turn up in the queerest places. Now, for the skin and stomach complaints there are various salves and tinctures. These are recipes that have been passed down for generations. Almost always effective, and when it's not, we'll try something else. There's often a special charm for your own situation. And of course you must send your earnest prayers to Almighty God, too.

Yes, the last wee while has been strange. Since Margaret Small was found a witch we've all been troubled. There haven't been any witches round here for years and we're a good village of righteous churchgoers, so we were very upset to discover such a one nearby. We have to keep attending the kirk and apply ourselves to the Lord's word. If we follow the minister, I'm sure we'll be safe.

No, of course I'm not worried personally about the accusations. Why would I be? No, no, you've got it wrong. I only do good Christian charms, wouldn't go near anything dark-hearted. Absolutely not. That's a very different practice altogether and I have no time for it. What you're talking about is witchcraft, plain and simple, and I'll discuss it no further.

2

HOW TO START A WITCH-HUNT

It stands to reason that before you kill a witch, you first have to find a witch. Despite their devilish powers of deception, once you look for them, they are really not so hard to find. And once you find one, you find many, for witches rarely work alone.

Throughout history, it appears that witches thrive in times of social unrest. In good times – where people have enough to eat, adequate health care and social harmony – what does the Devil have to bargain with for someone to relinquish their eternal soul? In times of strife, however, when hunger and disease are common, the Devil preys on the weak to relinquish themselves to him, and do his evil bidding with promises of money, food and good health.

In Scotland between the 16th and 18th centuries, the Devil had just the right fertile soil in which to plant his seeds. Of course, witches were not purely a Scottish phenomenon – the Devil had bigger plans than that – but we focus on Scotland here to show how the Devil managed to work his way into the very heart of Scottish society. It was only by the strenuous efforts of godly people that we managed to all but banish ~~quarrelsome women~~ – sorry, we mean witches – from our society.

Draw up a chair, grab some paper and make some notes. You never know when the next witch infiltration will arise.

First, though, a bit of historical background.

By the middle of the 16th century, Catholicism was losing its charm for the Scottish folk. Back in 1533 in England, King Henry VIII, still then inconveniently married to his wife Catherine, had decided he wanted to wed his (possibly already pregnant) paramour Anne Boleyn, who was in turn described as a witch who bewitched the poor King. By doing so, Henry initiated a break with Catholicism in England. Admittedly, it might all have been a bit more complicated than that, but the point is this: there was a decline in the Catholic faith not only in England but also in Scotland, and by the late 1550s Protestantism was very much on the rise.

The Protestant faith was founded by Martin Luther, a German priest who had become disillusioned with the corruption in the Catholic Church. Aside from his view that the Bible itself was the final word on God's law and not the Pope, his main complaint, well founded to the modern eye, was that the Catholic Church's highly profitable trade in 'indulgences' was problematic. The granting of indulgences, which had been taking place since the 11th century, was the practice of the church granting a reprieve for the amount of time you spent repenting of your sins – in heaven or earth – in exchange for a sum of money. This system proved to be a veritable goldmine for the church for five centuries. However, Luther, in the famous list of grievances that became known as the *Ninety-five Theses* (1517), concluded that he thought this practice of people paying to cleanse themselves of the punishment of sin was open to abuse by unscrupulous clerics, who were making pots of cash from even more unscrupulous sinning folk.[†]

Enter, in 1559, a Protestant Scottish preacher called John Knox (1514–72), whose fiery sermons inflamed such passion that Catholic priests' homes were attacked, and Catholic statues toppled. Toppling statues is far from a new thing. In spring that year, Knox was the driving force behind an armed revolt that ultimately led to the Scottish Reformation. The people of Scotland were whipped up into a religious fervour and, having become disillusioned with the old papist ways, gladly turned to the new religion of Protestantism. The fact that the state was also making it very difficult for Catholics to exist in peace no doubt also

† In our view, if anyone should have been annoyed it should have been the Devil, tempting people to do wrong only for them to buy their way out of it.

assisted the conversion of the religiously apathetic. After all, it was the same God and, let's face it, anything for a quiet life.

Problematically, the Queen in Scotland remained obstinately Catholic. In 1560, the Catholic Dowager Queen Mary of Guise, who had been ruling as Queen Regent, died, leaving her daughter Mary Queen of Scots, then 18 years old, to reign alone† (Mary's first husband, the King of France, also died later that year aged 16). Mary was Catholic, like her mother, but she tolerated the rise of the new religion. The Protestants took full advantage: those in favour of the Reformation quickly convened the new Scottish Parliament and passed two important pieces of legislation (although they were not technically ratified by the new Queen). The Confession of Faith Ratification Act of 1560 identified 'the trew Kirk' as the religion of Scotland and the Papal Jurisdiction Act of 1560 removed the authority of the Pope in Scotland, citing the fact that in 'tymes bipast [it] hes bene verray hurtful and prejudiciall to our soveranis autoritie and commone weill of this realme'. These two pieces of legislation solidified the Protestant faith in Scotland. At the same time, six Protestant ministers called John, known somewhat unimaginatively as 'the Six Johns', wrote the new rules for the Kirk of Scotland. John Knox was their leader. Somewhat oddly, therefore, Scotland had a Catholic Queen and a Protestant parliament.

Fast forward three years, and this new Parliament was busy getting to grips with passing legislation to further cement the power of the church in people's lives. It was against this background that the Witchcraft Act of 1563 was passed.

Usually, an act criminalizing behaviour is passed because there is some pressing social need for it. Which begs the question – was Scotland overrun with witches in 1563? It would appear unlikely. The Reformation Parliament was, however, very keen to ensure that Scottish folk did not indulge in any

† Mary Queen of Scots was only six days old when her father James V died and she formally inherited the throne.

extracurricular quasi-religious tomfoolery. God was a man (naturally) who had no truck with charms or spells, Catholic idolatry or indulgences. The new church would be a one-stop shop for all your religious needs and there was no requirement to seek communion with Himself via anyone but a minister. Also, and perhaps somewhat unfortunately for the evil rich, you could no longer buy your way out of the effects of sinning with indulgences. In these new enlightened times, you no longer had any choice but to follow a religious life, praise God, and be good. Don't, whatever you do, look to any other source for charms or help, consult anyone claiming to have the power to speak to the dead, or carry out acts of witchcraft yourself. The church has you covered.

The challenge for the new church, the state and, as a subtext, the patriarchy, was how exactly does one legislate against Catholics, witches and the Devil all at once? You do it by passing legislation outlawing acts of witchcraft. There was a precedent for this south of the border – there had already been two Witchcraft Acts in England in 1541 and 1562. Clearly the Scots legislators needed to keep up. And so it was that the Witchcraft Act was passed and placed on the statute books in Scotland in 1563.

This is a transcript of the original text, to give you a flavour:

June 4, 1563: Anentis Witchcraftis

Forsamekill as the Quenis Majestie and thre Estatis in this present Parliament being informit, that the havy and abominabill superstitioun usit be divers of the liegis of this Realme, be using of Witchcraftis, Sorsarie and Necromancie, and credence gevin thairto in tymes bygane aganis the Law of God: And for avoyding and away putting of all sic vane superstitioun in tymes tocum:

It is statute and ordanit be the Quenis Majestie, and thre Estatis foirsaidis, that na maner of persoun nor persounis, of quhatsumever estate, degre or conditioun thay be of, tak upone hand in ony tymes heirefter, to use ony maner of Witchcraftis, Sorsarie or Necromancie, nor gif thame selfis furth to have ony sic craft or knawlege thairof, thairthrow abusand

> the pepill: Nor that na persoun seik ony help, response or cosultatioun at ony sic usaris or abusaris foirsaidis of Witchcraftis, Sorsareis or Necromancie, under the pane of deid, alsweill to be execute aganis the usar, abusar, as the seikar of the response or consultatioun.
>
> Which, translated from old Scots, reads as follows:
>
> 4 June 1563: Against Witchcraft
>
> The Queen and her Estates, in this present parliament having been informed that several types of heavy and abominable superstition are being used by the subjects of this realm, that being witchcraft, sorcery and necromancy, and credence is being given thereto as was in bygone times, against the laws of God. For the avoiding and putting away of all this vain superstition in times to come:
>
> It is put into statute and ordained by her Majesty the Queen and her Estates that no manner of person or persons, of whatever estate, degree or condition they may be of, take upon hand in any times hereinafter to use any manner of witchcraft, sorcery or necromancy, nor to give themselves further to have any craft or have knowledge of it, thereby abusing the people [of the realm]: Nor should anyone seek any help, response or consultation from any users or abusers of the aforesaid witchcraft, sorcery or necromancy, under the pain of death, as much as to be executed against the user and abuser as the seeker of the response or consultation.

So, in precis: the practices of witchcraft, sorcery and necromancy are banned. Anyone who practises, or consults those who practise, will be executed.

What is especially interesting about the Act, at least to us, is that it does not give any guide as to what constitutes the unholy triumvirate of witchcraft, sorcery or necromancy. One has to understand that, at the time, the descriptions were so commonplace that everybody knew what a witch, sorcerer and necromancer was. It was plain to anyone that acts of witchcraft were carried out to cause harm to another person or their property (this was known as 'maleficium'). Sorcery was the act of casting spells. And necromancy was speaking to the dead. Notice, too, that the crime legislated against is not being a witch per se, but committing an *act* of witchcraft.

In any case, the overall meaning was clear, and the lawmakers could rest easy, knowing they had God on their side. The Bible does not have a lot to say about witches, but what it does have is not favourable to them. In Exodus 22:18, the Bible warns: 'Thou shalt not suffer a witch to live.'

From that, the legislators made it clear that the crime would be committed 'under the pain of death'.

So what was the common understanding of what a witch was? The answer is that the definition changed over time. When the act came into force in 1563, a witch was a person who used magical powers to assist people. By the time the act was being enforced with a vengeance in the 1590s, 'witch' had a definite meaning: a person who had powers given to them by the Devil. The centrality of the Devil to the definition was something Mary Queen of Scots's son King James VI personally endorsed: a witch was a person who had given themselves to Satan; who had turned from God and had promised their eternal soul to the Devil in exchange for his power. The witches themselves were conduits of Lucifer.

The eagle-eyed reader may have noticed that nowhere in the legislation does it mention that witches were most likely to be women. Indeed, the wording is entirely gender-neutral. How odd, then, that of the 4,000 or so people accused of witchcraft in Scotland between 1563 and 1736 (when the act was repealed), 85 per cent of them were women. It's almost as if there was some inherent bias against women in this patriarchal society.

The question as to why more women were accused than men is one King James VI himself sought to answer in his book examining the study of witchcraft and other malevolent creatures, *Daemonologie* (which we will look at in more detail later). He posed the question: 'What can be the cause that there are twentie women given to that craft, where there is one man?'

A Witch Sailing to Aleppo in a Sieve, Charles Turner, 1807

The patriarchal answer was clear, if not spelled out. If you were the Devil in those days, who would you go for? The fine upstanding members of the community? The men who were morally, intellectually, physically and spiritually better than women? Or the women who would literally sell their soul for a chance at finding some financial or personal gain?

But the act would put a stop to all this evil corruption. From 1563 onwards, then, it was illegal to commit acts of witchcraft, talk to the dead or cast spells. But it wasn't until the 1590s, during the reign of James VI, that the first big witch purge took place north of the border.

James VI was born to Mary Queen of Scots and her second husband Henry Stuart, Lord Darnley, on 19 June 1566, three years after the passing of the Scottish Witchcraft Act. James was the son of the Scottish Queen and, on his father's side, a great-great-grandson of Henry VII of England. Such impressive parentage allowed James to claim rights to the Scottish and English thrones, and ultimately unite the crowns as James VI of Scotland and I of England.

Lord Darnley, his father, had been a jealous man and when Mary fell pregnant with James, Darnley was suspicious that her private secretary, an Italian named David Rizzio, had sired the child. A man of action, it is widely believed that Darnley conspired with a group of Protestant noblemen to accuse Rizzio of adultery and to murder him. Whether Darnley was the catalyst or not, the plan was executed on the evening of Saturday 9 March 1566 when the rebel noblemen, led by Lord Ruthven, pounced on Rizzio when he was with Mary and her attendants at supper. Ruthven and the others stabbed him some 57 times with a dagger while Mary, six months pregnant with James VI, was held at gunpoint.

As so often is the case, one violent act precipitated another. On 10 February 1567, when James was only eight months old, Darnley was staying at Kirk o' Field in Edinburgh when there was a terrible explosion. Darnley was found dead, though it was not the explosion that killed him – he had been smothered. Fingers were immediately pointed at the Queen. Outrage – which had not been similarly exhibited for the foreign private secretary's murder – was nursed into outright religious rebellion against the Catholic Queen. The Queen sealed her fate when, on 15 May 1567, she married the man who was said to have killed Darnley, James Hepburn, the Earl of Bothwell.† Her wedded bliss was to last less than a month. In June 1567, rebel Protestant lords arrested Mary and imprisoned her in Lochleven Castle near Kinross. James VI, by then 12 months old, was never to see his mother again.

On 24 July 1567, Mary was forced to abdicate in favour of her infant son, and the Earl of Moray was appointed James's regent. Poor Mary's extraordinary story didn't end there. After miscarrying twins, she escaped from imprisonment; raised an army; fled south after being defeated; was taken into custody by her cousin Elizabeth I; became embroiled in various plots; and was eventually executed in 1587. Dramatic to the end, the first blow of the axe missed her neck – and when the deed was eventually done, the executioner held her head aloft and her hair promptly fell off, revealing it to be a wig.

With the Earl of Moray as regent, however, the Protestant lords had their young king-to-be under their control and, until he came of age, a total of four regents were appointed to rule in his stead. John Knox preached the sermon at his coronation and remained an important figure in the life of the young James in relation to his religious learning.

James grew up as the Protestant King in a time still fraught with religious tensions. He was, of course, by his divine right, God's envoy on earth. As such he had to be on the lookout for the Devil, whom he understood would very much be plotting his downfall at every turn. It's hard to overstate how much the Protestant

† Although prior to the marriage Lord Bothwell stood trial for the murder and was acquitted, he too met a sorry end. He fled Scotland to Norway, but found himself in Denmark where he was imprisoned for ten years, tied to a pillar. A mummified body that was said to be his was repatriated to Scotland and shown in the Edinburgh Wax Museum in 1976. Incidentally, this museum, located on the Royal Mile in a former commercial bank, served a dual role in its heyday in the 1970s and 80s: by day it was a wax museum and by night it became the Castle Dracula Theatre, starring its owner Charles Cameron, the self-styled 'Godfather of Bizarre Magic', in his 'Gothic House of Terror'. If ever a footnote deserved to be a book in its own right it is this one. Currently, and much more mundanely, it is used as the Faculty of Advocates' consulting rooms where Claire has conducted many a meeting, although not with mummies, vampires or bizarre magicians, although she would very much like to.

faith permeated every part of Scottish culture. The church was the provider of education, moral guidance, enforcement of the law, alms and protection from the Devil. In much the same way as God was central to the lives of those in Scotland, his opposite number was similarly very much present.

It was widely understood that the Devil could, and did, take on human form – by compressing air to the shape of a man – to prey on the vulnerable. By all confession accounts (which we will detail later), the Devil was a flaneur enjoying wild parties, bountiful buffets and devilish sex with the women who had given themselves over to him as witches. He was a well-dressed man who occasionally enjoyed a bit of transmutation into the form of a dog or cat and, when he was trying to seduce honest women, husbands. Alas, many a good woman was undone by having sex with the man she thought was her husband, only to find out it was the Devil in disguise. But more of that later.

Raised in this atmosphere as a young and impressionable orphan, it is not surprising that James grew up hyper-vigilant against the threats of the Devil. His fears were crystallized in 1589 when he elected to marry a Danish princess (Denmark was by then, like Scotland, a Protestant country). Anne of Denmark was 14, the older sister of the 12-year-old King Christian IV. Now considered old enough to marry, she was promised to James and the couple married by proxy on 20 August. James was 23.

Now the bride needed to actually meet the groom. The plan was for Anne to travel to Scotland from Copenhagen, in the care of the Danish navigator Admiral Peder Munk, in order to meet her new husband. But despite Munk's best efforts, the voyage was thwarted by repeated bad weather and her flotilla of ships was driven back. This was a seriously embarrassing setback for Munk and a scapegoat was urgently required. As it happened, Denmark was under the grip of its own witch-hunt at the time so Munk was immediately suspicious that witchcraft was the cause of the problems in getting his precious regal cargo across the waters to Scotland. He certainly had no truck with the idea that his seafaring prowess might be to blame.

Rather than return to Copenhagen, Munk and his ships had been forced to dock in Oslo. From there, they sent word to James of their problems, telling him that they would try again when the seas calmed. James, impatient to meet his young bride, instead marshalled his own ships and sailed to Oslo to meet her in a somewhat grand romantic gesture. They were married again (in person this time) on 23 November 1589. The newlyweds stayed abroad for a number of months, during which period James met Niels Hemmingsen, an influential Danish Protestant theologian who in 1575 wrote a thesis warning against the practice of witchcraft. It is recorded that they had a long talk on all things theological just before James set sail with his new bride to return home to Scotland.

Hemmingsen had a nuanced stance on witchcraft. He believed that it existed, but he was concerned that many of the accusations of witchcraft against 'simple folk' could not be fully trusted, and may well have been unfounded. Sadly, this more thoughtful position did not seem to be adopted by James VI.

But it was not only Hemmingsen who had spoken to James on the subject during his Danish trip. Witchcraft was the talk of the Danish court, in particular the witch trials that were currently being held in Trier, an independent Catholic diocese that is now part of Germany. Proving that Catholics were equal to Protestants when it came to witch-hunts, the newly appointed archbishop of Trier, Johann von Schönenberg, had immediately set himself the task of ridding the area of witches (along with Protestants and Jewish people). Over 12 years between 1581 and 1593, witchcraft trials took place with great frequency, and at least 360 people were burned alive as a result. The total number of executions, including those within the diocese who lived outside the city, might be closer to 1,000.

A pamphlet from the trials, a copy of which is still available at the British Museum, detailing the accusations and confessions was distributed far and wide. It consisted of six short columns of text under a huge etched illustration depicting witches carrying out acts of witchcraft on their hapless victims, the style resembling the work of Hieronymus Bosch. It was no doubt pored over with fear, excitement and prurient interest, and was believed to have directly influenced what was to follow in both Copenhagen and North Berwick in Scotland.

On 1 May 1590, James and Anne at last returned to Scotland, having once again battled fierce weather on the crossing, and the pair settled into a long, fruitful and reasonably harmonious marriage (though there was much speculation – even at the time – that James' relationships with his male favourites were sexual).

Meanwhile, back in Denmark, a row was brewing about the royal travel fiasco, and fingers of blame began to be pointed at various players in the whole embarrassing saga. Peder Munk – still suspicious that witchcraft was behind the bad crossing but presumably keen to raise a case against a defender he might get some money out of – launched a legal case against the Minister for Finance Christoffer Valkendorff about the state of the ships which had, he argued, placed Princess Anne in danger during the crossing. Ironically, Valkendorff then promptly played the witchcraft card in his defence, claiming that the problems experienced by the fleet had nothing to do with anything as straightforward as lack of proper funding of the Admiralty and insufficient investment in the ships. The true cause, he said, was the result of the work of witches, who had sent little demons in barrels to the ship to cause bad weather.

Yes, you read that correctly. As we will come to see when we look at witchcraft accusations and confessions, witches and demons travelling in small barrels and sieves was a commonplace witch activity.† But notwithstanding the fantastical nature of these accusations, it would be very reasonable to ask, where on earth was the evidence for this witch-based defence?

As it happened, someone had confessed to exactly this crime. In May 1590,

† So common in fact that when Shakespeare wrote *Macbeth* – aka 'The Scottish Play' – in 1606, he drew on the image to curry favour with the new witch-obsessed King (James VI had taken the English crown three years earlier). In Act 1 Scene 3, one of the witches explains how she would intercept a ship at sea, 'but in a sieve I'll thither sail'. See Charles Turner's *A Witch Sailing to Aleppo in a Sieve* (on page 27) for a great artistic representation of this. The engraving is held in the Metropolitan Museum but is alas not currently on view.

a Danish woman called Ane Koldings was accused and convicted of witchcraft, in relation to matters at the time unrelated to the royal sea crossing. Awaiting sentence, she had become something of a reluctant celebrity in Copenhagen, where she was put on display for important people to come and visit in jail. Valkendorff, clear in his mind that it was not his fault that the ship transporting James and his queen had faced peril in the rough crossing – and perhaps even looking for an easy scapegoat (perish the thought!) – asked the Mayor of Copenhagen to interrogate Ane Koldings to see if she had anything to do with it. As chance would have it, Ane Koldings confessed – under torture – that she, along with several other witches, had met at the home of Karen the Weaver† and had cursed the crossing and Anne's ship. They had summoned demons to sail in empty barrels to intercept the royals' ship and cause the bad weather in an effort to sink it.

Ane Koldings was executed for her original crimes in July 1590. A further five trials of women named by Koldings took place and each was convicted of bewitching the royal crossing. In total, 19 people, mostly women, were convicted and executed.

Back in Scotland, when he heard of the witches' work, it dawned on James that his return trip had also been bedevilled by bad weather, quite literally it seemed. As the ancient Romans did, James asked himself *cui bono?* – to whom did it benefit if James and his new wife were to perish in a watery grave leaving no progeny? The obvious answer was, of course, the Devil. What better way to disrupt God's plans for Scotland than to leave it without a future king or, failing that, a queen? When the results of the Koldings trials filtered back to him, it was proof that the Devil had taken the opportunity to attempt to thwart both the godly king and his new wife on their respective outbound journeys, so clearly the same thing must have been attempted on the return leg. James knew that the Devil did not usually work directly, but instead called in the services of witches to do his bidding. And so,

† An early example of the demonizing of women named Karen.

the question remained: *which* witches had cursed the return royal trip and how would one go about identifying them?

James's very beginnings, upbringing and his entire history had led him to this point, and this had only been reinforced by his recent experiences abroad. Through a combination of religious zeal, political paranoia and influential advice, he had become obsessed by the thought that witches were bedevilling his reign. Now he swept into action.

James became the 'complainer' in several ensuing witchcraft trials, which is the term in Scotland for the person who is the subject of the criminal charge – but he far exceeded that role in these trials. He heard evidence; he listened to confessions; he watched the trial process; he consulted his own lawyers. None of this was the normal way to proceed in a trial process – but who was going to challenge the King, as close to God as any man *and* the foremost expert on witchcraft to boot?

And as a result, the first major Scottish witch-hunt was underway.

PORTRAIT OF THE ACCUSED

EUPHAME MACCALZEAN

NORTH BERWICK 1590

Euphame MacCalzean was born around 1558 into a privileged family. Her father, Thomas MacCalzean, was a judge in Edinburgh, a senator of the College of Justice and a provost of the city. Euphame married Patrick Moscrop and, as she came from a family of greater standing, he took her name in order to preserve the MacCalzean line. They had at least five children.

Despite this relatively powerful position in society, in 1590 Euphame was dragged into what became known as the North Berwick witch trials – the first of the major witch trials in Scotland – when a maid named Geillis Duncan accused her and several others of witchcraft. In the most shocking allegation, Euphame was co-accused of planning to murder King James VI. Unusually for an influential and strong woman (we jest), she was accused of having a controlling personality and of using witchcraft to domineer over her husband. She was also accused of murdering her godfather and bewitching a judge to 'bear goodwill' to her daughter. Interestingly, among all this self-serving murderousness, she was further indicted for helping to relieve women of the pain of childbirth.[†]

Alongside her co-accused, John Fian, Agnes Sampson and Barbara Napier, Euphame was alleged to have attended a get-together with the Devil at a beach called Atkynson's (or Acheson's) Haven in East Lothian, where they passed around a picture of the King with the intent of bringing about his destruction. At this meeting, the group of 'witches' were said to have engaged the Devil to

† You might be asking why assisting someone in easing their labour pains would be denounced as witchcraft. It seems it was down to the outrageous lack of humility displayed in the attempt to go against God's will: pain was the price of childbirth, after all.

interfere with the weather in order to impede the King's sea crossing. Some of the accused were brought before the King and a council of nobles to the Palace of Holyroodhouse in Edinburgh, where they were tortured until they confessed.

Euphame was convicted in 1591 and executed on the hill below Edinburgh Castle on 25 June that year. She was burned alive rather than strangled: the gravity of the crime of attempted regicide meant the most painful death was reserved for her.

The King disposed of her estate, Cliftonhall, to one of his allies, Sir James Sandilands of Slamannan, and her house on the High Street in Edinburgh to an officer of the royal stables, John Shaw. The patriarchy had once again what was rightfully theirs and the dreadful witch was ash.

KING JAMES'S LAWYER

NORTH BERWICK WITCH TRIALS

I have been watching His Majesty from my place in the makeshift court and I have realized it is an intellectual game to him. He has always had a reputation as a clever man, and why wouldn't he be? He was raised at Knox's knee. But it is fascinating seeing him getting his teeth into the questioning. Especially with this particular accused, who is a clever one. She claims to have witnessed the intimate moments between our King and his delightful new wife in their bedchamber.

The look on the King's face when she uttered this was quite something to behold. I saw there a combination of shock that someone, some little thing from the countryside – a woman no less – would dare to speak so boldly to the King. There was also naked curiosity about what on earth the woman might claim to have witnessed.

The King took her away into an antechamber and questioned her more closely in complete privacy. The King insisted upon no one accompanying him, though this caused some consternation and disquiet amongst the religious men in court. If the accused is a witch, and there seems very little doubt on that point from the King, then is it not very dangerous for our King to be on his own with the Devil's assistant?

However, the King insisted and declared that as he was put on Earth by our Lord Almighty, surely he had the greatest of protection. Which I found rather an interesting logical argument considering we are all gathered here today precisely because these witches are so very dangerous to our King. But the King knows best, naturally.

Having questioned the woman, King James is satisfied that she did, seemingly impossibly, witness those private, tender moments between the King and his bride. Thus, proving Agnes Sampson's witchery. Of course, as no one else heard the evidence given (which I don't need to tell you is highly unusual, but as it is the King, all bets are off), we will never know exactly what was said. However, there was quite the look of satisfaction on the King's face upon his re-entry into the court, so one must assume it was a happy enough outcome for his eminence.

Now we must see what will happen next, but it seems most likely there will be several executions and then the burnings. What this means for Scotland and her people remains to be seen, but if I was a betting man – naturally I am not, I use this merely as a figure of speech – I would lay odds on it spelling for trouble for Scotland, but useful for King James's ascendancy to the throne over all of us in these disparate countries.

3

KNOW YOUR ENEMY PART I: NEWES FROM SCOTLAND

North Berwick is a small town on the coast of East Lothian in Scotland, which, at the time of James VI's return from Denmark, was suffering a major witch outbreak. David Seaton, a local bailiff, had come to notice that his servant, Geillis Duncan, had what he considered an unnatural ability to heal those who sought her help. What power could this young woman possess other than witchcraft? This God-fearing master was not to know that his observation would spark the biggest witch trial Scotland had ever seen, uncovering a supposed coven of over 70 witches who were said to be intent on killing the King.

To examine these events, we have the best of all teaching tools: an apparently contemporaneous record of events in a 24-page pamphlet entitled *Newes from Scotland*, published the year after the trials in 1591. It is believed to have been written by a Protestant minister named James Carmichael, who became a later adviser to King James VI. So supportive of the King is it, we suspect the King had a hand in the writing of it himself! Two copies of this short book exist, one in the University of Glasgow, the other in the Bodleian Library in Oxford. To find out how the witch-hunt started, we decided to visit the Bodleian and consult the source information in person.

We arrived at the library on a warm, sunny morning. The University of Oxford was established centuries before the witchcraft trials, in 1096, so this great place of learning was witness to those times. After a little faffing filling in forms, we tiptoed through the cold hallways of the first floor to find the book that had been set aside for us to read. Lining the walls was a parade of busts and portraits of various men, silently watching over us. Ushered into a large library, even colder than the halls, we were shown to a table and waited for the 430-year-old document to arrive. Laid before us was a book cushion for the precious pamphlet to rest on as we read it, to protect its spine. Gloves donned, we received the book from the silent librarian who left us to our research.

If you want to read *Newes from Scotland* in its original form, it is possible to find it online. However, be warned, you may find this heavy going. For the purposes of this book we've produced an edited precis below in modern-day language. It is an extraordinary document, giving a unique insight into the beliefs and worldview of the time. From the perspective of nearly half a millennium after its publication, it is clear it is also a nightmarishly extravagant piece of Jamesian propaganda – watch out for the obsequious flattery to the King throughout. Reporting the news, it seems, has never been an impartial business.

NEWES FROM SCOTLAND[†]

INTRODUCTION

Here you will find the testimonials of Dr Fian and the witches, as they were uttered in the presence of the King James VI. It is the true story of the apprehension of various witches who have been recently arrested in Scotland, some of whom are already executed and some of whom are still imprisoned.

God in His omnipotence has lately overthrown the wicked intentions of a great number of 'ungodly creatures' who had allowed themselves to be enticed by the Devil. These people served the Devil and studied the detestable art of witchcraft, enticing others to join them by means of their sorcery. They all resided in the Lothians, the area in which the King's primary residence was located [. . .].[‡]

---

† Possibly one of the first examples of 'Fake News'.

‡ Immediately we can see that the writer draws a link between the coven of witches identified and the fact that they lived in the very area where the King resided. The introduction concludes that God has revealed their terrible intent to harm the King and country and invites the reader to find out how by reading the tale.

Newes from Scotland,

Declaring the Damna-
ble life and death of Doctor Fian, *a*
notable Sorcerer, who was burned at
Edenbrough in Ianuary last.
1591.

Which Doctor was regester to the Diuell
that sundry times preached at North Bar-
rick Kirke, to a number of noto-
nous Witches.

With the true examinations of the saide Doctor
and Witches, as they vttered them in the pre-
sence of the Scottish King.

Discouering how they pretended
to bewitch and drowne his Maiestie in the Sea
comming from Denmarke, with such
other wonderfull matters as the like
hath not been heard of at
any time.

Published according to the Scottish Coppie.

AT LONDON
Printed for William
Wright.

Newes from Scotland frontispiece, 1591

THE ACCUSED

In the town of Trenent in Scotland, there lived a David Seaton. He was a deputy bailiff, and he had a maidservant by the name of Geillis Duncan.[†]

Geillis aroused the suspicion of her employer by leaving home every other night and acquiring the ability to heal the sick and infirm by performing 'matters most miraculous'. David Seaton began to suspect that these healings had not been performed in a natural way but rather by 'some extraordinary and unlawful means'. Seaton became very inquisitive and demanded to know how she was able to achieve these miracles. She gave him no answer.

In order to find out the truth, David Seaton and others tortured Geillis with the use of pilliwinks on her fingers, 'a most cruel torment', and also by thrawing – 'binding and wrenching her head with a cord or rope'. Yet still she did not confess.

At this, Seaton, along with his friends, made a diligent search of the maid's body, and there they found the Devil's mark on her throat.[‡] Upon this discovery, Geillis confessed that she was indeed a witch and that all her 'doings' were achieved by means of witchcraft.

While awaiting trial in prison, Geillis pointed the finger at several other 'notorious witches', all of whom were apprehended. This list included the following people:

Agnes Sampson, the eldest of the witches, living in Haddington

† *Outlander* fans: this is the real woman accused of witchcraft and not the time-travelling Scottish independence fan.

‡ A Devil's mark (or witch's mark) was a blemish such as a mole, skin tag, wart, scar or unhealed area on the body. It might not bleed or hurt when the skin is 'pricked'. The mark was said to be physical proof of the Devil's pact with his initiate. We'll look at this idea in more detail later.

Doctor Fian, alias John Cunningham, schoolmaster at Saltpans in Lothian
George Mott's wife of Saltpans
Robert Grierson, skipper
Jennifer Bandilands
the porter's wife of Seaton
the smith at the Bridge Halls
'innumerable others'[†]

Some of these people are already executed and the rest remain in prison, awaiting His Majesty's pleasure.

Geillis Duncan also caused Euphame MacCalzean[‡] to be apprehended. She conspired and caused the death of her godfather, and she used her art on one of the local judges to cause him to look favourably on her daughter.

In addition, Geillis caused the apprehension of a woman called Barbara Napier for the crime of bewitching to death Archibald, the last Earl of Angus. At the time of his death, it hadn't been suspected that he had been killed by witchcraft; it was just thought he had died of a disease so strange the doctor did not know how to cure it.

Of all the witches mentioned, Euphame MacCalzean and Barbara Napier had previously been thought to be as honest and civil as any women that lived within the city of Edinburgh.[§]

---

† Academics estimate that after all the accused were interrogated and had given the names of others – who in turn gave the names of more – at least 70 people were accused as witches and possibly as many as 100.

‡ Euphame MacCalzean is spelled Euphemia Maclean in the original document. Names, and all else, were spelled phonetically at the time and this name in particular lent itself to several artistic interpretations. Other names, such as Agnes Thomson's surname, are similarly spelled various ways within the document. Claire continues to subscribe to this form of spelling.

§ This of course shows the power of the Devil – that even those thought the most virtuous could be turned to his bidding. No one, not even the most seemingly godly women, were above suspicion.

THE ALLEGATIONS

Agnes Sampson, the elder witch, was taken to Holyroodhouse before King James VI and various other noblemen of Scotland, where she was 'strictly examined'. However, it was to no avail – none of the 'persuasions' that the King and noblemen tried worked. She confessed nothing, and 'stood stiffly in the denial' of all of which she was accused. As a result, she was taken away to jail, to be tortured.

It has lately been found that the Devil generally marks his witches with a private mark, as the witches have confessed themselves. The Devil licks them with his tongue in some private place of their body before he receives them as his servants. The mark is commonly given to them under their hair on some part of body, so it is not easily found when searched; generally, as long as the mark is not discovered, the person who has it will never confess anything.†

By special commandment, Agnes Sampson had all her hair shaven off, on every part of her body. Her head was bound with a twisted rope, according to the custom. Yet still she would not admit anything. It wasn't until the Devil's mark was found on her private parts that she immediately confessed all.

She was then brought before King James VI and his council and was examined about the witches' meetings and their 'detestable dealings'. She testified that on the night of All Hallows' Eve she was with a great many other witches, 200 in total, and that they all went together to sea in a sieve. They drank from flagons of wine and made merry while they sailed to the kirk of North Berwick in Lothian. After they landed, they joined hands and danced a reel or short dance, singing with one voice:

Cummer go ye before, cummer go ye,

† Positively fiendish work! The Devil made it difficult for anyone innocent to be believed – the examiners would naturally assume the person had a Devil's mark that hadn't yet been found and that was the reason for the failure to confess.

Gif ye will not go before, cummer let me.

Agnes testified that Geillis Duncan went before them, playing a reel or dance upon a small trumpet, until they entered the kirk at North Berwick.

The King was astonished by these confessions and sent for Geillis Duncan, who duly played the trumpet and performed the dance before the King. He took great delight in witnessing these strange testimonies.

Agnes Thomson also confessed that the Devil had come to North Berwick Kirk in the form of a man. The witches had taken too long to arrive, and the Devil said that they had to pay him a penance: they had to kiss his buttocks, as a sign of their duty to him. He showed his bare buttocks over the pulpit and the witches did as they were required.[†] Having made his 'ungodly exhortations', the Devil spoke with great hostility against the King of Scotland. The witches asked why he bore him such hatred. The Devil responded that the King was the greatest enemy he had in the world. This particular fact is stated in all the witches' confessions and depositions on record.[‡]

After receiving the witches' oaths for their good and true service, the Devil then departed. The witches returned to the sea and so to home.

Returning to Agnes Sampson again, it seemed her confessions were so various, strange and miraculous that the King thought she and the others who had confessed must be lying. Agnes Sampson said she did not want the King to think her a liar.[§] To prove this, she took the King aside and told him the very words that had passed between him and his new Queen at Oslo in Norway on the first night of their marriage.

† This was known as the 'osculum infame', literally the shameful kiss. Could this be where we derive the insult 'kiss my ass'?

‡ The subtext here is that the King of Scotland must be exceedingly virtuous and godly if he is the Devil's greatest adversary. How lucky the people of Scotland are to have such a holy man to protect them from the Devil and his minions. And how lucky the English would be if he were to become their King too!

§ Quite why she would be so keen to prove herself a witch is not known.

The King was greatly amazed and swore by the living God that he believed all the devils in hell could not have discovered these words: acknowledging her words to be true, he therefore gave more credit to the rest of the confessions.[†]

Agnes Thomson, meanwhile, was under the direction of the Devil himself to plan and execute the King's assassination. She confessed she took a black toad and hung it by the heels for three days, collecting and gathering its venom as it dropped into an oyster shell. She kept the venom close and covered it until she could obtain a piece of 'foul linen cloth'[‡] belonging to the King, such as a shirt, handkerchief or napkin. She proposed to get these items from John Kers, an old acquaintance who was an attendant in the King's chambers. He refused, saying he could not help her.

Agnes Thomson further confessed that if she had obtained any such piece of linen cloth that the King had used, she would have bewitched him to death and put him to extraordinary pain, as if he had been lying on sharp thorns and the ends of needles.

Moreover, she testified that when his Majesty was in Denmark, she, along with those she had previously named, took a cat and christened it. Afterwards they bound to each part of that cat the 'chiefest'[§] part of a dead man along with several joints of his body. The following night the cat was taken into the middle of the sea by witches sailing in their sieves. They left the cat in front of the town of Leith in Scotland, and as a result there arose a huge tempest at sea, the likes of which had never been

---

† Note the fact that the King of Scotland had put his credibility on the line by swearing to this, which meant that few would doubt the veracity of what was 'confessed' by the witches. His royal seal of approval would surely change the mind of anyone who was in any doubt about the truth of them. The fact that he was the only one who could verify this story was of no moment.

‡ The fouling of clothes is unlikely to have meant the King's soiled undergarments! Rather it meant any clothing or items he had worn or used.

§ If the chiefest part of a man is what we are imagining it is, that must have been pretty hard to attach.

seen before. This tempest caused the sinking of the boat coming from Burntisland [in Fife], which was carrying all the various jewels and rich gifts that should have been presented to the new Queen of Scotland on her arrival at Leith.[†]

Agnes claimed that the aforementioned cat was the cause of the King's ship facing a headwind on his return from Denmark. The King acknowledged it was true that the other ships in his flotilla had enjoyed a fair and good wind, whereas the wind continually blew against his own ship; Agnes further testified that his Majesty the King would never have come safely from the sea had his faith not prevailed above their intentions.[‡]

Agnes was then asked to explain what the Devil would do with the witches when he was in their company. She said that he received them as his servants and that he would 'carnally use them, albeit to their little pleasure', due to his cold nature.[§] He would repeat this at various times as it suited him.

In respect of Doctor Fian, also known as John Cunningham, his testimony shows the great subtlety of the Devil. He was apprehended after Geillis Duncan's confession named him; she claimed he had been the register keeper for all the witches, and that he was the only man called to the Devil's meetings.

The doctor was taken and imprisoned and subjected to the same torture as the others. First, they tried thrawing[¶] his head with rope, but he

† Call us cynical, but it seems a little too convenient for a ship of riches and jewels to have disappeared in this way. Also, how fortunate it must have been for the captain of the Burntisland ship that, as with the Danish captain, all his problems at sea could be blamed on witchcraft!

‡ Again: how virtuous and brave the King of Scotland is, whose faith is so strong it saved him from the Devil's fiendish plan to kill him, etc etc. You get the idea.

§ Although the Devil's manner was probably not the warmest, this is not what the witches are speaking of when they describe his cold nature. At this time, it was known that the Devil was made of vapour, like a spirit. For him to take corporeal form, he had to compress that air. Such a transformation would leave him looking like a normal human being, but he would be cold to the touch.

¶ The wrapping of rope round the head, which is then twisted and turned to tighten it, causing great pain.

would not confess. Secondly, they tried to persuade him to confess 'by fair means', but that did not work either. Lastly, he was put to the most severe and cruel pain in the world, called bootikins.[†] After he had received three strokes, he was asked if he would now confess his damnable acts, but his tongue did not allow him to speak. The other witches present told the interrogators to search his tongue, under which was found two pins thrust up into his head. On this discovery, the witches said, 'Now is the charm stinted [stunted].' The witches showed that those enchanted pins were the reason that he could not confess anything: at this revelation he was immediately released from the bootikins and brought before the King, where his confession was taken.

First, he said, whenever the witches met, he was always present: he was clerk to all those who were in subjugation to the Devil's service. It was he who took their oaths of service to the Devil, and he wrote down such matters as it pleased the Devil to command him to do.[‡]

He confessed that using his witchcraft he had bewitched a gentleman who lived near to Saltpans, where the doctor worked as a schoolteacher, because this gentleman was enamoured of a woman whom the doctor also loved. By means of sorcery, witchcraft and devilish practices, he caused the gentleman to fall into lunacy once every 12 hours and for this fit of madness to continue for one whole hour each time. To prove the truth of this, the man was brought before the King in his chamber on 24 December last year. When he was there, the man suddenly gave a great screech and fell into madness, sometimes bending himself over and sometimes stretching up so high that his head touched the ceiling of the chamber, to the great astonishment of His Majesty and the others present. All the gentlemen in the chamber were not able to hold him until they called for more help,

† Despite their nursery-rhyme name, bootikins were indeed a dreadful form of torture. They were wooden boards encasing the lower limbs and designed so that wedges could be hammered into them, crushing the ankle and foot. A bit like pilliwinks for the feet.

‡ It appears that the patriarchy is doing well in hell, what with the only man getting the desk job.

and together bound him hand and foot, and he had to lie bound until his fury passed. Within an hour he became himself again. When the King asked him what he saw or did during that hour, the man replied that he had been asleep.

The doctor also confessed that he had tried at various times to obtain his 'purpose and wicked intent' with the gentlewoman, but he was not successful. Being thwarted in his intentions, he decided to use sorcery to obtain the outcome he desired. He did this in the following manner.

It so happened that this woman had a brother who went to the doctor's school. The doctor called this boy to him and demanded to know his sleeping arrangements, in particular whether he shared a bed with his sister. The boy answered that he did. The doctor thought that this would serve his purpose, so he secretly promised the boy that he would teach him without whipping him if he obtained three hairs from his sister's private parts, when the opportunity presented itself. The boy promised to carry out this task faithfully, and took from the doctor a piece of conjured paper to put the hairs in once he had obtained them. Thereafter the boy practised nightly to try to carry out his master's instructions when his sister was asleep.

But God, who knows the secrets of all hearts and reveals all wicked and ungodly practices, would not suffer the intents of this devilish doctor's plan.[†] God declared that He was most gravely offended with this wicked scheme, and He worked through the gentlewoman to defeat it. One night when she was asleep next to her brother, she woke and suddenly cried out to her mother, declaring that her brother would not leave her alone to sleep. The mother, who was quick-witted, acted speedily, as she very much suspected Dr Fian's intention, because she was a witch herself! She wanted

† Here we see the omnipotence of God, even over the Devil's plans, and His willingness to intervene when an innocent young woman was preyed upon. We'll come to look at God's power and interventions later.

to know what the boy had been doing, and she beat him a number of times until eventually he told her the truth.

The mother, being well practised in witchcraft, thought it would be clever to play the Devil at his own game. So she took the enchanted paper from the boy, went to a young heifer that had never borne a calf or been put to the bull, and with a pair of shears she clipped off three hairs from the cow's udder and wrapped them in the paper. She gave the package to her son, telling him to give it to his master, which he immediately did.

As soon as Dr Fian received the hairs, thinking them to be the maid's, he performed his sorcery on them; but the doctor had no sooner done so than the heifer whose hairs had been clipped came to the door of the church, where the schoolmaster was, and went in. The heifer made straight towards the schoolmaster, leaping and dancing upon him, and following him as he ran out of the church. The cow followed him everywhere he went, to the great astonishment of all the townspeople of Saltpans and all who beheld the sight. The report of these extraordinary occurrences made everyone suspect that the Devil must have been behind them. From then on, the name of Dr Fian – who was still a young man – became notorious among the people of Scotland, and it was said that he was a 'notable conjurer'.

Although at first he denied being a witch, after he felt the pain of the bootikins he confessed that what had been said was true. In front of the King, Dr Fian signed the confessions with his own hand, and the truth of this remains upon the record in Scotland.

After the depositions of Dr Fian (alias Cunningham) had been taken, he was remanded in prison and appointed to a cell by himself. There he renounced the Devil, announcing that he was forsaking his wicked ways, acknowledging his previous ungodly life and admitting that he had followed the allurements and enticements of Satan, and had practised his dark arts. He now vowed to lead the life of a Christian and seemed to be newly connected with God.

The day after his conversion, he stated that the Devil had appeared to him the night before, dressed all in black with a white wand in his hand, and that the Devil had demanded to know if he was going to continue his service to him, as he had promised in his earlier oath. Dr Fian declared that he utterly renounced the Devil to his face, saying to him, 'Avoid, Satan, avoid, for I have listened too much unto thee, and by the same thou hast undone me, in respect whereof I utterly forsake thee.' The Devil responded: 'That once ere thou die thou shalt be mine.' As he said it, he broke the white wand and immediately vanished from sight.[†]

All that day, Dr Fian spent time alone, and seemed to be concerned about his soul. He called upon God, showing himself to be penitent for his wicked life. Nevertheless, that very night, he stole the key to his cell and the prison, and escaped to Saltpans.

When the King became aware of Dr Fian's sudden departure, he ordered him to be apprehended, and to aid this process he sent public proclamations to all parts of the land. By means of 'hot and hard' pursuit, Dr Fian was soon recaptured and brought to prison where he was again called before the King and re-interrogated on his escape, and all that had happened before.

But this doctor, despite his written confession having been taken in the presence of the King himself and a number of his counsel,[‡] now denied its truth.

The King, seeing how stubborn Dr Fian was, came up with the idea that during his time on the run he must have entered into a new agreement with the Devil. If this had happened, he would have been newly marked – so Dr Fian was closely searched once more. However, no mark could be

---

† A white wand may be symbolic of the breaking of Dr Fian's pact with the Devil. A broken wand appears similarly in other ceremonies: at Queen Elizabeth II's funeral on 19 September 2022, the Lord Chamberlain broke a wand over her coffin to denote the end of his service to the Queen.

‡ The reference to the King and his counsel is where we get the term 'King's Counsel' from. These were the senior lawyers/advisors who assisted the King.

found. As a result, a 'most strange torment' was devised to make him confess.

First, the nails on all his fingers were riven and prised up with an instrument that in old Scots is called a 'turkas', otherwise known as a pair of pincers. Then under every nail two needles were thrust in up to their heads. These tortures notwithstanding, the doctor never failed in his courage and continued to refuse to confess to witchcraft.

With all due haste and on the commandment of the King, Dr Fian was then subject to the torment of the bootikins once more, in which he continued to suffer for a long time. He withstood so many blows that his legs were crushed and beaten 'as small as might be', and the bones and the flesh so bruised that the blood and marrow spouted forth in great abundance, so that his feet were made useless for ever. Notwithstanding all these terrible pains and cruel torments, he would not confess to anything. So deeply had the Devil entered his heart that he utterly denied all that he had vouched for before and would say nothing about his confession other than this; that all he had done and said earlier was due to him being tortured.[†]

The King and his Counsel gave great thought to this, for as well as wanting to serve due justice upon such a detestable criminal there was a need for an example to be made of him to strike terror in all others who might think to deal in the ungodly practice of witchcraft.[‡] So Dr Fian was soon arraigned, condemned and adjudged by the law to die, and then to be burned according to the law of the land. He was strangled, placed in a cart, then his body was immediately put into a great fire, which had been set up for that purpose on Castle Hill in Edinburgh. This took place on a Saturday at the end of January last past, in 1591.

† Note that the idea he might have been telling the truth now and he had confessed before due to the torture is simply not entertained as a possibility.

‡ Exemplary sentences are still used today, to send messages to the public about the dangers of becoming involved in serious crimes, although thankfully we no longer have the death penalty.

The rest of the witches that are not yet executed remain in prison till further trial and in knowledge of the King's pleasure.[†]

THE CONCLUSION

Having heard this strange story, the reader may perhaps think that the King would not risk putting himself in the presence of such notorious witches, as in doing so he might have faced great danger to himself and to Scotland. But let this answer suffice. First, it is well known that the King is the child and servant of God, and the witches are mere servants to the Devil. He is the Lord's anointed, and they but vessels of God's wrath. He is a true Christian and trusts in God; they are worse than infidels, for they only trust in the Devil, who brings them to utter destruction.

But here it is evident that the King possesses a truly magnanimous and undaunted mind. He was not afraid of the witches' enchantments; he was resolute in the knowledge that so long as God is with him, he has no fear of who is against him. Truly, this whole treatise makes plain the wonderful providence of the Almighty. If the King had not been defended by God's omnipotence and power, his Highness would not have returned from Denmark – so there is no doubt that God would as well defend him on the land as on the sea, or wherever the witches carried out their damnable practice.

THE END

So what can we take from this extraordinarily detailed document, other than it was a very effective pitch for James VI of Scotland to achieve his lifelong ambition of unifying the country and becoming James I of England?

Certainly, it's no surprise that stress is put on the fact that if you are truly godly, then God will intervene in any plan the Devil seeks to carry out against

† The writing of the pamphlet was contemporaneous with the trials, as this comment shows some were still awaiting trial.

you. So if a witch casts a spell on you and it works, then maybe you were simply not godly enough. Did your cow die after a witch cursed you? Maybe had you remembered to say your prayers, then God would have intervened to stop it. The lesson is that the church provides safety from the Devil; the godlier you are, the less you have to fear.

Further, the Devil was very cunning at hiding his work. If you were accused but had not confessed, that is because a Devil's mark had not been found on your body, which was why you were able to withstand torture. So, confession or no confession – either way was proof you were a witch.

Finally, where you find one witch there will doubtless be more. The Devil ensures that if one witch is discovered and executed, he has many more that can be called upon to do his satanic service.

By the time the Berwick witch trials were concluded, King James VI was an expert in witches. Happily, for our present purposes, he thought it was important to record that information for others so that they would be better prepared to deal with the problem themselves if/when it arose again. Thus in 1597 he published a work titled *Daemonologie* – the King's own treatise on demons, spirits, witches and all that is unholy. We will come to that in the next chapter.

PORTRAIT OF THE ACCUSED

ALLISON (OR MARGARET) BALFOUR

ORKNEY ISLANDS 1594

Allison Balfour lived in the Stenness area on the Orkney Islands, off the north coast of Scotland, towards the end of the 16th century.

Orkney has quite a different history to the rest of Scotland and was, in fact, officially still under Norwegian law until as late as 1611, although it had been ruled by Scottish earls from the late 15th century onwards. In 1594, the archipelago was under the control of the 2nd Earl of Orkney, Patrick Stewart, whose nickname was Black Patie due to his tyrannical nature.

The paranoid earl was convinced that his three wee brothers, led by John, Earl of Carrick, were determined to kill him in order to seize the reins of power. It seems the Stewarts had a long, troubled and highly adversarial relationship with each other. The earl searched John's servants and on finding poison among the belongings of one man, Thomas Paplay, he proceeded to torture Paplay for 11 days. He was placed in a metal cage known as a 'caschielaws', which gradually heated up to cause horrific burns, and stripped and lashed with ropes. Somewhat unsurprisingly, Paplay broke and named, among others, a local natural healer called Allison Balfour as a co-conspirator.

The autumn before the accusations, Paplay testified, Allison had been approached by the earl's brothers and their associates to cast a spell on Black Patie. However, whatever spell she used, it didn't seem to have the intended outcome, as the earl was clearly in good health. Physically, at least.

In December 1594, entirely under the personal authority of the earl rather than under the usual legal commission, Allison was taken to Kirkwall Castle where she was accused of witchcraft. Allison was questioned and tortured for two days by the earl's close associate, Henry Colville of Orphir, who was an ordained minister.

The treatment that Allison experienced was absolutely hideous, not least because after 48 hours with no result, her husband and small children were also brought in and brutally tortured in front of her. It's hard to imagine a man of the cloth instigating and directing these actions, but it's not the first or last time that religion has been used to control and dominate.

First, Allison's legs were put into the 'caschielawes' and burned, as Paplay had been. Every time she blacked out, they would revive her and repeat the treatment.

Then, as this strategy wasn't getting Colville the desired results, he began to torture Allison's elderly husband, possibly by crushing him under 50 stones of weight in what was known as the 'iron langs'. Despite this horror, Allison did not confess. Colville then started on Allison's little boy, whose legs were put into an iron boot and mutilated by being smashed with a large hammer. Still Colville wasn't satisfied. It was only when he tortured Allison's seven-year-old daughter, by crushing her fingers in thumbscrews, that she finally broke and admitted to practising witchcraft.

Allison had been told she wouldn't be executed if she confessed, but you may not be surprised to hear that this turned out to be a lie. She was tried, found guilty and sentenced to death. Just like Paplay, she retracted her confession before her execution and told those gathered about the torture she and her family had suffered at the earl's hands.

Allison Ballfour was executed at Gallow Ha' in Kirkwall on 16 December 1594.

4

KNOW YOUR ENEMY PART II: DAEMONOLOGIE

The rare books section of Edinburgh's National Library of Scotland is, as you would expect, a quiet place. Readers sit at tables, manuscripts are spread about, and books are piled up. So much antiquity in one room, with people beavering away, extracting history from the written word.

One Thursday afternoon, the two of us were brought into a quiet conference room – which incidentally, has one of the best views of Edinburgh, with Arthur's Seat looming over the tops of buildings in the Old Town – and seated at a table. We didn't enjoy the view for long: metal blinds are fixed at the windows to protect documents and ancient books from any dangerous sunshine. The blinds duly closed, one of the librarians checked that the air conditioning was working, presumably so the books didn't spontaneously overheat and burst into flames. Once we were fully air-conditioned, we were supplied with small beanbags to lay the books on to support their spines.

All these precautions having been taken, the librarian brought us in two books. Two versions of King James VI's book, *Daemonologie.*

The first was dated 1597, which was the version written in Scots. The second was the English translation from 1603, republished to coincide with James taking the English throne. What struck us both immediately is that they are very small volumes, much smaller than a modern-day paperback. We had imagined that a book with a name like *Daemonologie* would be like a big bumper Disney book of spells à la *Sorcerer's Apprentice*.[†] The smaller one, the London edition, is a little fancier than the other, with embossing on the front, gilt down the edges

† The 1970s Disney one with Mickey Mouse as the hapless magic trainee, not the 2010 Nicolas Cage one where the book unfolds from a thin pamphlet to an enormous tome.

of the pages and marbled endpapers, no doubt to suit the more refined tastes of a metropolitan London audience.† Both books are in very good condition.

The work itself is divided into three parts. Book One concerns itself with magic and, in particular, the practice of speaking with the dead – necromancy. Book Two covers sorcery and witchcraft. And finally, Book Three is a discourse on all remaining ghosts and spirits that bother folk.

Book Two, which we are specifically interested in here, is presented in the form of a dialogue between Philomathes and Epistemon, 'to make this treatise more pleasant and facile'. Philomathes (Greek for 'lover of learning') is new to the subject, curious and quite sceptical. Epistemon (meaning 'understanding, knowing') is wise and clearly comprehends the real and present danger of witches. This part of the book is divided into seven chapters, and each chapter proposes a question that is discussed by student and teacher and resolved in an answer.

Approaching the volumes felt to some degree transgressive and dangerous. It is one thing to know – from our modern-day perspective – that witchcraft does not exist; it is another to immerse yourself in a world in which it is entirely real. It seems for a moment to invite that dangerous history to come alive in the 21st century by resurrecting the beliefs of the times. But as we studied the pages, it felt as if we were peering directly into the past. Here we could read James VI's very own words and get a tantalizing insight into his mind. For any keen student of the patriarchy, interested in tracking down and prosecuting witches, *Daeomonologie* is an essential guide. What follows here is our summary of the contents of the work, focusing on Book Two, interwoven with our own commentary.

The book begins with a Preface in which the King explains that this is not a vanity project to display his 'learning and ingenuity', but that he has written the book because he was moved to warn people about the detestable slaves of the Devil, witches.

He further explains that it is a response to the 'damnable opinions' of an

† Plus ça change, eh?

DAEMONOLO-
GIE, IN FORME
of a Dialogue,
Diuided into three Bookes.

EDINBVRGH

Printed by Robert Walde-graue
Printer to the Kings Majestie. An. 1597.

Cum Privilegio Regio.

Daemonologie frontispiece, 1597

Englishman named Scot, who had denied the truth about witchcraft,[†] and a German doctor called Wierus,[‡] who proposed a public apology for people accused of this crime, and thus 'plainly shows himself to be one of their profession'.[§]

The King's intention, he says, is to warn his subjects that the Devil and his servant witches are very real and that they should be punished. He couldn't hope to categorize every example of the Devil's 'infinite' power in the book, of course: therefore he has categorized the work into different topics. Witches, he notes, have the power to cure or cause disease – and by this we can infer that the Devil has power over diseases in general, and this can also be proved in other ways such as 'weakening the nature of some men to make them unable for women'; and making it 'abound in others, more than the ordinary course of nature would permit'.[¶]

The King signs off his introduction, making it clear that this book is to be used, in contrast with weighty academic tomes of the time, as a practical guide, for the reader.

Now, what were the literally burning questions of the day?

---

† Reginald Scot, an English MP, wrote *The Discoverie of Witchcraft* in 1584, which proposed that most witchcraft and magic were nothing more than stage magic that could be debunked. Myth has it that when James VI took the English throne, he had all the copies that could be found collected and thrown on the pyre.

‡ Also known as Johann Weyer or Wier, he was in fact Dutch and wrote *On the Illusions of the Demons and on Spells and Poisons* in 1563 – coincidentally the same year that the Witchcraft Act was passed in Scotland. He suggested that the crime was virtually impossible and that most people who confessed were mentally ill, or 'melancholic'. As we come to see, King James VI had no truck with this excuse.

§ Ahem, just for the avoidance of doubt, although some centuries later the Witches of Scotland campaigned for the public apology, we are not witches.

¶ We pause to note that it's interesting that women – sorry, witches – are blamed here both for male impotency and for men being oversexed. It's almost as if women were being blamed for things over which they had no power at all.

1. DO WITCHES ACTUALLY EXIST?

Of course, this is the most important question of all and readers may be unsurprised to learn that the answer, according to *Daemonologie*, is a resounding yes. To test this, three arguments are posed against the existence of witches for those who think that people thought to be witches have nothing but 'imagination or melancholic humour' causing them to mistakenly believe they are in league with the Devil.

The first argument against their existence is that the scriptures don't speak of witches, rather they speak of magicians and necromancers. This is dismissed because the Bible plainly prohibits anyone from consulting with the Devil, whatever they are called. Second, are witches not, in truth, 'simple raving creatures' suffering from 'melancholique imaginations'? Again, no, and here we find some 16th-century body-shaming given as the reason. Apparently, those who have a 'natural humour of the melancholie' are lean, pale and 'desire of solitude', but, in sharp contrast, a great number of witches are 'rich and worldly-wise, some of them fatte or corpulent in their bodies, and most part of them altogether given over to the pleasures of the flesh'.

Thirdly and finally, if witches, through the power of the Devil, can kill people, why haven't they just killed everyone who is not a witch? The answer is simple: the Devil's powers are limited, as was set down before the foundations of the world were laid. Ultimately, God has the power to rein in the acts of the Devil. The righteous have nothing to fear, as God will protect. This argument has important ramifications, not least of which is it gives us an explanation for why people stood by and allowed others to be executed: the woman on the pyre must indeed be a witch, otherwise God would surely have intervened to prevent an injustice occurring.

OK, witches are real. What next?

2. WHAT IS A WITCH AND HOW DO YOU BECOME ONE?

Sorcery, James tells us, is a Latin word, which is taken from the casting of the lot that determines fates, and it has come to be applied to practices and charms that derived from witchcraft. Both magicians and sorcerers (and by extension, witches) serve the same master, i.e. the Devil.

So how does the Devil ensnare a person to do his bidding? The Devil bases his decision on whether the prospective witch is 'riche and of better accompt' or 'poore and of basser degree'. Perhaps unsurprisingly, to those in poverty he promises 'greate riches, and worldlie commoditie'.[†] For those who are rich but want revenge on someone, 'he allures them by promises, to get their turne satisfied to their hartes contentment'.

Even if you are poor or vengeful and filled with despair, though, the Devil still might not find sufficient leverage to insinuate his way in. You also need to be an ungodly person. This is a central tenet of James VI's thinking – if you are conned by the Devil into becoming a witch, it's only because your own contempt for God created an easy route for him to get to you. Conversely, of course, the godlier you are, the less likely it is that the Devil will try his chances with you.

When the Devil has found his prey – what then? In terrible behaviour, as expected of this 'old and craftie enemie of ours', he fills his prospective witches with more and more despair until he finds the right time to show himself to them.[‡] When he has them at their lowest and weakest, he gets them alone – perhaps walking in the fields or lying in their beds – and either by disembodied voice or in the likeness of a man he inquires what troubles them. At this first meeting he proffers an immediate remedy to their problem, provided that the poor dupe follows the Devil's orders. Sneakily, the Devil doesn't identify who he is at this first meeting. It's only at the second meeting that he persuades them to give themselves to his service and reveals himself to be none other than Satan. By this time, of course, it is too late; the new witch has renounced their baptism. The Devil then places a mark on some secret part of their body, which remains unhealed, and furthermore he takes all feeling away from the wound, regardless

† Note, he just promises them – so far in our research we've not actually found one poor soul whom the Devil has made good on his promise with.

‡ The ole 'get 'em when they're down' trick. In fact, what follows we would probably now describe as the use of coercive control.

of whether it is 'nipped or pricked'. This is powerful proof that the Devil can hurt or heal them at will, and that their wellbeing is now wholly dependent on him. At the final meeting, fearing they might forget him because they are new to the job as apprentices or not resolute enough in their fiendish folly, or else (perhaps the most likely) they are scunnered[†] with the deal they had done, the Devil makes a show of keeping his promise , either by teaching them ways to achieve their revenge, or by showing them how 'they may obtaine gaine and worldlie commoditie' through 'vile and unlawfull means', whichever is their preference.[‡]

3. WHAT DO WITCHES DO?

We have seen that people become witches to benefit themselves, but what's in it for the Devil? The answer is simply world domination – 'to wit, the enlargeing of Sathans[§] tyrannie, and crossing of the propagation of the Kingdome of Christ'.

To understand, we have to think of the Devil as 'God's ape' ('ape' meaning to mimic, often mockingly). God's ape requires the same service and adoration to him that God requires of His servants. Just as people go to church to worship God, so witches convene to praise Satan, albeit in secret. In order to become one of God's servants, baptism is required, so for the Devil, they must receive his mark, as described above. As ministers teach how to serve God in spirit and truth, so the Devil teaches his disciples how to work all types of mischief. Finally, that he may 'more accurately counterfeit and scorne God', the Devil often makes his witches convene in the very places that are ordained for God's people, namely churches.

† This is a great old Scots word still in use in the present day, meaning feeling aversion to something. 'I'm scunnered with this weather' is, perhaps unsurprisingly, a relatively common phrase in Scotland.

‡ The Devil appears to be an adherent of the three-date rule.

§ In *Daemonology* Satan is also referred to as Sathan, which has the unfortunate effect of making him sound more friendly.

4. HOW DO WITCHES TRAVEL?

Travelling anywhere during the 17th century was done on foot, hoof or boat. Ordinary folk were unlikely to do much more than walk. There was a fascination, therefore, with how witches travelled and whether they could really transport themselves to distant places, or if these journeys were 'mere illusiones of Sathan'.

Daemonologie explains that witches will say they can transport themselves to distant places because their senses are deluded into believing it, although as a matter of fact it is not true. Witches can convene to meet Satan by conventional means, but they can also be carried swiftly by the force of the 'spirit' over land and sea. In scripture it is recorded that God was able to do this, so the Devil, by aping him, will be able to do an approximation of it. There is a drawback, however, to this form of transport. 'In this violent forme' they can only be carried short distances, for the same length of time as they can hold their breath.[†] The reasoning given for this is that when someone falls from a height they are injured as a result of that person's breath being 'forceablie banished from the bodie, before he can win to the earth, as is oft seen by experience'.

Why, we wonder, do we not see the skies full of women holding their breath as they leap over our heads? The answer is given that the Devil is able to form any impression he pleases and can 'thicken and obscure' the air so that man's eyes can't pierce through it.[‡]

So witches cannot travel great distances. And for the avoidance of any doubt, a few other things witches claim but cannot do are listed: they cannot turn themselves into 'the likenesse of a little beast or foule'. They cannot squeeze into any house or church via any route that air can get in. And they cannot lie in bed, verified by 'witnesses that have seene their body lying senseles', while

† This may be the origins of the superstition that you should hold your breath as you go through a tunnel.

‡ An invisible force-field for flying witches.

simultaneously being transported from one country to another.[†] Well, these are some things we can all agree on.

5. WHAT DO WITCHES DO AND WHY ARE THEY MOSTLY WOMEN?

Witches usually convene for the 'adoring' of the Devil in churches at a time and place set by him. When they meet him, they let him know what 'wicked turne' they have done or propose to do for obtaining riches or revenge. He then gives them advice and assistance with their plans. As for the 'little trifling turnes that women have ado with', the Devil 'causeth them to joynt dead corpses, & to make powders thereof, mixing such other thinges there amongst, as he gives unto them'. What those little trifling turns are, we can only guess at. Not big important things that men would do, though, that is clear.

Now we come to a central question in our investigations. Why are there so many more women accused than men?

Daemonologie supplies the answer: 'The reason is easie, for as that sexe is frailer than man is, so is it easier to be entrapped in these grosse snares of the Devill.'

Short but damning. In so few words, the patriarchal mission of the period is laid bare. Women are the frailer sex so they are easier to entrap. Since Eve ate that apple, the Devil has found his closest allies in women.

So what does the Devil teach his witch women?

To some, he teaches how to make images of people from wax or clay, which, when roasted, will cause the person to suffer 'continuall sicknesse'. This will cause them to sweat and have stomach aches so that eventually they wither and die. To others, he gives stones and powders to help cure sickness and disease.

Witches can make men or women love or hate one another, as the Devil

† The example of the witch lying in bed while at the same time being elsewhere was cited as evidence in the Salem witch trials in the US, when one witch thought to prove her innocence by having witnesses swear they saw her asleep in bed. The menfolk of the parish saw right through that ruse. We'll come to this later in the book.

knows how to persuade the 'corrupted affection of those whom God will permit him so to deal with'. They can also lay the sickness of one person upon another.

Witches can raise storms and tempests in the air, either upon sea or land, within prescribed boundaries. The storms can be differentiated from naturally occurring weather events as they are sudden, short and violent. The Devil has an affinity with the air as he is a 'spirite'; James reminds us that in the scripture the Devil is known as the 'Prince of the Air'.†

Witches can also make folks become frenetic or manic,‡ or they can cause sprites to follow people or to haunt certain houses.

The book addresses another key issue. Will God allow witches to trouble anyone who believes in Him?

The answer is that there are three types of people that God allows to be tempted or troubled: the wicked for their horrible sins, the godly that are weak in faith, and even some of his most holy to test their patience.§

Who, then, might be free from these practices?

The answer doesn't give much hope. 'No man ought to presume so far as to promise anie impunitie to himself.' Essentially, if God has preordained it, tough luck.

And there is more bad news. Readers might want to know, not unreasonably, if they could ask a witch to remove a spell cast upon them by another? Again, the answer is clear: absolutely not. The only way to be lawfully cured was by praying even harder, amending your life – and by 'sharp persewing' every witch to their death.

---

† In Ephesians 2:2, Satan is described as 'the prince of the power of the air'. This wording is found in the King James (yes, the same one) translation of the Bible.

‡ We saw Dr Fian cast such a spell on his love rival.

§ On reflection we can't help thinking it would just have been faster to say, 'everyone but for different reasons'.

6. WHY DON'T WITCHES USE THEIR WITCHCRAFT AGAINST THOSE WHO PROSECUTE THEM AND KEEP THEM IN JAIL?

If witches can do such terrible things to people, why are prosecutors immune from their spells? Or as *Daemonologie* puts it much more eloquently, 'but who dare take upon him to punish them, if no man can be sure to be free from their unnaturall invasiones?'

Well, the most godly and zealous of those who pursue witches are doing God's work, so they should go about this business knowing that they will be protected.†

And what of when witches are in prison? Does their witchcraft work? Intriguingly, that is dependent on the form of their detention. 'If they be but apprehended and deteined by anie private person . . . their power no doubt either in escaping, or in doing hurte, is no lesse nor ever it was before.' So if the witch had been apprehended in what we now call a citizen's arrest – when a member of the public steps in to detain a criminal – then a witch's power remains intact. But if they're detained by the lawful magistrate, witches will be robbed of their powers. In other words, leave it to the lawmen.

Does the Devil ever come to visit witches when they are imprisoned? Apparently so, but his response may depend on the state that these 'miserable wretches' are in. If he visits and finds them 'in anie comfort', he then tries to 'fill them more and more with the vaine hope of some maner of reliefe'. Alternatively, if he finds them in deep despair, he will encourage such thoughts, and seek to 'perswade them by some extraordinarie meanes to put themselues downe, which verie commonlie they doe'. The only relief can be obtained by confession, after

† We paused to think of how important this philosophy must have been to a zealous minister, weeding out witches in the local community. What greater proof that he was doing the right thing, if he was immune from the powers of the witch that he was accusing? We can see why those who investigated witches did so with such fervour: their own safety from the Devil depended on it, and not just their mortal body but their eternal soul. The fact that the minister would also be immune from any behaviour of a perfectly innocent woman did not seem to worry anyone.

which 'God will not permit him to trouble them anie more with his presence and allurementes'.[†]

When in prison, what form does Satan take? It seems he appears to different people in different forms, as has been found by the difference of their confessions on this point.[‡] By deluding them with 'vaine impressiones in the aire', he makes himself seem more terrible to the worst of them, so they are moved to fear and revere him all the more, and 'les[s] monstrous and uncouthlike to the craftier sort, least otherwaise they might sturre [stare] and skunner at his ugliness'.

When witches say that he comes to them in prison, how can he touch them if he is made of air? Simple really: he may make himself 'palpable' either by assuming the form of a dead body,[§] or else he may delude their senses of seeing or feeling. And what of the other people imprisoned – will the Devil appear to them too? The answer is not definitive. 'Some-times they will and some-times not, as it pleases God.'

7. WHY WERE GHOSTS AND SPIRITS MORE COMMONLY SEEN PRIOR TO THE REFORMATION?

Finally, we come to the last chapter, which poses the interesting question: why have ghosts and spirits gone out of fashion?[¶]

---

† Sadly, many women died before they ever made it to the courtroom, because of the conditions they were kept in; their poor health; the torture; or more likely a combination of all three. Doubtless there were suicidal deaths attributed to the Devil that were much more man-made.

‡ Sneaky work by the Devil here. Of course, the alternative explanation, not to be countenanced, is that everyone was making up what he looked like and that is why there are so many different descriptions.

§ A revenant, more of which we will deal with later.

¶ Book Three of *Daemonologie* deals with demons, spirits, ghosts and spectres in more detail. These were seen as other manifestations of evil. Four broad definitions are made: first, there are spectra, which appear in homes and in quiet nooks and crannies. Then there are ghosts that only appear at certain times, such as incubi and succubae, who come at night to try to have sex with sleeping women and men, respectively. Then there is possession, in which spirits enter people's bodies and occupy them, and finally faeries, of whom we have already spoken. God was of course seen as omnipotent, so it was believed that none of these entities have any power to do evil without His concurrence. The Devil is not master of them; he is just a different form of evil.

The question James VI poses is a thinly veiled opportunity to make absolutely clear his express rejection of the Catholic faith. Remember that his mother, Mary, had been a devout Catholic, and no doubt it would be important to emphasize his very different view. In the time of 'blind papistry', he says, ghosts and spirits had been seen more often. Why? 'Our fathers erring grosselie, & through ignorance, that mist of errours overshaddowed the Devill to walke the more familiarlie amongst them.' In short: papistry allowed the Devil to flourish but the Reformers have now got the Devil on the run.

And with that, James VI concluded his Q and A on witches.

Daemonologie is a remarkable document. Firstly, it was a bestseller of the time, written by the King about the most scandalous crime short of treason of its day. This was not an academic resource, but a practical guide to keep the King's subjects safe. But more than all of this, this was James VI's personal statement of his knowledge of all that was unholy, and how he alone was the man who had the correct lineage and the divine knowledge to unite the crowns and to keep the kingdoms safe. It was a calling card to every other good Protestant on the isle, introducing him as their only safe choice as King.

The English translation of *Daemonologie* was published in 1603, the year James VI took the English throne (as James I). This is no coincidence, of course, as James wanted to tackle witchcraft accusations in his newly acquired country. Those in charge of the legislature followed his lead and in the same year the Witchcraft Act of 1603 was passed as 'An Act against Conjuration, Witchcraft and Dealing with Evil and Wicked Spirits' in England. With its renewed focus on the demonic and evil nature of witchcraft, you can see the influence of James's beliefs throughout. The aim of the act was to define witchcraft and its relation to the Devil more clearly, and to ensure a 'better restraining of said offences, and more severe punishing of the same'. There would be no mercy for witches either side of the border.

Reading *Daemonologie* was nothing short of transformational for us. We had up to this point, quite wrongly as it transpires, thought that the Devil and God were believed to be equal foes, like good and evil Marvel characters, battling throughout the universe for supremacy. Once we realized that God was seen as omnipotent and infallible and that anything the Devil or witches did was because He allowed it, it provided a completely new perspective on how we viewed the witchcraft accusations.

Have you been cursed by a witch? The fault lies not only with the Devil and his handmaiden, but with you – had you been more godly, God would have protected you. You need to go to the minister; you need to pray more; you need to be more chaste; more demure; more mindful. In modern parlance we hear the phrase 'God sends his toughest battles to his strongest soldiers'; so even if you have regularly attended church and prayed fervently, then God might just decide to test your resolve for goodness and holiness by sending witches to torment you. The Devil and his witches are as much the servants of God as the minister and his flock, and in tempting you into evil, they are, strangely, being allowed to do so by God.

This revelatory information about the philosophy underpinning the beliefs about witchcraft and the work of the Devil gave us a whole new perspective on the thought processes of the populace at the time. Of course witch-hunters and ministers did not fear the Devil – they were the holiest of folk doing God's work, so God wouldn't allow them to be harmed! The converse, of course, was true of the poor souls accused, convicted and sentenced to death for their blasphemous acts of witchcraft – if they were not truly witches, God would never allow such a heinous thing to happen. James VI wrote his book to educate ordinary folk into the world of witches and magic, and here we were in the 21st century, learning the very same thing.

After turning the last page, we headed back out of the National Library of Scotland into the sun, our minds filled with images of these 'wicked instrumentes' of the Devil and the terrible fates that awaited them.

PORTRAIT OF THE ACCUSED

JANET WISHART

ABERDEEN 1597

On Halloween 1596, a witches' sabbath was supposedly held at the Fish Cross in Aberdeen, the site of the old fish market. The witches sang, played musical instruments, and danced up and down the length of the high street at midnight. This event saw the beginning of a witch panic in the Aberdeen area, which led to the accusation and ultimate execution of 23 people, including Janet Wishart.

Janet had a 25-year reputation as a 'witch' in her community and had 31 dittays against her (a 'dittay' is a Scots legal term for an indictment, in other words the charge that is read out before the court). When Janet was accused, so too were her husband, John Leys, her son Thomas and her three daughters, Violet, Elspet and Jonet. Her associate, Isobel Cockie from Kintore, was also accused at the same time.

During her trial, Janet was accused of many things, including being involved in an incident in 1572 where she was witnessed by a group of men leaving her neighbour's yard in a suspicious manner in the middle of the night. The witnesses immediately alerted the occupants of the house. When confronted about her actions, Wishart cursed them. Later that day, two of the witnesses drowned.

Janet was also accused of using spells to cause her victims to shiver and shake, making them so ill they nearly died, and also of killing people through her magic. Furthermore, she was accused of interfering with the weather and using a cat to invade people's dreams. But it was the High Street witches' hooley that proved to be the final straw and led to Janet being formally accused of witchcraft.

During their imprisonment, it was said that Janet and her son were visited by the Devil who advised them to 'deny everything' and await his return. At her trial, Janet was found guilty of 18 of the accusations made against her and was likely executed on that same day, 17 February 1597. Unusually, Janet was burned to death rather than the much more common strangulation or hanging. The cost of Janet's execution was just over £11, and this covered the costs of burning her plus the fee for the executioner.

Isobel Cockie and Janet's son were also found guilty, but her husband and daughters were found innocent. However, due to their association with Janet, they were banished from the area.

JOHN KNOX

LEADER OF THE SCOTTISH REFORMATION

Allow me to quote from my most important work, in which I expound on my belief that rule by a woman is contrary to the holy teachings of the Bible:

> *Aristotle, as before is touched, does plainly affirm, that wheresoever women bear dominion, there the people must needs be disordered, living and abounding in all intemperance, given to pride, excess, and vanity; and finally, in the end, they must needs come to confusion and ruin.*†

Let me elaborate.

Because woman is our mother, our succour and our refuge, she is also naturally and most obviously weaker than us. Contemplate Eve in the Garden of Eden. Adam and Eve found themselves in the most abundant creations of God's unfathomable imagination. They were surrounded by beauty and ease. They wanted for nothing.

Yet...

Yet...

Eve fell prey to the temptations of the serpent, whereas Adam did not. And why was she entranced by the Devil's appalling charms?

Because she was designed that way.

As we all know and is clear in our everyday dealings, man is superior not only in

† This is a real quote from *The First Blast of the Trumpet Against the Monstrous Regiment of Women*, written by John Knox in 1558.

physical size and strength, but in every conceivable manner. Even the most intelligent of women can never be a true match for man. This is true from the humblest of homes to the highest stations in the land.

Though women may learn a great deal from the Bible and their ministers' teachings, there will always be a blind spot, a weakness in their moral structure, where the Devil can insinuate himself into their hearts, minds and spirits.

As we all know, not unlike the jackdaw, women are easily enticed with shiny items and fripperies. They look not into the depths but seek only the surface reflection.

And this is as it should be.

Women were made by God to be man's inferior in order to assist and support their men and fulfil their physical potential unto the glory of God.

This is their greatest attribute and yet their biggest failing.

However, fear not. We as proper, morally upright, biblically learned men, can and will protect them from the enticements and entrapments of the Devil. But we must stay vigilant and imperturbable in the face of the wicked temptations unto which women are vulnerable. We must keep a close eye on their Bible studies and their social interactions.

If women are kept busy in the home and in the kirk, and are watched carefully outwith, then we may keep the Devil at bay and protect ourselves, the King and indeed Scotland.

5
HOW TO BELIEVE IN A WITCH

Now you are a little better prepared to understand the hyperbole, fervour and theological justification for the trials, you may find yourself asking what it was that made the public at large buy into these witch-hunts? Was it simply an abuse of a largely illiterate population by a powerful elite working to their own religious and political ends? Or was there something about the specific environment of 16th–18th-century Scotland that made it a fertile ground for accusation and persecution? The witch-hunts are so alien to us today that it's hard to understand how things got out of control so quickly – how were people so content to let these obvious injustices occur again and again?

And also – and we kept returning to this question – seriously, why were so many of the accused women? We've heard James VI's view, but was there more to it?

To help us answer these questions, we spoke (via a Zoom call) to esteemed Scottish historian and one of the founders of the Survey of Scottish Witchcraft,[†] Doctor Louise Yeoman. Louise has written and researched extensively about the witch trials and has paved the way for many non-historians to become passionate about the subject. She also tells a great story: her speech is peppered with lots of Scots language and she made us feel as if she were gathering us in around her to tell us something special. We began by asking her what ordinary folk would have believed at the time.

† We cannot overstate how useful this painstaking resource and interactive database is to those interested in the witch trials.

'An ordinary person in a fishing burgh like Pittenweem or Anstruther[†] might believe that people could do magical harm,' she told us. 'They could sink ships and bring ill luck on the men fishing.'

Life, she continued, was often incredibly hard in the close-knit little villages that dot the northeast coast of Fife. Families made a precarious living from fishing the treacherous North Sea, and many superstitions and beliefs were woven into the fabric of the villagers' inner worlds. At the same time, the involvement of the church, or kirk, was incredibly important in these communities' lives and the minister was quite literally seen as being a direct connection to God. Everyone attended the kirk on a Sunday and communities were quick to point the finger of blame at anyone who deviated from the societal norms.

If someone in the village had been paying close attention to the minister and perhaps had even witnessed a witch trial, they would likely believe that people could indeed sell their souls to the Devil to secure power and then use that power maliciously against other fishermen and their ships. Remember, men died frequently while away at sea – in fact, many mariners at the time would refuse to learn to swim, as they believed it was better to succumb to death if they fell in the water, rather than fruitlessly battle against it. All the rage and grief villagers felt about losing fathers, husbands and sons had to end up somewhere. Couple that with a culture where the church constructed a framework of belief as to why things happened and who should be blamed if thing went wrong, and you end up with a perfect storm. As we see time and time again, humans need scapegoats.

Louise elaborates. 'If you lose your livelihood or if you're malting grain[‡] for

† These coastal settlements are located in Northeast Fife, where many witches were killed. This is where Zoe is from. Fife was the seat of the Scottish monarchy for around 600 years; several monarchs were buried at Dunfermline Abbey and St Andrews was a vitally important location for the Scottish Reformation. The latter is also hailed as 'the home of golf'.

‡ Leaving grain in water until it starts to germinate, so it can be used in the production of beer or whisky. People often drank weak beer instead of water. Perhaps we should take this up again.

brewing beer and it spoils, this is bringing people into hunger and want and danger. And if you think an ill-willed neighbour can do that to you, you'd be very frightened.'

There was no back-up support system such as we (supposedly) have today. Life was brutal and short. Diseases and malnutrition routinely killed children and people grieved their lost babies just as much as they do nowadays. It makes a certain kind of sense that if you identified the person who you believed had deliberately hurt your loved ones, you would want to punish them to the fullest extent of the law. And remember, this was all sanctioned, encouraged even, by the King and the church – the two most powerful forces in shaping society's ideas and actions.

Louise tells us the story of a woman called Anna Tait who she had come across in her research. Anna was a miller's wife who lived in Haddington, near Edinburgh in the 17th century.

'This case has always stuck with me. Anna is found trying to end her life. She is found trying to hang herself with the strings of her headdress. Of course, 17th-century society doesn't have compassion for people in these situations of despair. It thinks if you do that, you're motivated by the Devil. Suicide is a terrible crime [in their eyes] and you'll not get a normal burial. They have really horrible beliefs on this. So once Anna is caught trying to kill herself, the first thing people say to her is, "Did the Devil come to you?" And of course this is somebody in despair, so she says, "Yes, yes, the Devil came to me," but she also gives a horrifying, sad, tragic confession.'

As we will see time and time again, when a person is distressed, they will often admit to anything to make the pain stop. It would appear that during Anna's testimony she also used the opportunity to make a broader confession about things that she had done in her life, some of them quite shocking. First, she admitted that she had in fact poisoned her first husband with foxglove leaves in order to marry her second husband. Then, when her daughter became pregnant, Anna had helped her to terminate the pregnancy, but tragically, her daughter had died as a result. This was what had led Anna to such distress.

Anna was arrested and imprisoned at the end of 1634 and executed soon after, but we do not have an exact date of her death.

While many of the confessions have great similarities, the fact that Anna's confession is so unusual and unique is striking. Generally, they were fairly formulaic, as the interrogators were looking for specific information such as how the Devil approached the accused, what he said, what he promised, and what nefarious acts the witch and Devil then indulged in. In Anna's case, however, she unburdens herself of her very personal, heartbreaking story, which, though criminal, was not exactly what they were interested in.

'These are not the kind of things the people interrogating you want to hear,' says Louise. 'The people who are interrogating you want to hear you made a pact with the Devil. You had sex with the Devil, the Devil gave you a mark, and then you went and did horrible things. They don't want to hear your life story.'

Louise suggests that sometimes the accused thought they were going to die anyway so they might as well use the opportunity to straighten things up with God.

'I know of another case where a woman talks about her young son dying and she talks about it in the context of fairy changelings. The fairies took the son, and they left a log in the cradle and the log was thrown in the fire. You think, what actually happened to that wee boy?'

Louise has read many dozens of confessions to witchcraft, and it seems that often what is detailed is not the voice of the accused, but the voice of the person asking the questions. When we do hear from the accused themselves, they sometimes seem to be scrabbling for anything to say or, perhaps more commonly, they just say anything to get the horror over with. They'll say they don't know who the other people present were; perhaps they were wearing masks, or they've all died since.

Many of the confessions were so basic and similar they read like an early version of a 'cut and paste' job. In the story of the woman's dying son, there is deeply personal information that is unlikely to have been made up by the interrogators. It is here where we are likely to have the best insights into the real stories of women at the time. As Louise says, when a story breaks through that is personal, you know as a researcher that you are hearing the person confessing's real voice.

It is no wonder, when we get these glimpses of the very real hardships of these people's lives, that beliefs about witchcraft took such hold.

One thing that we have discussed at length since the inception of the Witches of Scotland campaign is why in Scotland (and most other countries) so many more women were accused than men. It is true that in some places, namely parts of Scandinavia and Russia, witches were generally believed to be men, but this derived from specific local traditions. In the far north of Scandinavia, for example, shamans were all men, so it was they who were accused of working with the Devil.

However, in Scotland, the belief systems of the 1500s to the 1700s were particularly disposed to a patriarchal solution to the problem of witches. Women were seen as weaker and therefore dangerously susceptible to the Devil's wicked and often sexy charms.[†] They were also more likely to misbehave and not follow God's (read man's) rules; more likely to be grasping and greedy; more likely to be jealous and weak. In short, women were stereotyped long before the witch-hunts as being the perfect quarry for the Devil.

What's particularly interesting to us is that then, as is largely the case now, women weren't the ones wreaking havoc on battlefields or in street brawls. Women had no legal power or professional standing. They weren't sitting at the side of the King or presiding over legal cases. What we think this led to is men (with power) being desperately scared that those without power (women) would try and grasp it by any means possible. It makes a twisted kind of sense, therefore, that they would create a fantastical means by which they could keep the powerless down. But that, we would argue, is where Scotland found itself from the 1500s onwards.

---

† Note that women alone weren't dangerous; they still needed a man to actually activate their dangerous tendencies.

One of the greatest moral architects of the period, the Reformer John Knox, had a particular interest in women not holding power – and, in fact, Louise's colleague, Professor Julian Goodare, has argued that Knox may have been one of the authors of the Witchcraft Act. But is there any evidence that he drove this desire to accuse and punish women?

'No,' thinks Louise. 'John Knox is an interesting case. He's somebody who really loves and respects the women in his life. He spends endless time counselling them on their spiritual problems. He's somebody who, within what he thinks is the sphere for godly women, thinks women are great.'

This is a somewhat surprising response, given what we know of his thoughts about female rulers (which we'll come to in a minute). But according to Louise, what Knox was most interested in was idolatry, and this is where it's another leap to get into the mind of the 16th-century believer. Idolatry – the worship of images and idols, very much part of the Catholic tradition – was seen by Knox and his contemporaries as so much more than superficially important. The Protestants had thrown out their idols and worshipped God directly, not via images, portraits and holy objects. The new thinking was that if you didn't follow the Bible to the letter, then you might find you're not worshipping God but, rather, the Devil.

Because here was the problem: if individuals couldn't get it right, then an unintended consequence could be that they might bring down the wrath of God upon Scotland, upon the whole nation. For this reason, Knox was concerned – to the point of obsession – with people not going against the word of the Bible. This is shown in the wording of the Witchcraft Act: there must be absolutely no necromancers – *everyone* must be following the rules of the Bible perfectly.

Despite Louise's take on Knox, his sexism, to us, runs very deeply. In 1588, he published a tract with the ferocious title *The First Blast of the Trumpet Against the Monstrous Regiment of Women* ('regiment' meaning rule or government). In it, Knox argues that female monarchs are contrary to the Bible's teaching and an affront to God – a direct attack on the monarch of the time, Mary Queen of Scots. It always struck us as very interesting that Knox wrote that, although as

God's envoy on earth she had been put into power by Him, he still believed that the country would be better served with a male king. That seemed very bold, even treasonous, to us. Perhaps it just again shows the temerity of men.

However, as is sometimes the case with this kind of grandstanding, Knox gets caught bonny. When the Protestant Queen, Elizabeth, was crowned in England in 1559, Knox's colleagues received elevated positions in the Church of England, but Elizabeth refused to do the same for Knox. It is said that she never forgave him.

It's small comfort, but we'll take it.

We first came across the historian Professor Marion Gibson on what was still known then as Twitter, as she fiercely battled misinformation and nonsense espoused about the witch trials under her fantastic handle @witchesetc. Marion is a great communicator whose warmth and knowledge must surely make her very popular with her students at the University of Exeter where she is Professor of Renaissance and Magical Literatures.†

When Marion was at university, it was accounts of the witch trials that drew her towards the field. As she learned more about the confessions of the witches and she thought about the women behind the stories, the truth about these persecuted individuals really began to matter to her.

As soon as you start reading confessions, you notice that there are certain themes and ideas, even phrases, that get repeated. Was it a case of these stories getting into the national consciousness? Or were the accused simply repeating what their interrogators were saying to them? Were they even accurate accounts of what the accused had actually said at all? Perhaps most perplexingly for us as a modern audience is the question of why on earth did people confess to witchcraft?

Firstly, we have to think about why ideas become a part of the culture.

Marion leans in. 'Why did somebody one day decide that people might keep

---

† Imagine having 'Magical' in your job title!

a small animal familiar† who was in fact a devil and that this would suck their blood? Who had that idea? That's a very strange idea indeed. But then when you think about how it enters into culture, you think about the rumours that fly around today – not only on social media but also in ordinary life.'

It's true, of course: we often see today how ideas or stories that are clearly without foundation can become normalized the more they are talked about – see the rise of conspiracy theories during the 2020 pandemic, or flat earthers, or chemtrail believers, or those who deny the Moon landings.

'Although coming to explain how these ideas originated is really difficult, how they spread is quite easily understood,' Marion continues. 'It is by gossip, but it is also by writing. The more people write these things down and the more people talk about them in court, and then the more people print the confessions and the more people take the pamphlet down to the pub and they read it to their friends – you can see how once people got hold of these ideas, they circulated in the culture.'

During the witch trials, publications appeared that were widely distributed, a bit like the penny dreadfuls of the Victorian era that we're perhaps more familiar with (serialized and sensationalized stories sold at a penny an issue). As we have seen, the most famous of the witch trial publications was the *Newes from Scotland*, which was printed in England in 1591 then circulated across the whole of the British Isles. While the advent of print is of course an indisputably positive development – the Age of Enlightenment could not have happened without it – it also had a dark side. One example is the widening distribution of the idea that witches were hidden (or not so hidden) among the ordinary population. Seeing these stories written down legitimized these beliefs and also encouraged communities to take action against witches as a way to make themselves safe.

---

† Familiars are a small part of the Scottish witch trials story, but a big part of the overarching idea of witches. They might be an animal such as a cat, dog or bird (sometimes it could even be a child) that would drink the witch's blood from a 'witch's teat'. One belief was that familiars suckled the witch as a kind of evil, female holy communion. Sometimes the familiar would consume the blood then would 'work' for the witch by doing evil deeds such as killing people or livestock to settle a score.

Of course, the vast majority of people in Scotland were still illiterate in the 16th century; reading was a privilege of wealthy males (anyone seeing a pattern forming here?). Scotland actually passed three education acts in 1616, 1633 and 1696 to try to establish schools, but a shortage of teachers and the expense of the school fees meant literacy rates remained low, especially for girls. The elite men who were literate were powerful, educated and in charge of the country. Their authority gave their views legitimacy to the lower orders. No doubt servants would pick up snippets of information from their masters, and they would tell their friends, who would tell their friends. With no internet or Netflix (other streaming services are available), these stories would not only provide entertainment, but would also be where ordinary folk got their information from – outwith, of course, the sermons of the minister at the kirk.

Ironically, considering where we first encountered Marion, we see the same thing happening daily on platforms like X, Facebook and TikTok. Ideas – often harmful – are spread worldwide in seconds and, sadly, as humans are so often fearful and blame-seeking, this is a perfect means of transmitting hate.

But it's not the mode of communication that is the problem. It's the humans who want to be scandalized by gossip and hear stories of aberration that then create cultures of accusation and punishment.

'These are persistent human fascinations, and we can't get rid of them,' Marion says. 'We wouldn't have folklore and fantasy without these kinds of beliefs, but of course they also have these terrible consequences of persecution.'

This leads us to a discussion about some of the broader beliefs about witches that seem very bizarre indeed to us now. One of these beliefs has become one of the central pillars of the contemporary culture's idea of a witch – the act of 'ducking' or in this context more accurately 'swimming' a witch.

Ducking witches – or 'dooking' as it would be described north of the border – was very rarely practised in Scotland and was more of a phenomenon in England. But ducking women into water as a public punishment long precedes the witch trials, as it was used as a form of humiliation from the 13th century onwards. Women were plunged into water to show them the error of their ways if they had been scolds or gossips, and sometimes it proved fatal. King James deemed it to be a good test of witches in *Daemonologie* in 1597 and the first recorded example in England is in Northamptonshire around 1612.

You might ask yourself, what was the logic of this 'test'? The thinking behind it was that if you had undergone a proper Christian baptism, you were under the protection of God's holy water and therefore, if you were thrown in, you would be accepted by the water – as in, you'd sink (and quite possibly drown, but that's by the by). But if you had renounced your baptism in order to sign your soul to the Devil, the water would refuse your entry and you would float on top. This curious logic is a source of fascination to our modern minds, and is perhaps the reason why the image of witches being thrown into water is so enduring† – even though it didn't happen anywhere near as often as you might think.

If ducking wasn't used as a means of flushing out witches, another possible test was to weigh the accused. Weigh stations – essentially large public scales in trade halls – existed across many towns in the mediaeval period for the purposes of commerce, with regards to grain or livestock and so on. However, as the witch-hunt mania spread across parts of Europe in the 1600s, these stations were put to a different use when they were employed to see if accused people were lighter than an honest woman and, therefore, witches. Sadly, there was a great deal of corruption at worst and incompetence at best, and many people were found to be suspiciously light and then executed in these weighing sites. One notable exception was at the Weighing House in Oudewater in the Netherlands, where the scales were reputed to have been verified by the Holy Roman Emperor Charles V himself. As a result, no one is thought to have been found guilty there – indeed, accused witches would travel to Oudewater to prove their innocence, as the scales had a reputation for being fair. The scales were built in 1482 and, remarkably, still exist today. If you so desire, you can go and get weighed there and receive a

† It's also, perhaps, partly due to the famous scene in *Monty Python and the Holy Grail* where the villagers argue that because witches burn, just like wood, and wood floats, just like ducks, so, if a woman weighs the same as a duck, she must be a witch. People don't remember the particulars of this scene outwith a mob shouting, 'She's a witch!' and that it has something to do with witches floating, yet it is a part of our inherited knowledge about the witch trials and, actually, a great example of the transmission of nonsense.

certificate proving that you aren't a witch. We'll leave that up to you to decide how grim that is for various reasons.

All these ideas sound bizarre to our ears, but did we not say we shouldn't write the people of the past off as foolish or ignorant? We must have the humility to realize that the people of the future may find some of our own current ideas equally as flawed. Yes, the logic behind swimming or weighing a witch does seem tremendously bonkers to us now. But spend a couple of hours on X and you will not have to go far to see equally lunatic conspiracy theories with equally ugly consequences for the real world. Plus ça change!

Another idea that permeated the culture of the time was the binary idea of good and evil. Marion explained: 'Their entire world was structured by this binary idea that there's God on one hand, with His people, so on the other hand there must be the Devil and his people. There must be witches and they must have certain laws that apply to them, and they must have certain behaviours that are often a kind of parody or an inversion of Christianity.'

Many witch confessions focus on their making a pact with the Devil, an inversion of the holy sacrament of confirmation. People took different vows and oaths to be confirmed, depending on which sect they belonged to. In Scotland, people generally made a 'covenant' once they were an adult and had the maturity and understanding to enter into the agreement with free will. They would pledge to follow the church's laws in order to be protected by God. It was a major tenet of their faith: as Psalm 105:8 says, 'He hath remembered His covenant for ever, the word which he commanded to a thousand generations.' A covenant was literally signed like any other contract.

Witches, by extension, would sign up to the dark side – they would make a pact or 'covenant with the Devil'. There are many variations on what that looked like. Sometimes people were offered money or sexual success or revenge in return for their soul. Then we see the actions they performed to harm: ruining crops; killing neighbours; causing illnesses; manipulating weather.

And this binary thinking of God on one side and the Devil on the other with no grey areas is what contributed to there being so many more women being accused than men, Marion believes. If men were on God's side as they were cleverer and stronger morally, then who must be on the other side with the Devil? Silly, inferior women, that's who! Women in their gullibility would easily fall for the Devil's sophistication. There was suspicion, too, when women spent time with other women. What did they talk about all day? Were they making plans to meet the Devil? Were they casting spells?

It seems ridiculous to think that thousands of people were accused or murdered all for these quite silly ideas. Women could be malicious, and they gossip. They must be up to something.

'When I started off my career in academia,' says Marion, 'I thought, it can't be as simple as that. But it's one of the great truths. This is about people hating women and it's really important to keep saying that. You can say all sorts of other things – it's about economic circumstance and, yes, that's important – but gender's part of that. Or you can say it's about domesticity and it's about people fighting over domestic spaces and boundaries and yes, it is, but gender is a part of that. And you can say it's about medical knowledge and who's supposed to have it, yes, but gender's a part of that too. It's about gender. And I think we sometimes forget to say it because we're so busy looking for other explanations, which are contextually very important. But that central truth? It's about women.'

We wonder whether we shy away from this truth because we modern women don't want to seem like harpies. It's the 21st century and you're still banging on about gender equality? Yes. Yes, we are. And we're going to keep banging on about it until it's sorted. It's a massive disparity – 85 per cent of the people accused as witches were women. We feel terrible for the 15 per cent of men accused, of course, as well. But we do have the sense that many of the men were dragged into it by the accused women. Quite often the men are relatives of the women. Perhaps their mother or wife has been accused and they are guilty by association or they are used to pressure the women into naming other witches. Even the men who escaped direct accusation themselves were harmed by the ordeal.

'These men suffered terrible fates, too,' agrees Marion. 'Imagine if you were one of the men left behind? Imagine if your wife is accused and you can't save her, you can't protect her? This is a universal tragedy.'

It is indeed a terrible set of circumstances that tore whole families apart. But, as Marion puts it, 'There is often a truth that you have to talk about and then the other truths fall into place around it.' And that truth is that this is about women – and as a result, it is a feminist issue.

The sexual dynamic to the accusations and confessions in Britain seem to be a key part of the witch trials. It's men who question and torture and examine the accused's bodies. It's men who decide their fates and then dispatch them. Once women are cast as witches in collusion with the male figure of the Devil, a sexual element to the confessions is inevitable. The witches meet up with the Devil, at night, in the woods or behind the town. What else would they be getting up to? The Devil is described as handsome and being nicely dressed. He's charming and persuasive, a fantasy lover. Life was hard and life expectancy was around 35, so who could blame a woman for having a little fantasy about someone who could take her away from all that? As women were viewed as being difficult and foolish as well as being sexually dangerous,[†] they were the perfect targets for all of society's fears.

One interesting case with a strong sexual element was that of Isobel Duff from Inverness, whose trial took place on 17 July 1662. This was during one of the five peaks of witch-hunting that experts generally recognize as happening between 1590 and 1662. In fact, Isobel's trial took place during what's seen as the biggest peak anti-witch fervour in Scotland, during which around 600 people were accused and nearly half were executed. Previous to this, the Highlands hadn't been involved greatly with witch trials.

Isobel's trial is of particular interest as it lays bare (so to speak) the underlying sexual dynamics of the pact with the Devil. Isobel's confession goes into great detail about the Devil tricking her into agreeing to have sex with him by his taking the form of a man called 'Tailiour', a soldier with whom Isobel was having an affair. Apparently, Isobel could tell the difference between the Devil and Tailiour by 'the length of his wand'. Isobel also described the Devil as being

† Riddle us this: men were morally stronger than women, but they also had to be on their guard not to be tempted to sexual impropriety by those sneaky sex pots.

unnaturally cold and not having any feet.[†] There are also descriptions of the mechanics of the copulation, namely that the Devil penetrated her 'after the manner of beasts' at Isobel's 'back parts', which would seem to be either sex from behind or possibly anal sex.

At any rate, Isobel's confession clearly paints her as an immoral, sexually voracious woman, which was most strongly frowned upon at the time. Still is, some would argue. The confession records that Isobel agreed to be part of the Devil's coven as she wished to seek revenge on her local enemy, John Robertson, but her use of magic for evil purposes, or malefice, extended to others too: she was accused of being involved in the deaths of several local people, as well as John Robertson. There was also an interesting case of magical curing when she helped a child recover from whooping cough. Another child apparently advised her to tie a ribbon around the affected child's neck – this cured the sick child, but the child that gave her the idea died soon after.

Isobel was tried and declared guilty on 17 July 1662 – and why wouldn't she be with such a sexually explicit and damning confession? The court instructed that Isobel 'be taken to the usual burning hill beside Inverness . . . and there to be strangled to a stake . . . and thereafter your body to be burned to ashes as a notorious and known witch.'

Once again, we see the fear of female sexuality taken to its deadliest conclusion.

So why did Isobel – and so many others like her – confess, if they were innocent?

Naturally, it's not hard to see why eventually, after being tortured (whether by physical means or in later years with sleep deprivation), the vast majority of people will say anything to make it stop. However, Marion has an interesting theory about why some of the women gave false confessions.

'There's something in the stories that's satisfying to tell. If you're in a situation where you're tired and you've been physically assaulted or put under stress in some

† Walking with no feet would seem a pretty clear indication to us that he wasn't a human, but we suppose the difference in penis size made for a more interesting story.

way, you're frightened and you want to go home, and this wealthy gentleman is asking you questions and you live in a society where your job is to agree with the wealthy gentleman, you can see why you might end up coming up with a story to please him. So you might say, "Yes, I was a witch, and I quarrelled with Goodie So-and-So next door and I decided I wanted to hurt her. So one day this strange man came to me and offered all this wealth and happiness. He said that I was special, and I was going to be his and that he would reward me if I took revenge on Goodie So-and-So, so I did and I felt fantastic about it. Now I can see that this was wrong. Please can you absolve me and then we can all go back to where we were?" But of course it doesn't work like that. By the time you've made the confession, you're in such deep trouble that you're probably not going to get out of it.'

And yet, we see a kind of agency in telling this story, in being able to threaten that you had been in cahoots with the Devil, so people had better watch how they treat you or something bad might happen to them too. Women were given the opportunity to talk at length and have men – powerful men – listen and even write down what they had to say. Not only that, but these men were often frightened of these women because of the power they thought they had.

As Marion puts it: 'That must have been a wonderfully satisfying position of power. Even if it only lasted for, say, half an hour. It must have been transformative.'

PORTRAIT OF THE ACCUSED

MARGARET AITKEN

FIFE 1597

Margaret Aitken, who became known as the Great Witch of Scotland, was arrested in April 1597, setting into motion a devastating chain of events that led to hundreds of people's deaths. Margaret was arrested in the parish of Abbotshall, south of Kirkcaldy in Fife. She came from a tiny village called Balwearie, which had a long history of magic and superstition. According to legend, many years before in 1539, King James V suffered a disturbing nightmare during which he was visited by devils and the Laird of Balwearie's son.

When Margaret was accused, she was tortured and, it seems, concocted a story in order to save her own life. She told her interrogators that she had the uncanny ability to discern a witch just by looking into their eyes. A commission was approved in May 1597 by King James VI and she was duly toured around Scottish towns in a form of horrific judicial roadshow, picking out those she identified as witches. The commission even went so far as to utilize the rarely used swimming test. Margaret and her clerical entourage eventually reached Glasgow where things began to fall apart.

Initially, a minister called John Cowper, reputed to be particularly unpleasant, was very keen to condemn any women based on Margaret's testimony and the number of accused and executed is suspected to have reached several hundred. But in August 1597, some sort of legal justice finally prevailed when one of the prosecutors, unconvinced by Margaret's claims, arranged for a group of people condemned by Margaret one day to be presented again the next, but dressed in different clothing. Lo and behold, Margaret proclaimed them innocent and unwittingly sealed her own fate.

Margaret made one final confession – possibly her only true one – where she admitted to fabricating her special powers. A Glasgow widow called Marion Walker, an active resister of the witch-hunts, printed and shared Margaret's confession in which she had blamed Cowper for his part in the frenzy, which brought this particular bout of witch trials to an end. Margaret was sentenced to death by burning at the stake and was taken back to Fife to face her end.

Following this embarrassing disaster, King James put an end to the commission and there were no further witch panics for more than 30 years – though they were to start up again with a vengeance in the 17th century.

PART TWO: BUILDING A CASE

ELDER ACCUSER

Never have I had the misfortune to meet somebody as unpleasant as the Guthrie woman. Nasty old bachle. Always getting herself involved in everyone else's business. Never a good word to say for anyone, and if on the rare occasion she doesn't say what she's thinking, the look on her crabbit auld face tells you clear enough.

When I was a young laddie, I remember her standing with a few of her cronies laughing at me and my father as we walked to a kirk meeting. You would not believe it looking at the man I am now, but she made me feel like a silly wee boy in the shadow of his father and that the pair of us were pretending at being important men.

I'll never forget it and she never has either because she always makes bold comments when she sees me about my business. Impertinent asides about how smart I look or what a marvellous baillie I am.

Of course, I can do nothing because the words she is saying are seemingly respectful. But everybody knows she is a twister of words and perverts meaning.

In these terrible times where the Devil is abroad, it all makes sense. She and her cronies. We see it now for what it is. She is the big black spider at the centre of it all, surrounded by her coven of slatterns, drunks and whores.

It all started with that first wee lassie. Lo and behold, when she confessed, who did she name but auld wife Guthrie? Always arguing with folk, always muttering something or other. Always around when someone takes ill. Drunken behaviour.

It's been said that one day at market she walked past Robert Miller's milk kirns and the whole lot turned. He didn't make a penny that day. And it wasn't long after that that Miller's daughter became ill.

She moves around, leaving disharmony behind her. Well, no more. We've got her now.

We will spare no effort in questioning her, and then we'll have the names of the others in the coven, though we all know who they will be. All the lowest sort, drinking in the woods and making an unholy racket as they pass through the town in the wee hours.

We'll have no more of that ungodly behaviour.

So far, her tongue will not serve her to speak, but once a few more days and nights have passed I have faith we will get past the Demon, and she'll be forced to tell all.

She's standing now in the corner and still as bold as ever, head tipped back, as if she judges us! We'll soon cure her of that. I can see Davy McLean coming through from the kirk with the collar[†] *and the rest.*

She will soon know whom she serves, and it is not the Devil.

† The so-called 'witch's collar'. This was a device made of iron, often with spikes around its lower and upper edges. It was attached to a chain, which in turn would be fastened to the kirk wall or gate.

PORTRAIT OF THE ACCUSED

AGNES FINNIE

EDINBURGH 1644

Agnes Finnie was a notorious money lender and shopkeeper who lived in Potterrow Port in Edinburgh in the mid-1600s. Unusually, according to writer Mary Craig in her book about Agnes, she described herself as a witch and conducted her business openly and bad-temperedly in her shop and the surrounding neighbourhood for many years. Despite her poor bedside manner, many locals consulted her to heal the sick, particularly children. However, as life became harder in these difficult years, several of her customers and patients didn't recover, or indeed they fell ill or became injured following some of her characteristic harsh words. Eventually, Agnes's bad reputation caught up with her.

It has been argued that her denouncement worked as a kind of release for the community under all the pressure of the time. Certainly, it was a thorough condemnation. On 8 July 1644, at around the age of 48, Agnes was arrested and ultimately charged with over 20 offences, spanning some 16 years. It was said she was in 'cumpany with the Devill, in consulting wi him', and that among other things she 'tried to remove witches' malice with a gift of ale'. The records also indicate that her malice was partially caused by 'social slight', and she sought revenge for a godchild not being named after her.

Agnes's prosecution was very dragged out. The trial was on 18 December 1644, and she was held in Edinburgh's tolbooth for five months beforehand. Then the case was deliberated until 8 February 1645 and her date of execution was set a month later. In total, she was incarcerated for nearly nine months.

Eventually, on 6 March 1645, Agnes Finnie was strangled and her body burned on Castle Hill.

6

HOW TO ACCUSE A WITCH

So, you have a suspected witch in your community. What happens now?

One of the aspects of the witch trials that makes them so compelling is that these horrific events were not enacted by some sort of out-of-control mob who were taking to the streets with pitchforks, as perhaps we might be led to believe from portrayals in film and TV. Rather, the whole process was considered, thought-out and organized by the two arms of the society that should have kept people safe: the church and the law. It is perplexing to reflect on what happened then and understand that these were laws and beliefs that were seen as rational and approved by the King and God. The accusations and the trials followed a strict protocol that was punishable if communities deviated from the law.

Interestingly, the execution rates in the lower courts were much higher than those of the higher courts. This changed somewhat in 1597, when the kirk sessions (local church courts) largely took over. These kirk sessions were made up of local parish bigwigs and were more open to abuses, such as attacking Catholics and those deemed to be superstitious.

We spoke to independent scholar Judith Langlands-Scott about what happened in the kirk sessions. Judith has been a great supporter of our campaign, and it has been fascinating seeing her uncover more and more cases of the accused in the Forfar area[†] through her relentless detective work in the local archives. Judith is passionate and couthy and incredibly engaging. It's fair to say that researching the witch trials in Scotland, particularly in her home turf, has

† Forfar is a small town in the county of Angus in the east of Scotland, five miles from Glamis Castle, birthplace of the Queen Mother.

become an all-consuming passion for her. So much so that Judith has designed an incredibly beautiful and striking sleeve tattoo on her right arm that shows a stylized portrayal of one of the Forfar 'witches', Girzell Simpson, who was accused and convicted in 1661. Done in greyscale, the tattoo shows Girzell's face surrounded by the different lunar phases and various images from nature including a fox, wolf, trees and rowan berries. Alongside her co-researcher Shaun Wilson, Judith has galvanized local interest in the Forfar witches, discovered previously unknown names, headed up a local memorial, and more besides. There are many people in the area whose family have been there for hundreds of years so there is a tangible connection to these people's names – they aren't just historical details, but real people, and we think this is the vital key for engagement with history.

We were curious about exactly what occurred from the point of view of a person being accused through the trial and up to the point of conviction and execution. Our understanding through representations in popular culture implied that the community would just round on someone, literally pointing the finger. The reality was far more subtle.

Forfar saw its first witch-hunt under the Witchcraft Act in 1568–9. This trial collapsed for reasons unknown, but in July 1574 the Earl of Argyll held several more trials that saw the executions of men and women under the accusation of 'common sorcery'. Decades of relative peace followed until a spike in cases occurred in 1649–50, after the passing of the new Scottish Witchcraft Act (essentially extending the powers of the original 1563 act to deal with consulters of 'Devils and familiar spirits'). There was then a much bigger peak from 1661–2, where at least 53 people in Forfar, and some 660 people across Scotland, were accused in the space of 16 months – more than at any other time in Scottish history. It is believed around 120 were burned during that time period.[†]

† As a comparison, in the two centuries of England's witch-hunt years (between 1541, when Henry VIII made witchcraft a capital offence in England, and 1735 when the Witchcraft

This flood of cases occurred – not uncoincidentally – during a very unstable period in Scottish history. In the years prior to the events of 1661, there had been failed crops, a mini ice age, waves of death through sickness, and also the invasion of Oliver Cromwell's troops, which led to huge civil changes and unrest. In 1650, in his desire to bring the Scottish Presbyterian Church into line, Cromwell sent his forces up north to put Scotland under martial law. The Scots had proclaimed Charles I's son Charles II as king, which did not go down well with their English neighbours. After Cromwell defeated the Scottish army at Dunbar, and again at Worcester, Scotland remained occupied by an English force until Cromwell's death. This turbulent time in British history is known as the Wars of the Three Kingdoms.

Following the Restoration of King Charles II in 1660, Scotland again became an independent kingdom and regained its system of law, parliament and kirk. The Presbyterian Church of Scotland once again dominated all aspects of life. Sundays were completely given over to the community's attendance at church with hours-long sermons and sometimes as many as three services a day. The biggest peak of the Forfar witchcraft trials took place against this background of intense religious focus.

Before church, the minister would meet with his 12 elders – the apostles to his Jesus – to find out if there was any news to report of his parishioners.

'Imagine that you were an elder, you might feel a certain amount of pressure to have something juicy to tell the minister as, after all, your role is to enforce the religious code,' says Judith. 'It's your job to keep an eye on the parishioners and make sure they are toeing the line and living godly lives. You wouldn't want to appear to not be on top of things and not know everyone's business. Also, everyone in the town knows that the kirk session meets on a Sunday, so if anyone has an accusation, they'll bring it to an elder to tell the minister on their behalf.' See it, say it, sorcery.

Village life is notorious for being a place where there are no secrets, and

Act put an end to convictions across the whole of Great Britain), it is estimated that around 500 people were executed. And, of course, England has a much bigger population.

everyone knows everyone else's business.[†] This was particularly true in those days when everyone in society was a God-fearing Christian who was expected to follow a strict moral code. It would be very easy, when heightened fears of the supernatural were added to this mix, to conclude that anyone who didn't comply with these societal rules might be possessed by the Devil. Say someone was being a quarrelsome dame, cursing at people in the market, not attending church frequently enough, enjoying an inappropriate relationship – or maybe simply being 'different' to the norm, or to the gender stereotypes, or showing signs of mental illness or a learning disability or alcoholism. If a woman's behaviour is unacceptable or suspicious, could it be that she is a witch?

It's one thing for there to be scurrilous gossip, though, but how did it find its way from the minister in the kirk session to the local courts?

'Ah,' says Judith. 'It was because the elders weren't only in the church, but they were also the magistrates and the baillies. They had power at a civic level. It wasn't just the church court, but their other day selves were the law.'

Baillies were essentially the heavies for the minister enforcing his edicts and decisions. From a modern perspective it is shocking that there was no proper separation of powers. It really begs a question about who kept a check on fairness or impartiality, and whether or not such trials could be just.

'Exactly,' says Judith. 'They elected each other. It wasn't put to a vote in the town. No one asked, "Who do you want to be your magistrate?" These were men elected by other men – it was definitely not democratic.'

Although baillies weren't lawyers, they had a lot of power because everything was dealt with at local level. These men would hear the accusations and decide if the kirk session should seek a commission from the Privy Council to proceed to a trial.

This was a particular weakness of the system, according to Judith. 'If you were a baillie, it would be really easy to stitch someone up if you had a grudge. Think about how disliked politicians can be just now. If you think about what it was

† This was true even in the olden days before the advent of Facebook.

like back then, if someone was difficult towards a baillie (essentially like a local politician) then the baillie had the power to punish them.'

The kirk session met between sermons on Sunday. If someone was accused it usually happened at the first session, then they would be questioned between sermons. Sometimes the accused would be humiliated in front of the congregation before they were taken away. The aspect of public humiliation was critically important as it served as a reminder to the community of who was in charge and the consequences for not being obedient. Once the accused was taken away, he or she would of course be questioned and pushed for a confession.

In 1661, Girzell Simpson of Forfar – the subject of Judith's tattoo – was accused of being a witch.

There are no records remaining that say exactly how old Girzell was, but she wasn't married and was not described as a 'girl'. As the average age of marriage for a woman was between 22 and 26 at the time,[†] Judith's hypothesis is that Girzell was therefore probably in her late teens. After she was found guilty, she was publicly hanged from the tollbooth window in August of that year.

There is an incredibly interesting aspect to Girzell's case, which is that Judith has discovered that, unlike other 'witches', she was buried after her public execution – as Judith's research develops, she will hopefully discover exactly where. Most convicted witches' remains were destroyed without burial. Judith knows this as Girzell's parents were called to collect her remains, eight days after her death. Judith imagines that this variation from the usual turn of events is

† This average marrying age for women has largely stayed the same until more recent years when the age has gone up. We were very surprised by this as we had assumed that women married much younger. However, Judith explained to us that the labour of unmarried girls played an important part of the financial security of many families (they might work on the family's smallholding and take produce to the market, for example) and the family might therefore be reluctant to relinquish that extra pair of hands any earlier than necessary.

down to the big gap that had occurred since the previous witch trials. It leaves us with the impression that perhaps there was not enough public appetite to go on to destroy Girzell's remains after her execution, and that the townspeople were perhaps regretful after the fact.

No details remain of exactly why Girzell was accused and, again, Judith has had to fill in the gaps using other pieces of evidence. She surmises that as Cromwell's troops had not long left, Girzell was probably accused of having taken part in dalliances at best, paid sex work at worst, with the soldiers. This, of course, would have been seen as completely immoral and unacceptable, although it was quite common in Scotland at the time.

But any scandals would have sufficed to attract an accusation. Literally, 'any scandals': Judith found this wording in the archives of Inverarity, a village in Angus. Women were accused of the following acts of witchcraft in 1661–2 in Forfar: being beautiful; digging up a dead baby to eat in a pie to give themselves special, demonic powers; using cantrips and charms; causing a cow to no longer give milk due to being cursed; causing people to become ill or die due to receiving curses from the accused. This list is by no means exhaustive.

Following Girzell's execution, a flurry of further accusations ensued and several people were brought in for questioning. When the notorious witch pricker John Kincaid[†] arrived in town, all the accused confessed.

Agnes Spark, one of the first accused, had already faced public disgrace when she had been punished for being a nagging wife, and was paraded through town by her husband wearing a scold's bridle. She perfectly fits the bill as a 'troublesome dame' who was disliked locally for being a woman with too much to say for herself – the type of person on whom suspicion would naturally fall during times of strife.

Another woman accused in this group was Isobel Shyrie, an older woman who relied on the charity of the church to survive. When taxes were reintroduced after the English forces' withdrawal, a baillie, George Wood, demanded payment from Isobel. When she couldn't pay up, he took literally the only thing she owned – a

† See Chapter 7 for a fuller picture of what this involved and Kincaid's part in it.

cooking pot.[†] He would not relinquish the pot until he had his money. When Wood died some days later, Isobel was accused of witchcraft as people believed she had cursed him in revenge.

As the number of accused started to snowball, the community would no doubt have had in mind that no witch worked alone. It was popularly believed that they operated as a coven of at least 13 people, usually with one person at the centre.

At the centre of Forfar's accusations was a woman named Helen Guthrie. Although she had a tragic life, she sounds like she would be someone it would be hard to have sympathy for in real life. She was socially problematic and roundly disliked by her whole community. Her role was central to the case, as it was her testimony that implicated so many of the other accused witches.

'I don't believe I would have liked her,' says Judith. 'It would be so easy to try and claim her as some sort of feminist hero, but she isn't.'[‡]

It seems that Helen had accidentally fatally injured her sister as a child and, quite understandably, she had never recovered from the tragedy. Her mother refused to forgive her, even on her deathbed, and this perhaps hardened Helen into a difficult, cantankerous person who drank too much and caused a nuisance in the town.

In today's terms we would see Helen as someone who had experienced trauma as a young girl and we would, hopefully, have had some sympathy for her anger and self-harm. However, in the early 1660s, the issue was much more clearly linked to the Devil.

And the number of accused only continued to grow. At this time in Forfar, there were approximately 1,000 people living in town and probably around 2,000 people spread out over the surrounding countryside. Shockingly,

† She literally didn't have a pot to piss in. The origins of this phrase lie in the fact that the poor sometimes sold their urine to tanneries, so you must be truly poor if you didn't even have this means of making money. See also the phrase 'piss poor'.

‡ This is where sometimes we see the modern reclamation go awry – see, for example, the T-shirt slogan 'We are the granddaughters of the women you couldn't burn'. As well as being temporally wrong, this theory doesn't bear much scrutiny.

52 people ended up being accused, a significant percentage of the local population.

'Following the extraction of the confession, the town leaders would send for a commission to take the case further,' explains Judith. 'A commission wasn't merely a piece of paper; it was also a body of people – magistrates, baillies and so on – who would then be involved in the case. A delegation (or sometimes an individual) would be dispatched by horse to Edinburgh to go to the Privy Council.'

The Privy Council initially met in Holyroodhouse and then in the College of Justice after it was founded in 1532. This later became known as the Court of Session, which, as an advocate, Claire is very familiar with and which still looks very similar today. The Privy Council was in place from around 1490 until the start of the 18th century and it was initially created to advise the Scottish monarch. It was heavily involved in the running of Scotland, having responsibility for the administration of the law in the kingdom and various other aspects of Scottish life, including dealing with outbreaks of the plague, regulating shipping and trade, banishing gypsies and beggars, tackling criminality in the further reaches of Scotland and – crucially for our interests – managing witch epidemics.

Once at the Privy Council, the delegation would appeal to seek a commission in order to proceed to trial at home. The details of their case would be laid out and they would communicate that a confession had been secured. Usually, the commission would be brought in respect of one or two named individuals. However, this wasn't always the case and sometimes special circumstances were granted for a specified number of accused to be tried along with 'others' – allowing for a broader number of people to be tried. This meant that effectively anyone who was problematic could be swept up in the trial.

Meanwhile, back in Forfar in 1661–2, the accused were held in custody, awaiting their fate.

As neither the Privy Council nor the local court contributed anything financially, the family of the accused often had to pay for aspects of the trial such as paper, tobacco, and food and drink for the guards and questioners. This is one of the areas that Judith has studied in order to uncover new cases. She says she 'follows the money' and it's these often scrupulously kept parish financial records that shed light on who was imprisoned and executed and when. Record-keeping of confessions and court happenings often haven't survived or are incomplete or damaged. We believe that, in some cases, records were deliberately destroyed to cover up what had become an embarrassment once the witch trials had stopped.

Life was often hard for ordinary people during the two centuries of the witch-hunts. In the latter half of the 16th century the traditional wool trade declined, so in response Scotland increased its exports of salt, herring and coal – all of which were hard, dirty, dangerous and precarious industries. There were also frequent famines and outbreaks of plague. All of these factors naturally meant that money was frequently tight.

If the accused's family couldn't afford to pay the costs of the imprisonment and interrogation, the debt would fall on the town council and most likely the local burgesses would organize the payment. The burgess was something like a police commissioner – he had quasi legal power too. He'd have the power of arrest and he'd be allowed to sit on a commission. Usually, he would have gained the position through having money and connections and being voted in by his peers. The position was often also hereditary. Judith says: 'Burgesses received certain privileges in exchange for promising to protect the burgh and further its economic interests. It's likely that the position's clout and prestige would be why people did it. The guards, however, were paid a salary in various areas as it was more of a regular job. The costs of the holding of the accused and their time in custody was listed in the accounts.' It is these financial accounts that have provided Judith with so much information about the logistical aspects of the trials.

And what of the trial itself? Once the commission had been arranged and the trial agreed, how did it actually proceed?

Whereas generally a minimum of five people was needed to hold a commission, in the case of Helen Guthrie in Forfar in December 1662, 30 men sat on the commission. It would appear that all the high-status men of the town wanted to be involved in this high-profile case.

Judith explains, 'People wanted their name put to it because they very much believed they were doing the Lord's work, and they wanted the world to know. Of course, being seen to be involved in ridding Scotland of witches would also help them curry favour from those in power – hopefully even the King.'

Certainly, in this case, their work was very successful. In total, 22 witches were strangled and burned in Forfar, including Helen, who was the last woman to be executed in the town. Her 13-year-old daughter, Janet, who had also been accused, managed to escape the death sentence but was kept in prison for four more years. Her final fate is unknown.

As we have seen so often in these stories, it was the confessions of the witches themselves that led to their swift executions – in this case, it was the evidence of Helen Guthrie in particular that led so many innocent people to their death. The obvious question is: how were these incriminating confessions extracted?

Enter the witch pricker.

THE WITCH PRICKER

It is always like this. You come into town and they are all there, the great and the good, bowing and scraping before you, desperate to be seen to be on the side of the minister, of the baillies, of the men of the town. Of God, ultimately.

You are escorted to the place where they are holding the accused, usually the tollbooth, sometimes the church itself. You are led into a room and shown a woman who sits small on the ground, looking up at you, knowing her troubles have only just begun. Usually, her eyes look huge because her head has been newly shaved in preparation for your arrival.

You tell her to stand, and she does, of course she does, because no one refuses the witch pricker. The other men (and there are always other men, there is always an audience) line the room and try their best not to push forward to allow you to do what you have been summoned to do. You examine the woman with your eyes first of all. It's remarkable, over the years there have been so many women (and it's almost always women) and they all look the same. This must be down to the presence of the Devil, his creeping taint all over their pitiful faces.

You tell her to remove her clothes and she does, slowly, sometimes needing a rough help to complete the process.

Then you take out the tools of your trade. You need several bodkins even though it's usually only necessary to use one. To take the time to lay out an array of the sharp instruments creates fear in the eyes of all that behold them – especially the witch, who knows her time is running out.

You would never know the pain of the needle, of course, but you have pierced the flesh of many another whose flinches and wailing tell the tale of how painful it can be. It is worse in bonier places and satisfyingly bloodying in more fleshy areas.

It is important to give the witnesses, the accusers, the aforementioned great and good, the performance they are paying for.

You approach the accused slowly with a great show of eye contact. You must convey that you are going into a battle with the Devil through this once-human creature. Though she is now cowed and quieted, there is no knowing what she may do when cornered by one such as you. However, you are doing God's work, you must approach with the knowledge the Lord will conquer even the most heinous of opponents.

Holding the bodkin before you, you must judge if the witch will attempt to scuttle away and if you need to ask for assistance in holding the wretch down. On this occasion, the miscreant looks at you with wide, bloodshot eyes and seems frozen in place. Though it is cold in the cell, when you lay your left hand on her shoulder, her skin is hot to the touch and clammy as well.

You start with one arm. There is a small amount of blood, and the witch does not move a great deal though she is not the fleshiest of subjects. You move on to the other arm, and are still not satisfied with the witch's response or the certainty of the marks you have pricked.

The woman's trunk is next and still she does not call out. But then you spy a promising blemish under her wizened dugs and, finally, she cries out.

The men in the room all breathe out at once. You know your job here is done and the money owed to you will be forthcoming.

7
HOW TO PRICK A WITCH

In Scottish parishes and towns in the early modern period, there were two men who would hold much of the authority in the local area.

The magistrate was the man who would deal with prosaic crimes and misdemeanours such as poaching or fighting. The minister, meanwhile, would uphold the spiritual and moral values of the parish, ensuring his flock toed the line.

However, there was one man who people feared much, much more. He would sweep into town and send the populace into an immediate and febrile state of fear.

Had you offended someone or acted suspiciously? Had you a reputation for being awkward in the marketplace or for scolding your husband? Did you drink too much or beg too often?

With this man in town, would you find the finger of suspicion pointing in your direction and, ultimately, would you pay with your life?

The witch pricker had arrived and his power was absolute.

One of the most unsettling features of the witch trials was how guilt was 'proved' by searching for and (almost always) finding the 'Devil's mark' somewhere on the accused's body. This evidence was viewed the same way as today's DNA, in that it was believed to be a compelling proof of guilt. The idea of sin showing up physically on the body goes back to ancient times: you see it in mediaeval descriptions of 'leprous' skin and beliefs that warts and other skin irregularities were outward signs of evil. When Anne Boleyn was executed, there was much discussion about how many warts she had; rumours abounded that she had an extra finger (a certain sign of witchcraft). The prevailing belief was that God created us and we were made in His perfect image, so if a person had a non-perfect body, it was therefore a clear outward sign that you had been touched by the Devil.

If there was an inherent sexism in these judgements – with men inspecting women's bodies and finding them wanting – there were also issues of class and privilege at work. People of a better class had more nutritious diets and healthier lifestyles and would be less likely to suffer physical impairments than the lower classes, whose poor diet, sanitation and working conditions would show in their physical health. Either way, for anyone whose body displayed any scars, calluses, unusual moles, extra nipples or other 'deformities', there was much to fear.

The idea of the Devil's mark was first seen in the 16th century and reached a peak in the middle of the following century. It was taken up very enthusiastically in Scotland – much more so than in other countries. We would argue that this is down to the fact that different religions had different concepts of where witchcraft came from: in Catholic countries, witchcraft was believed to be a result of heresy, whereas the Protestant Church of Scotland was particularly obsessed with the Devil and his connection to witchcraft.

Certainly, the idea was strongly endorsed by King James VI, which only added to its popularity. When his book *Daemonologie* was published in 1597, one of its most compelling aspects was its description of how the Devil took people over into his employ. James describes the Devil performing a reverse baptism whereby the person would renounce their Christianity and the Devil would make his mark on their body, an indelible sore that only he could cause or cure:

> At which time, before he proceede any further with them, he first perswades them to addict themselves to his service: which being easely obteined, he then discovers what he is unto them: makes them to renunce their God and Baptisme directlie, and gives them his marke upon some secreit place of their bodie, which remaines soare unhealed, while his next

meeting with them, and thereafter ever insensible, how soever it be nipped or pricked by any, as is dailie proved, to give them a proofe thereby, that as in that doing, hee could hurte and heale them; so all their ill and well doing thereafter, must depende upon him.

James VI, *Daemonologie*, Book 2, Chapter 2

Given that this idea became such a central part of the witch accusations and trial proceedings, it is perhaps unsurprising that a profession soon evolved to facilitate it. A handful of individuals were believed to have special powers of identifying and confirming the guilt of the accused. It's generally held that the role of witch prickers is largely responsible for the exponential growth in prosecutions and executions in Scotland and England during the 17th century.

Matthew Hopkins was born in England around 1620, and his demeanour and attitude have come to embody how we think of a witch finder today. Born in Suffolk, he was the son of a Puritan minister so had some childhood training in speech-making and using the Bible to prove a point – many thought he was a lawyer due to his writing and verbal prowess, but there's no evidence he ever trained as one. He must have spotted a gap in the market, given the demand for witch prickers at the time, and realized he could use these skills to make some serious money. His career really took off during the English Civil War: although he wasn't actually appointed by Parliament, he proclaimed himself the 'Witchfinder General' – a neat bit of early self-marketing – and proceeded to oversee an extraordinarily fanatical witch-hunt in East Anglia.

Over the three years of his witch-finding career, from 1644 to 1647, it's thought that Matthew Hopkins was responsible for more witchcraft hangings than all of the previous trials of the preceding century and a half – hundreds, in fact. It is Hopkins and his colleague John Stearne who are portrayed in the 60s cult classic film *Witchfinder General*, where they are shown sweeping into town and creating a reign of terror for their own ends – an image that still holds firm in the popular imagination hundreds of years after the fact.

Hopkins and Stearne's behaviour has been described as 'weaponized belief' by the critic Adam Scovell in an article marking the 50th anniversary of the film, in reference to how the prickers created such an atmosphere of fear among the communities they visited. But paradoxically they were seen as necessary for a stable society – how better to achieve order than by having a strong authority figure who can identify those individuals working against the common good and who can rid society of their evil presence? All this while making a pretty penny too: the records at Stowmarket in Suffolk reveal they charged the town £23 (equivalent to around £5,000 today) plus travelling expenses.

Hopkins and his assistants would start their inspection by looking for the Devil's mark. The accused's body would first be shaved and then examined thoroughly. If the suspected witch had no such visible marks, invisible ones could be discovered by pricking the skin (often called 'brodding' in Scotland). The witch finder would employ specialist 'witch prickers' – instruments such as needles or sometimes knives – to pierce the accused's flesh. It was thought that a witch would have areas on her body that would not bleed – either because they were the place where the Devil had kissed her to seal their pact, or because this was the spot from which she suckled her 'familiars'.[†] Therefore if the skin did not bleed after it had been pricked, this was 'proof' of her guilt.

Hopkins supposedly had a trick to help ensure success with this aspect of his craft: it is believed he had a special pin made with a retractable blade, the point retracting into the handle when it met resistance. Overleaf is an illustration from Reginald Scot's sceptical book, *The Discoverie of Witchcraft* (1584), which proposed that most witchcraft was nothing more than stage magic. We have tried in vain to find surviving bodkins but there seem to be none in any public museums in Scotland.[‡] The 'false bodkins' that Scott features look to all intents

† Here we see differing folkloric traditions to explain the same idea. Magic is the opposite of the bureaucratic process: it has no rules and regulations.

‡ We did, however, discover that there are some strange people who acquire instruments of torture for their own private collections. We do not approve of this and think they should be held by bona fide museums just as the ephemera from, say, concentration camps or notorious

and purposes like the real things but could be used by unscrupulous 'witch prickers' to 'prove' the existence of a witch and collect the pay. We spoke to Scottish historian and writer Mary Craig to see what light she could shed on the practice of witch pricking. Mary, a former Carnegie scholar, has written extensively about the history of Northern Europe from Mata Hari to Anne Frank. She also has a wry sense of humour and a gift for describing history in vivid, realistic terms. It was Mary who introduced us to the concept of 'quarrelsome dames' and how this could be considered one of the first 'tests' of being a witch. Mary, herself, would no doubt have been seen as a quarrelsome dame had she been alive in the 17th century, and we mean this as the highest of compliments.†

Surely, we suggested, pricking had a sexual element to it? After all, the accused were stripped naked, had their heads shaved (thereby reducing their femininity), and were then searched all over and in their most intimate areas by the men of their community (usually led by the minister) in an act almost guaranteed to prove their guilt of sin.

Mary nodded and drew the contrast between Witchfinder General Matthew Hopkins and his assistant John Stearne.

'John Stearne was a devout, religious man. He was terrified by the Devil, and he was out to find witches and condemn them to death. Matthew Hopkins was a sexual pervert who went about grabbing young girls and making as much money as he could. Matthew Hopkins didn't give a monkey's. John Stearne is mainly remembered only for the fact that in 1648 he wrote a book called *A Confirmation and Discovery of Witchcraft*. But Hopkins was great at self-promotion and called himself the Witchfinder General, so he has made a far greater impact on the public consciousness.'

Hopkins was very young to have had such influence and was only around 27 years old when he died. So, could we see Matthew Hopkins as a 17th-century equivalent of the toxic male influencers of the 21st century?

---

murders should be. They are historical artefacts and should not be used as entertainment or for commercial gain.

† We would describe ourselves thus too, as anyone who listens to the podcast will know.

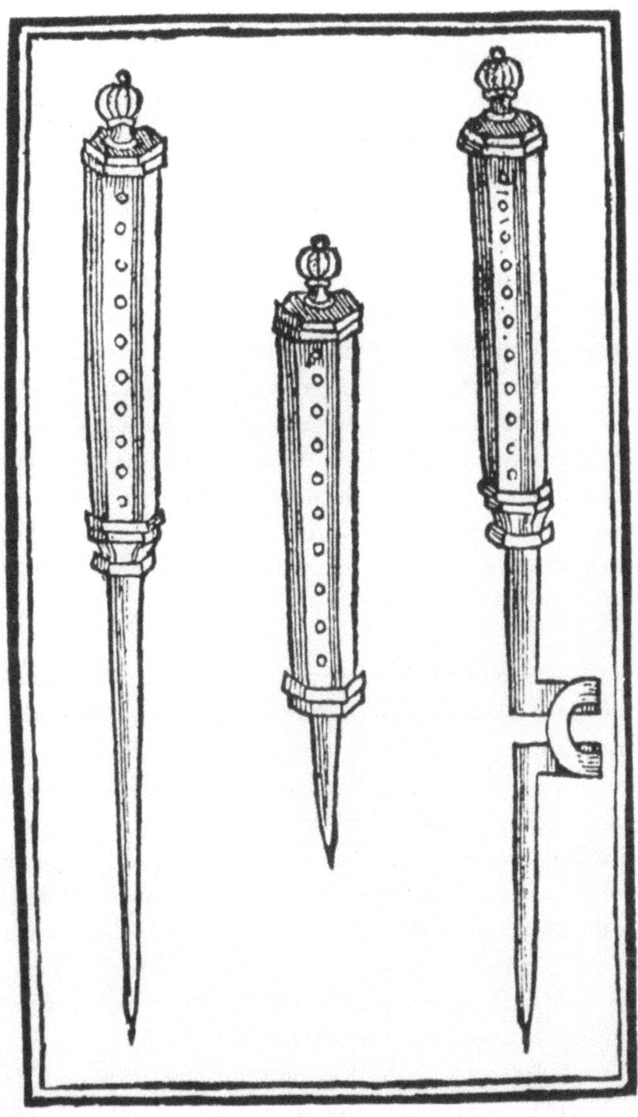

Engraving of retractable bodkins, from *The Discoverie of Witchcraft* by Reginald Scot, 1584

'Yes,' Mary answers. 'Matthew Hopkins was having a great time to himself. At the time people genuinely were frightened of the Devil and were trying to find his handmaidens. But it's a system where anybody could just pitch up and say, "I'm a witch pricker, and by the way, get your kit off so I can run my hands all over your body."'

There were of course, genuinely religious witch prickers who fervently believed they were doing the Lord's work. But others were driven by money and power, and others by sexual appetite or even sadism. Some will no doubt have been driven by a combination of all of these factors.

Money was certainly a corrupting influence. As prickers were paid by the head, there was nothing to discourage the unscrupulous from deliberately inflating the numbers of those found guilty. And they would always be paid, whatever the outcome: their evidence was essential for the Privy Council to proceed legally. There was also that implicit threat that if the pricker wasn't paid then the community would be at risk. And who's to say that the next person to be accused of witchcraft wouldn't be . . . you? It was the ultimate racket.

We were curious about whether there were differences between England and Scotland in the role of the prickers. Although there were witch prickers in Scotland, there didn't seem to be anyone of quite the enduring reputation as Hopkins. The nearest Scottish equivalent was a man called John Kincaid, but he was quite a different creature to Hopkins.

In Scotland, more moderate, and therefore perhaps more scrupulous, prickers (or 'brodders', as they were known north of the border) would put their hands only on the accused's head and neck, as that was where they believed the Devil would touch you, or where the reverse baptism occurred. There are records that Kincaid would ask for the accused to have their heads shaved and their shoulders bared, as opposed to requesting complete nakedness.

However, that's not to say that Kincaid was an honourable man. He made a great deal of money from his 'profession'. Very little is known about his background. It would appear that he was illiterate, as any papers he was involved with that have been found in archives bear just his mark or initials. Literacy proficiency aside, Kincaid was obviously a compelling pricker as over his career he was involved in anywhere between 150 and 200 executions. During the height of the vogue for witch prickers between 1648 and 1662, Kincaid was personally involved in two major surges in 1649–50 and 1661–2.

John Kincaid was based mostly in Tranent in East Lothian. Born somewhere between 1590 and 1600, he was already well into middle age when he first surfaces in the records in 1649, and evidence suggests he was already firmly established within his trade by that point. In June that year, Kincaid was called to Dirleton Castle in North Berwick to investigate the accusations made against Patrick Watson and his wife, Menie Halliburton. Tragically, it was the couple themselves who had requested Kincaid's presence to prick them, on the assumption that as he was doing God's work, he would know they were innocent. However, Kincaid announced that he had found Devil's marks on the couple and, damningly, when he pricked them, no blood was seen to appear. Watson was executed, closely followed by Halliburton, who confessed to acts of witchcraft and to having sex with the Devil. Knowing what the accused went through during questioning and that her husband had just been executed, it's perhaps unsurprising that Halliburton 'confessed' as she was likely a broken woman.

Kincaid mainly worked in the Lothian area, but he also travelled as far north as Aberdeen when he was requested by magistrates. He has been identified brodding as far south as Newcastle in the same year as the Dirleton case, where he earned 20 shillings for every witch he identified. That was a significant rate of pay and would surely encourage prickers to find more witches. There were other perks, too. Records indicate that when Kincaid worked for the parish of Dunfermline that same year, his accommodation costs were paid as well as a fee of 20 merks in the case of one Bessie Mourton who was found guilty and executed. In addition, he was paid by the Burncastle Estate for his role in the trial of a woman called Margaret Dunholm, who lived on the Scottish Borders and was also executed that year – £6 plus another £3 for food and wine for him and his assistant. It was nice work if you could get it.

Fast forward to 1659 and we come across the trial of Barbara Cochrane in

Kincaid's hometown of Tranent. Kincaid found two marks on her back near her left shoulder. The marks didn't respond to his brodding and therefore Cochrane was found guilty. It is said that when Kincaid declared her guilt, Cochrane cried out, 'Foul thief! Thou has deceived me!' Whether this recrimination was directed at Kincaid whom it's speculated she paid a sum of money to or at the Devil for forsaking her in her hour of need, we'll never know.

In that year in Scotland, 38 people were executed for witchcraft and nearly half were in East Lothian – with Kincaid recorded as the pricker in many of these cases.

Still, Kincaid's work continued. Two years later, a midwife from Newbattle in Midlothian, Beatrix Leslie, who was in her 80s, was accused of malefice and witchcraft. Two girls had died in a coal-pit accident after having an argument with Leslie over the killing of a cat; fingers naturally pointed at the old woman. Kincaid was called in to prick Leslie and, as the case involved the death of two children, he also performed a peculiar practice called 'bierricht' to assess her guilt.[†] This ancient ritual, also known as 'cruentation' from the Latin word *cruentare* meaning to make bloody, involved the accused being made to touch the body of their alleged victim, as it was believed that the corpse was still sentient for a short while after death, so would bleed or froth at the mouth when the murderer made contact. The girls' bodies supposedly bled when Leslie was brought to them, so she was found guilty and executed on 3 September 1661.

In fact, it was a busy year for Kincaid in 1661; he identified so many witches in Forfar, Angus (in the trials we discussed in the previous chapter), that he was given the freedom of the burgh as a reward.

However, even though Kincaid enjoyed a long period of prosperity and public approval, the tide turned on 9 January 1662 when the Privy Council received an application for his arrest. It seems the Council had become concerned about the lack of supervision of witchcraft trials and word of his abuses had reached their ears, which clearly did not reflect well on them. By now an old man of 60 or 70, Kincaid was imprisoned in the Old Tolbooth in Edinburgh, where he admitted

† A bier being the name for the stand that carried a corpse or a coffin.

that he had not only been using deception when pricking for the Devil's mark but had also been practising – almost more problematically from the authorities' point of view – without a Privy Council warrant. The official report submitted to the Privy Council concluded that Kincaid had strayed from his original religious fervour into cruelty and had harmed many innocents, concluding: 'There hath bein great abuses committed by John Kincaid.'

After some time, incarcerated, but not having been formally charged, the elderly Kincaid petitioned for his release. Upon posting a bail of £1,000 (equivalent to approximately £50,000 these days), Kincaid was released as long as he agreed not to work again without a warrant. However, seeing as he could afford such a huge bail fee, it seems clear that he had already made his fortune.

Despite the obvious miscarriage of justice that had occurred, there are no records of any appeals or releases taking place on cases founded on his questionable evidence. Kincaid slips back into historical obscurity again, though his name does appear once more in the records of a witch trial in 1690 when it is posthumously invoked as a threat. His reputation clearly left a long shadow in Scotland.

Not all prickers were men. Scotland's other most notorious brodder, Christian Caddell, was a woman, most likely in her late 20s or early 30s. In the early 1660s Scotland was whipped up into such a frenzy over witch activity that work was readily available for those who wanted it. It's believed, through oral history, that Caddell was inspired to take on the profession when she saw Kincaid at work in Newburgh, Fife, or she may even have started off working as his assistant.

Why would a woman want to do this work? The financial incentive was surely one reason – what other way could a woman earn such riches in this period? But also, the witch-pricking trade offered a certain amount of security in a febrile society. If you were the one pointing the finger at someone else, you were much less likely to be accused yourself. Arguably, and ignoring the moral dubiety, it was pragmatic and even clever of Caddell to pursue this career. She was able to keep herself safe, while making a very decent living out of others' misfortune.

There are, again, scant records of Caddell's career. What we do know is that she turned up in Elgin in March 1662, disguised as a man and calling herself John Dick or Dickson. It appears no one knew she was really a woman; after all, witch pricking was man's work. She was contracted by a John Innes, the baillie of Spynie in Moray. Innes signed Caddell/Dickson up for a year where she was to be paid a generous daily rate of six shillings with a further six shillings per identified witch. Men in those days earned about a shilling a day on average, so Caddell/Dickson was doing very well for herself indeed. Not surprisingly, she 'found' a great many witches. It's thought that it was Caddell who identified perhaps the most famous of the Scottish witches, Isobel Gowdie, who was accused in Nairn in 1662. (We will come to her story in Chapter 9.)

Caddell came close to exposure when she pricked a court messenger called John Hay in Tain. Hay's prestigious job bore the royal seal and, worse for Caddell, he had some legal knowledge and influence that he used to petition the government for his pricker's arrest. In his petition he described his treatment:

> Ane cheating fellow, named John Dick, to fix ane blott of perpetural infamie upon the petitioner by shaving all the parts of his body, and ther after pricking him to the great effusion of his blood and with much torture to his body.

There are no further records about what happened to Hay, although we are hopeful that, due to his standing, he was not condemned. Caddell herself seems to have moved on elsewhere, despite her arrest warrant, and continued to ply her trade. By June 1662, she was working in Strathglass in the Northwest Highlands, where a commission had just been issued for the so-called Strathglass witches. It was a case that was to prove her final undoing.

The accusations were cynical and corrupt from the start. It seems a Strathglass landowner called Chisholm of Cromer had formulated a plan to clear his land of a local tenant family called the Macleans, who had been living there peacefully for the past two centuries. Chisholm contrived to have a group of Macleans charged and questioned by the religious leaders of two nearby villages, Kiltarlity and Kilmorack. The accused, 14 women and one man, were taken to the church at Wardlaw. There, Caddell, now using the name James Paterson, aka 'Paterson the Pricker', shaved their heads in the churchyard, hid the hair in a stone dyke[†] and set to work.

In the words of the minister of the Wardlaw church, Reverend James Fraser:

> There came then to Inverness one Mr Paterson who had run over the kingdom for trial of witches, and was ordinarily called the Pricker, because his way of trial was with a long brass pin. Stripping them naked, he alleged that the spell spot was seen and discovered. After rubbing over the whole body with his palms, he slipt in the pin, and, it seems, with shame and feare being dasht, they felt it not, but he left it in the flesh, deep to the head, and desired them to find and take it out.

A contemporary witness noted the accused were horribly tortured:

> . . . by waking, hanging them up by the thombes, burning the soles of their feet at the fyre, drawing of others at horse taills and binding of them with widdies about the neck and feet and carrying them so alongst on horseback to prison, whereby and by other tortur one of them hath become distracted, another by their cruelt is departed this lyfe, and all of them have confest whatever they were pleasit to demand of them.

Faced with this torture, it is of course no surprise that all the accused confessed. Satisfied with this outcome, the Privy Council deemed the application secure

† Why was the hair hidden in the dyke? Perhaps it was to do with the old superstition whereby people would put bones, shoes and bottles of urine in the walls of their homes to protect from witchcraft, the idea being that the witch would become distracted and would focus on the items rather than the inhabitants. Or maybe it was just an extra layer of humiliation and dehumanization.

enough to award commissions to Chisholm, along with his brother and cousins, so they could conduct the trial.

However, the husband of one of the accused had the wherewithal to approach Sir Rory Maclean of Duart, a Maclean clan chief, who managed to convince the Privy Council that Chisholm was using the witchcraft accusations as a non-legal means to remove his tenants. Finally, the Privy Council saw sense and in October 1662 they sent a notary called John Neilson to examine the accused for evidence of torture. Unfortunately, the examination was skewed by the fact that Neilson did not ask directly if the accused had been tortured. In addition, and perhaps more unsettlingly, Caddell was allowed to stand at the door of the cell and watch proceedings.

Neilson must have had his suspicions, though, as the accused were set free (although, tragically, it seems other members of the Maclean family died while still in custody). Caddell was arrested and sent to the Old Tolbooth in Edinburgh. There – surprise! – it was discovered that Paterson/Dickson/Dick was actually Miss Christian Caddell. One can only imagine how this revelation was received by the local grandees, who had unknowingly been trusting a mere woman to do their work for so long.

Caddell – presumably grasping at straws to save herself – then bizarrely claimed that she had the power to discover witches by looking into her victims' eyes. But this time she was not believed. Her reign as Scotland's most notorious witch pricker had finally come to an end.

Unlike her victims, Caddell was not executed, but her punishment was to be transported to Barbados as an indentured servant. It was arranged that she would travel on the ship the *Mary of Leith* where she would be held with a number of other convicts.

During her brief spell as a witch pricker, Christian Caddell had become a rich woman. She had also been responsible for the deaths of at least six innocent people, although it is suspected that she was involved in at least ten convictions in total.

In a final, haunting coincidence, it's likely that on the day that Caddell set sail, 4 May 1663, her two final victims, Isobel Elder and Isobel Simpson from Forres in the north of Scotland, were being executed by strangulation and subsequent burning.

Looking back on it now, we wondered if it was clear to anyone that Caddell wasn't a man under her disguise or if it was a genuine shock for people when she was revealed as a fraudster woman.

'I think it was a case of the Emperor's new clothes,' says Mary. 'Because would you want to take the risk of saying she [Caddell] was actually a woman? What if you were wrong? Or what if, in fact, you were then accused of being a witch for suggesting such a thing?'

As we have found again and again, the fear that ruled the land through the early modern period simply meant that many people kept their heads down and turned a blind eye to things that seemed wrong. It was an atmosphere perhaps akin to the days of post-war East Germany when children were encouraged at school to report their own parents for misdeeds. The Maclean case in particular encapsulates the terrible dangers of people capitalizing (quite literally) on fear. It is the clearest example we have come across of how witch accusations could be used completely immorally as a cover for personal gain, from the appalling greed of Chisholm to the horrific sadism of Caddell.

Given the degree of her fraudulence, not to mention the severity of her crimes in sending innocent people to death, how was it that Caddell got off so lightly, after she was exposed? Mary says the reason is far from clear. 'I find it really weird that Caddell wasn't executed,' she says.

Claire speculates that perhaps it was because she had so much work through the legal structures of the day, that her exposure intrinsically undermined the whole system. How could the powers-that-be admit to the fact that her crimes had occurred for so long with their approval and without her being apprehended? Sending Caddell abroad meant that the Privy Council could avoid the inevitably notorious show trial where it would be revealed that a woman (a woman!) had most publicly pulled the wool over various communities of magistrates and ministers and other men of good standing.

Caddell had deceived the highest courts in the land and brought about the hideous, unlawful fates of many people. Much simpler just to ship her off abroad where she would disappear from the sight and imagination of the Scottish public.

'That ties in with my theory about John Kincaid,' says Mary. 'He was just arrested and quietly released.'

Furthermore, how could the Privy Council be sure they wouldn't be fooled by a charlatan again? After all, there were no formal qualifications for witch prickers.

'There are stories in parish records that witch prickers just appeared,' says Mary. 'You know, like Davy from the end of the street. So, when John Kincaid first got going, he just started witch pricking before he had a warrant from the Privy Council. It was only when he started doing it and people said, "Oh, he's really good," that he started to get a reputation and approval from the Privy Council.'

In the end, these great men had been taken in by Caddell's self-assurance, ironically a trait more often associated with men than women. There certainly must have been a certain element of showmanship to the pricker's art. People thought Matthew Hopkins was a lawyer because he spoke so well. This type of confidence goes a long way – behold the ongoing phenomenon of the temerity of mediocre men. If you act like you're right, people will generally believe the confidence even without evidence. We only need to look at recent British and American politicians to see how this confidence trick still works.

It was all rather embarrassing. Much better for all concerned to move the issue along by dealing with it swiftly and quietly.

The less said, the better.

In his book *Witch-Hunting in Scotland: Law, Politics and Religion*, historian Brian Levack argues that the Privy Council's decision to lock up Kincaid in 1662 for fraudulent and deceptive practices was a tipping point for the ending of the 1661–2 witch-hunt. Caddell's arrest the same year no doubt also contributed to the disquiet.

It seemed that finally the dark art of witch pricking was coming to an end, though it was still far from the end of the witch-hunts themselves, both in Scotland and abroad. In fact, across the Atlantic in America, a small town in Massachusetts was about to become the centre of the most famous witch panic of all . . .

PORTRAIT OF THE ACCUSED

TITUBA

SALEM 1692

Tituba was the first woman to be accused of witchcraft in the witch trials at Salem, Massachusetts, in 1692. Our knowledge of Tituba is limited, as she was an enslaved person and, as a result, her story has turned towards myth over the course of the trial itself, and certainly in the years since. What we do know about Tituba was that she was likely of Native American descent.[†] She had been working in a plantation in Barbados owned by a wealthy man named Samuel Parris, and he brought her to Salem when she was a teenager. In 1692, Parris became the Puritan minister of Salem Village, on the edge of the town.

The trouble for Tituba started when Samuel Parris's daughter Betty and her cousin Abigail Williams (age nine and 11, respectively) decided to play at fortune telling, a popular pastime in Salem at that point, but very much against Puritan rules. This had nothing to do with witchcraft and, more importantly, nothing to do with Tituba. The girls had been breaking an egg into water, the idea being that the shape that the egg took in the liquid enabled the participants to divine what was going to happen in the future. Unfortunately, what the children saw was the shape of a coffin. Immediately, the girls started barking, behaving hysterically, and having what looked like seizures. These continued to occur over the next month with no medical explanation, so the work of witches became the obvious solution.

† Tituba was described as 'Indian' 15 times in the court papers, although over time she became black in the public imagination. In 1952, the playwright Arthur Miller described her as a 'Negro slave' when he wrote his account of the Salem witch trials, *The Crucible*. But she may have been a native of South America, or since she was brought from Barbados, she might have had African roots. No one really knows.

Upon questioning, the girls named three vulnerable women: Sarah Osborne, Sarah Good and Tituba (Tituba had also tried to help the girls by making a 'witch cake' out of rye flour and urine). When Parris discovered Tituba's involvement, he was absolutely furious and beat her to elicit a confession that she was practising witchcraft. Tituba confessed to a detailed and fantastical number of things, including: having familiars (rats, cats, hogs, wolves, dogs and birds), signing the Devil's book, flying on a stick, and pinching the young girls of Salem. During her confession, she also claimed there were other witches in the town. This was enough to light the fuse of the infamous wave of paranoia and community panic known as the Salem witch trials. In total, over 200 people were accused and 20 executed, with at least a further five dying in jail.

Tituba's involvement in this story is interesting for several reasons. Firstly, despite the fact that she was accused of being a witch at least partially because of her ancestry, all her witch descriptions were of a European nature, rather than Native American, Caribbean or African. Secondly, Tituba was the only accused woman who wasn't white. And thirdly, despite her extraordinary confession, when she finally went to trial 15 months later, Tituba was not found guilty. Perhaps these last two facts are linked: there has been speculation that Salem society didn't see witches as anything other than white.

Eventually, the tide turned among the populace against the idea that witches had a stranglehold on Salem and the governor ordered an end to the trials and accusations. After her release, Tituba recanted her confession, revealing that her master had beaten her in order to confess.

Nothing is known of what happened to Tituba upon her release and, sadly, as she was enslaved, owned no property, had no rights and no one to speak for her, she slipped back into the shadows of history.

8

HOW TO KILL A WITCH THE AMERICAN WAY

Sarah Good, Sarah Osborne, Tituba.

The names seem so familiar, the Salem witch trials having worked their way into our consciousness over the hundreds of years since the notorious events took place in that Massachusetts town in 1692.

When people think about witch trials, they usually think of what happened in Salem. The common misconception is that this was 'the big one' – the most hysterical, brutal and iconic witch-hunt of them all.

But the truth is that the trials in Europe, particularly in Scotland, were far larger, more widespread and bloodier, with much greater death tolls. Thankfully, due to the work of several excellent historians and the debate thrown up by our own campaign and podcast – not to mention others that have been developed since – this pre-eminence of Salem in the league of witch trial shame is at last being questioned.

But Salem was always an unusual case and has thus always attracted attention. In many ways the Salem witch trials of 1692 were the exception to all the rules of colonial American witch trials. There had been trials of this nature in the English colonies before Salem, where a few people might have been executed, but this was of a different scale – albeit much smaller than the extreme purges of Scotland. Salem was a last gasp of superstition at the dawn of a new era.

What is fascinating to us about Salem is that these chilling events perfectly encapsulate what happens when a religious 'solution' is used to address social disharmony and anxiety, in a bid to regain control. So while Salem was not a typical case, it's incredibly useful as a tool to illuminate how and why witch trials functioned as they did.

And, arguably, it is also down to Salem that the modern positive reclamation of witches and magic has gained real traction. America took a grim episode in its history and in some ways redirected it, possibly through the swift recognition that there had been a miscarriage of justice, but also through commercializing the concept of witches and reframing the narrative.

When we spoke to Rachel Christ-Doane, the director of education for the Salem Witch Museum, she laughingly told us that the museum frequently has Scottish visitors who are fascinated by Salem but are completely unaware of Scotland's much bigger and deadlier trials. It's clear from our public engagement that this is an indication that the witch trials are rarely taught in Scottish schools, overshadowed as they are by world wars and the Industrial Revolution. Ask us anything you want about the benefits of farming Cheviot sheep after the Highland Clearances and we could name it. Witch trials? As school kids we knew nothing. Thankfully, we are now frequently contacted by educators throughout the United Kingdom who are teaching about the witch trials and who use our podcast as a resource. We are delighted by this turn of events as it is so important to understand your own country's history, no matter how uncomfortable or fraught.

And yet, Salem still exerts a real hold over the witch trial narrative. Why is this and why are witch trials generally still so relevant in the 21st century?

We initially spoke to Rachel via Zoom when she was in her office at the museum during the pandemic. Rachel is a relaxed and warm figure. She brings a modern sensibility and take on Salem and what it says about human nature, particularly in times of social stress.

Usually, of course, the Salem Witch Museum would have been incredibly busy, as is Salem itself. In October every year, the town, which normally has a population of less than 45,000, welcomes more than 100,000 visitors on the Saturday of Halloween alone. Over the course of the year, Salem receives in excess of two million visitors. This tourism is clearly a double-edged sword in that it brings in much-needed revenue to the restaurants, bars and witch-related attractions in the town, but is also hugely problematic for residents trying to go about their business. In fact, for many residents of what has come to be known as 'Witch City', Salem becomes a no-go zone in October. Part of the issue is that this huge influx of visitors is not coming to a custom-built theme park, but a small town with a historic infrastructure of little streets and not enough parking for tens of thousands of people. This Disneyfication of Salem is also problematic as historians and those who know the real story of the trials want, quite rightly, to focus on the miscarriage of justice and the people who lost their lives. How should we feel about hordes of people descending on a town for a diverting day out because it accused people of being witches 300 years ago? Accusations that ultimately lead to the executions of 20 people and more who died incarcerated?

The Salem Witch Museum is located on the land of the former home of the Reverend John Higginson, who was born in 1616 in England and came to Salem in 1629 with his father, Francis, the first minister of Salem. The young John Higginson followed in his father's footsteps by becoming a clergyman and he took a minor part in the Salem witchcraft trials himself when he interviewed a four-year-old child, Dorothy Good, who had been sent to prison. The trials came much closer to home when Higginson's own adult daughter, Ann Dolliver, was also accused of witchcraft for using poppets, small wax effigies. She admitted to owning the poppets but denied that she had meant to do any harm. Thankfully, she was eventually released without trial and returned to live with her father.

In 1844, the present imposing building that now houses the museum was built to house the Second Unitarian Church of Salem. It is a brownstone-and-brick Gothic Revival structure and it remained a fully operational church until 1902. The museum was opened in May 1972 – its mission to connect the thousands of visitors to the true facts of the case, and provoke thoughts about the very real ongoing issues with othering and justice.

'I've gotten really obsessed with why it's of such interest,' says Rachel.

'Gretchen Adams has written about how Salem became a "critical metaphor" in the years after the trials. You so often hear people say, "This is like the Salem witch trials."' Adams outlines how that idea of Salem being a metaphor for mass hysteria actually started almost immediately after the events occurred. 'You see people invoke the metaphor of Salem to criticize events of their time. It happens as early as the 1720s during a smallpox epidemic in Boston and it happens again and again. We tend to think of Arthur Miller's play *The Crucible* as the first time this critical metaphor is used and, of course, with this play he's criticizing McCarthyism and the Communist blacklist; American students learn that in high school.[†] But in truth it started much earlier than that.'

In fact, during the American Civil War, the Confederates attacked the Unionists in propagandist pamphlets, saying that the North had to get off their moral high horses about slavery because they were no better: after all, they had burned women at the stake. This, in itself, was a confusion of the facts, as women were rarely killed in this way – strangulation was by far the most common method of execution. And yet this Confederate accusation became the basis for the popularization of the trope of witches being burned at the stake.

It's all very messy. What did happen in Salem? What do we *really* know?

Let's start with the facts.

It all began in January 1692, when Betty Parris, the nine-year-old daughter of Samuel Parris, the minister of Salem, and the minister's niece Abigail Williams, who was 11, both became ill with a mysterious recurring ailment. What we would now likely call seizures struck both girls. They fell to the ground and made sounds that were described as 'animal-like' – surely very frightening to the adults around them, who were powerless and bewildered. Their families tried praying and fasting to help the girls, but a month later, the seizures were still occurring. The services of a doctor were called upon but he couldn't find any medical explanation for what

† It is also taught very frequently in Scotland and partially explains why many Scots know about Salem, but not their own connections to witch trials.

came to be known as 'the affliction', and instead he suggested it could be a case of witchcraft. In the late 1600s, just as in Scotland, Salem's inhabitants absolutely believed in the reality of the Devil and his ability to use witches to do his evil bidding. The townsfolk duly set about trying to identify who the witch was.

The girls were questioned, no doubt feeling under a certain amount of pressure or maybe believing this might end their suffering. Perhaps they even enjoyed the attention. In response, they offered up three names: Sarah Osborne, Sarah Good and Tituba. As we have so often seen with witch trials, the people named were isolated and vulnerable. Sarah Osborne was someone whom the community felt had disgraced herself by marrying below her station – she'd married a servant and had not been attending church as frequently as Puritan society demanded. Sarah Good was poor and often rude and aggressive; she would loudly curse those she begged from if she felt they were short-changing her.

And then there was the enslaved woman, Tituba, whom we have already met. Tituba was to all intents and purposes at the bottom of the pile in Salem society.

The three women were examined by the community's leaders. Both Sarahs denied any knowledge of witchcraft, but Tituba, for whatever reason, confessed. Moreover, as we also frequently saw in Scotland, she claimed there were other witches in Salem.[†]

Why did Tituba confess? Possibly because, as an enslaved person, she knew no one would help or defend her, and also, most likely, she was beaten until she said what they wanted to hear. But whatever the reason, with the idea that there were other witches at large in Salem, proceedings kicked up a gear.

Rachel explains, 'Things start to spiral out of control pretty quickly. Suddenly anybody you've had a problem with, anyone who you've had a border dispute with, anyone you think stole from you 20 years ago, or broke social taboos like yelling at your husband publicly – these are the people who start to get targeted.'

Also, Salem had recently lost its charter, basically an operating system for the town, which meant the town's leaders were in a state of flux while they waited to see how their legal system and courts would operate and who would be elected

† Perhaps those accused thought naming others might make the torture stop.

The Salem Witch Trials, Joseph E. Baker, 1892

to office. They lost their charter in 1684 and didn't get it back until 1692. It was an unsettling period for the townsfolk.

'They were in this weird legal limbo,' says Rachel. 'Without the charter they didn't know what their government would look like. Would they have a royally appointed governor? Would they be allowed to appoint their own representatives, which they had been doing up until that point? What would their taxes look like? Would they increase? Would the King take back the land they had tilled and distributed, so they would have to start again from scratch? You can see how this would be a period of extreme tension, especially for those ministers who came to Salem to start a city upon a hill where everything would be done right as they're God's chosen people. It really looked like it might all come crashing down.'

The Salem ministers were fearful that their great Puritan experiment would not only fail, but fail humiliatingly on their watch. And then on top of all this political and religious uncertainty comes a witchcraft outbreak.

'It's easy for them then to think the Devil has descended on Massachusetts and is waging war on them,' says Rachel. 'This is what they've been waiting for, in some ways. The leaders are in a state of panic.'

Salem couldn't carry out normal legal proceedings until the charter was arranged. As a result, there were already many people held in custody, waiting for their trials. An emergency court was put together to deal with the accused women. What this meant was that the Salem court was able to get away with importing some extraordinary legal practices from other countries like England that were not normally used. The precedent for the Salem trials is understood to have been the trial of two English widows called Amy Denny and Rose Cullender, which took place in Bury St Edmunds in Suffolk in 1662. The trial was presided over by Matthew Hale, later to become the Lord Chief Justice of England.[†] Evidence was heard from several children who said they were attacked

† If the name Matthew Hale is familiar, his opinion that abortion was a great crime was cited in a first draft opinion by Justice Alito in the case of Dobbs v Jackson Women's Health Organization in 2022, the case that overturned Roe v Wade.

and threatened by invisible spectres of the women. This was accepted as truth and the two elderly widows were hanged.

Despite its obvious faults, 'spectral evidence' was similarly admitted into the proceedings at Salem, as a result of the Bury St Edmunds precedent. Witnesses claimed to be able to see the spectres of the various accused people practising witchcraft and oftentimes physically attacking them in their spectral form. Just to be clear: it was accepted as evidence admissible in law for a witness to testify that they had had a dream or a vision of an accused person's spirit tormenting them, even though the accused's physical body was provably elsewhere.

As part of her confession and evidence in court, Tituba described her co-accused as having familiars that no one else could see, describing Sarah Osborne's and Sarah Good's as a yellow bird and two 'grotesque creatures'. There were also claims that witnesses had seen the dead in ghost form and that the ghosts had harassed them. Out of the total of 156 people accused and incarcerated, 79 of them had their charges based on spectral evidence alone.

It's hard for us to understand these days how this ever could have happened. Rachel agrees. 'It didn't make sense even in the 17th century. There was discussion about using spectral evidence at the time. There were letters from ministers saying, "We respect the court, but maybe don't use this evidence."' But the court carried on using it, because previously it had been very difficult to prove guilt and they had become fixated on finding guilt where they could.

Bridget Bishop was the first person to be convicted and she was hanged on 10 June on Gallows Hill in Salem Village. Nine days later another five people, among them Sarah Good who said that she was no more a witch than the judge was a wizard, were executed in the same place. On 19 August, a further five were executed. This group included George Burroughs who had been a minister in Salem until 1683 and who recited the Lord's Prayer as he stood at the gallows preparing to meet his maker. It's hard to understate how troubling this would have been to the sceptical in the community, as witch-hunt logic held that a real witch would be unable to utter God's word. However, 22 September saw another eight convicted people hanged. Among them was

Martha Corey, whose 81-year-old husband Giles had refused to submit a plea when arrested and who was subsequently pressed to death under stones. It took two days for him to die.

Tensions began to form between two groups of magistrates. One side were determined to see the 'due process' through to the end, while a more moderate group were starting to think that while there may have been witches, the rate at which they were executing meant that innocent people were likely being killed as well.

The tide began to turn in October, when Lady Mary Phips, the wife of Sir William Phips, the Governor of Massachusetts, was accused of being a witch. She had been named by one of the 'victims' using spectral evidence.

The governor, realizing that his wife wasn't a witch, finally came to the conclusion that spectral evidence was unsound, and he moved to halt the court.[†] It took a further several months to organize a new formal court the following January. Thankfully, this new court agreed that it did not accept spectral evidence. Most people still in custody ended up being acquitted, although a couple of guilty verdicts remained. The governor took decisive action, declared them all innocent, and (most) people were released from jail.[‡]

The Salem witch-hunt was over, but the story was a long way from ending.

What happened next in Salem is crucial to its place in our popular culture of today.

As the 17th century came to a close, social change was in the air. The survivors started pushing for a public, formal acknowledgement of how badly they'd been

† It's funny that it was only when matters were brought to his own door that he finally said, 'Wait a minute, are we absolutely sure we are not killing innocent women?'

‡ Though you couldn't leave until you paid your bill! You were charged for everything from food to clothes to chains and some people, deeply in debt, could not afford to settle up and died innocent in jail.

treated. This is in direct contrast to Scotland where we are still campaigning, 300 years later, for a legal pardon for those found guilty of witchcraft.

When Elizabeth Proctor was accused and convicted in Salem in 1692, she was pregnant. Her pregnancy saved her from being immediately put to death as the decision was taken to delay her execution until after she had given birth. Her husband John Proctor, not so fortunate, was executed. By the time the baby was born, the trials were over, but Elizabeth was left in a peculiar position. She had been found guilty of being a witch, and so she remained a witch in the eyes of the law. She presented herself to the court and made her case. They gave her a reprieve from execution, but in terms of her status there was nothing to be done – she was still legally a witch. Elizabeth knew she needed a court to fully clear her name. She knew, as well as anyone, that once found guilty of witchcraft, it was very likely you would be accused again, as your name had been tainted within the community. Although she initially got nowhere, other survivors and remaining family members came forward over the following years, also asking for the accused to have their names cleared and to be paid reparations.[†] Collectively, their voices began to be heard.

In Scotland, all the victims of the injustice, alive and dead, were swept under the judicial carpet. But in Salem, within two decades, the government had recognized that the convictions had been wrongful.

'This was quickly understood to be a miscarriage of justice,' says Rachel. 'It wasn't just that there had been so many people in jail, but also important men of the colonies were saying, "This is not right, or at the very least the evidence used was wrong."'

There was an understanding that innocent people had been held because of the insubstantial nature of the 'evidence'. Robert Calef's book *More Wonders of the Invisible World* was published in 1700 and was the first publication critical of the process of the trials, its title a cheeky response to Puritan minister Cotton

† Since starting our campaign for a pardon in Scotland, some people have accused us of chasing reparations. This would be impossible in Scotland as, unlike in Salem, we cannot prove who the descendants of the victims are.

Mather's book *Wonders of the Invisible World*. In fact, the book was published during a ban on publications covering the Salem trials, which had been ordered by the governor. We can only guess that the governor had decided that the trials weren't safe and that everyone needed to move on from them, quickly.

But what of Tituba, considering her extravagant confession in court?

'Tituba was never pardoned because she was never actually convicted,' says Rachel. 'The only people who received pardons were those that were convicted. Tituba is a really interesting case as she was one of the first accused and she confesses. Her confession is probably what saves her life because she's an important source of information; she languishes in jail through the whole trial. She was arrested in late February 1692 and not released until the spring of 1693. By the time of her trial they're no longer using spectral evidence. They've essentially said, "This whole matter is over and done with."'

So even though Tituba confessed, she was acquitted at her trial.

'It seems as though Tituba is sold by Samuel Parris for the cost of her trial fees,' Rachel explains. 'But we don't know who she was sold to and she just disappears. We have no idea where she goes after the trials.'

Tituba is really interesting to us as she is so 'other' in this setting. Of course, she is vulnerable and isolated in different ways, but the fact that her culture is used against her is very compelling and many of the visitors to the museum feel similarly.

'Tituba is one of the most fascinating people in the Salem witch trials, probably partially because of Arthur Miller's portrayal of her in *The Crucible*. That portrayal is very inaccurate and he doesn't do her justice at all, but he was basing his interpretation off older scholarship. When he was writing, that was the interpretation of her, that she was teaching the girls magic in the woods and the guilt from [taking part in] the magic was what caused the affliction. We now know that's not substantiated by primary sources but that was the original interpretation. But because she was one of the important characters in *The Crucible* she's very well known to people and she's fascinating because we don't know a lot about people of colour from the colonial period. Enslaved people of the colonies lived their lives "in the margins"; their names were literally often only recounted in the margins of papers, if recounted at all. The reason we know so much about her is because of the Salem witch trials. It's very unusual to hear a voice of a person of colour of that time even though the voice is through a filter of the people who believed she was a witch.'

In 1711, some people's names were cleared but this was purely down to certain families pushing for it. There were no automatic pardons. Following the American Revolution of 1765–83, the cases were essentially shelved for nearly 200 years and it was only during the 1950s that the family of Ann Pudeator, executed in 1692, demanded formal recognition of her innocence. Finally, in 1957, the Massachusetts General Court declared that 'Ann Pudeator and certain other persons' were cleared of all charges. As no other people are named, it took until 2001 and a great deal of community activism to clear the names of all but one of those convicted. Unfortunately, there was one woman, Elizabeth Johnson, whose name wasn't cleared as it was missed. It is speculated that this is because she was neither a wife nor a mother and had no one to advocate for her at the time. Her exoneration was finally accomplished in May 2022 when an eighth-grade class in North Andover Middle School learned about Elizabeth Johnson with their teacher Carrie LaPierre. The students researched the case and then involved their state senator, Diana DiZoglio, who introduced legislation. Finally, 329 years after Elizabeth's conviction, her name was cleared.

As the bill was passed, Senator DiZoglio said, 'Elizabeth's story and struggle continue to greatly resonate today. While we've come a long way since the horrors of the witch trials, women today still all too often find their rights challenged and concerns dismissed.'

The schoolchildren's fascination and passion reflect the way in which the trials continue to capture the public's imagination. And this isn't just a modern phenomenon. People have been visiting Salem since as early as the 1700s. John Adams, the former President of the United States, visited what he called 'Witch-hunt Hill' less than a hundred years after the trials.

'It speaks to what we call "dark tourism",[†] this fascination with tragedy and

† Naturally Scotland has a great deal of this, with all its castles, graveyards, battlefields, body-snatching and Queen-killing.

the macabre,' says Rachel. 'People have always been interested in sights of death and calamity – that's why people tour the Colosseum and the Catacombs and prison museums like Alcatraz. People find it fascinating because they are strange and disturbing. Salem held that draw from the beginning. People were coming to Salem and wanted to see where the hangings took place.'

The first tourist guide to Salem was published in 1880 and it instructed the reader not only where the hangings took place and but also where one could view the court documents. People came to town with the rise of train travel and would knock on locals' doors for information. The Spiritualism movement, so popular at the turn of the 20th century, added to Salem's appeal and the town's reputation grew. In April 1906, the man who would soon become known as Harry Houdini (real name Erik Weisz) visited the town and performed various feats of escapology.

'Salem tourism kept growing throughout the 20th century,' says Rachel. 'When *The Crucible* came out, and when the television show *Bewitched* was filmed in Salem in 1970 in an episode where the characters are coming to a witches' convention, both those things upped the ante of interest. In the 1970s you started to see modern witches moving to Salem like Laurie Cabot, who was very smart about publicity [even garnering national TV coverage when she opened its first 'Witch Shoppe']. It all comes together at that time – the Salem Witch Museum was inaugurated in 1972 – but it was in the 1980s and 90s that we saw that huge influx of tourism. That was when Salem started holding the "Haunted Happenings".[†] Salem is *the* witch reference in pop culture.'

But there is a flip side to all this. Tourism and infamy bring with them disinformation. So much of the Salem story is misunderstood, mis-told, misapprehended.

Many believe that the accused were ducked in water and that they were

† A series of Halloween-themed events, originally held over two days but now lasting the whole of October.

burned at the stake. Neither happened. With the exception of Giles Corey, all the 'witches' were hanged. The ducking test was not applied here; instead the two common 'tests' were having the accused recite the Lord's Prayer (the belief being that the Devil and his consorts could not utter the words) and searching the accused for the Devil's mark, specifically a witch's teat that the Devil could suckle from. This had the same inherent issue as the test in Scotland, as scars, moles, skin tags and so on could easily be described as something evil rather than natural.

Perhaps the most prevalent piece of nonsense about Salem is the idea that the town was suffering from a collective psychedelic trip due to wheat that had become mouldy and that caused ergot poisoning. This theory is a convenient excuse in some ways as it absolves accusers and prosecutors from responsibility, but there is no evidence for it and researchers are confident that by the 17th century farmers knew how to keep wheat dry and safe. In any event, the Salem events were not one isolated incident, which would lend greater credence to a poisoning theory, but took place for over a year between February 1692 and May 1693 – far too long a period for no one to notice that spoiled wheat was the cause.

But hyperbole and disinformation aside, the legacy of the tragedy of Salem has indirectly led to witches being embraced in modern pop culture, and the 21st century has seen a great rise in people (mostly women) identifying as witches. Naturally, the modern interpretation of witches is not about gaining power from the Devil or about practising evil magic. The modern witch is generally someone who connects with nature, identifies as a feminist and uses social media to her advantage to connect with witches worldwide. There have been many examples of witches working together to try and bring about political change[†] and influence world events[‡] and it's heartening to see these positive connections and new directions. We are delighted to see women owning

† Witches have assembled to collectively hex an unpopular, destructive politician in American elections.

‡ A group of Argentinian witches called La Brujineta worked 23 hours every day during the 2022 World Cup to send healing and protection to their team – who, of course, went on to win.

the word 'witch' and deciding on their own definition of the term, and we are equally happy when witches contact us and support us. They fully appreciate our distinction that while we support modern people's right to identify however they wish, in the times of the witch trials (and in modern-day witch accusations) there was no such thing as a witch. As we say in our campaign – they were women, not witches.

Sadly, the swing side of this positive move is that, of course, there will be some who will cling on to the old ideas; who see themselves as anti-witch. The most obvious proponents of clinging on to the old notion of witches as the Devil's handmaids are, surprise, surprise, rightwing religious types. Or at least people who declare themselves to be religious but are really just intent on controlling other people. And by other people, we mean almost exclusively women. The modern-day American pastor Greg Locke has tried to make a name for himself as a worthy opponent of the Devil by, among other things, naming 'witches' in his church. He also has a penchant for book burning and has burned so-called 'demonic' novels like the *Harry Potter* and *Twilight* series. In February 2022 he was recorded addressing witches in a sermon, telling them to 'get out' of the church or he would expose them. He even suggested that people who had fallen sick in the congregation might have done so as they had unknowingly befriended a witch.

Right-wing pundits and politicians also occasionally make use of the idea of witches either by trying to stir up a satanic panic, presumably to frighten voters into supporting them, or indeed the converse, by claiming to themselves be the victims of 'witch-hunts'. Two of the men most known for using this phrase are Richard Nixon and Donald Trump. We think that when politicians invoke this idea, on many occasions what they are really objecting to is being held responsible for breaking the law or the code of moral decency. It's laughable nonsense to see a man with power putting himself on an equal footing with someone accused of being a witch, facing execution.

The Salem Witch Museum team have gone to great lengths to create thought-provoking exhibits that encourage visitors to think about the causes of the witch-hunts and link them to more modern issues.

'The last thing our visitors see as they leave the museum is called our "witch-hunt wall" and it's a formula we use to break down former witch-hunts,' says Rachel. 'The formula is: Fear + a Trigger = a Scapegoat.'

Fear of the Devil was, in the case of Salem, triggered by a mysterious, incurable ailment that led to 150 people being scapegoated with accusations of witchcraft. The museum curators also draw parallels with more contemporary American historical occurrences: what happened to Japanese Americans during the Second World War; the McCarthy hearings and blacklists during the Cold War; the scapegoating of the gay community during the AIDS epidemic in the 1980s. The good news for those who can't make it to the Salem Witch Museum in person is that there is an excellent online tour, which anyone can access as long as they possess the heretical magic of wifi.

WATCH AND WAKE

It's been four days since they brought her in, and they think she's getting closer to confessing. I used to see her about the town, begging at doors, hanging about the market, waiting for scraps. She's always been someone you'd see but not really speaking much, just the hand held out, tired looking. I don't think she went to church over much, but I remember one time that she was that bowfin that she was told to leave. I felt sorry for her then, even though I was just a bairn and some folks were laughing at her behind their hands. It didn't seem right. But she was a midden.

She doesn't have any people or none that will claim her anyway. There have been a few times of late where she seemed drunk about the town and she was seen down on the steps of the tollbooth, asleep during the day.

The real trouble started when she asked at the Laird's house for alms and the housekeeper saw her off. They say she said something about how they'd regret their meanness before she disappeared off away down the lane. But then the housekeeper, Jean McInch, got sick, and even though they tried everything, she died. Then the Laird's best horse became lame, and the Laird himself hasn't been keeping too well, so people have been saying it was down to her. I don't know if it's true, but the minister says that this is what the Devil does. He gets ahold of someone and then they do his bidding. Everyone's saying it's true and what do I know? I've just been told to keep her awake through the night. So I'm sitting here in this chair keeping the candle lit and if she falls asleep on her wee pile of hay over there I wake her up.

It's tiring work and I know I have to start early tomorrow to help father with the deliveries, but mother says I must do it because we need the wee bit of pennies and it's God's work anyway and I should be grateful the minister thought of me.

She looks like she's drowsing now, so I get up and shake her shoulder. Her eyes roll up to me and then drop closed. This is no good. She can't fall asleep on my watch. I shoogle her shoulder but it's no good because she's been awake for days. She'll need to be moved. I pull her arm but she's a dead weight and I need to wrench her quite hard onto her feet. Even though she's skin and bones, it's not easy work.

'Come on, missus, come on.' I'm not speaking loudly. I don't want anyone to hear that I'm needing to waken her. I don't want to get into trouble. 'Come on, you.' She's awful hard to shift, but I pull her hand until she's sort of half standing, half leaning on me. I drag her around the wee cell and she's mumbling to me about Lord knows what. I can't really understand her. Maybe that's for the best. I think she's in a kind of a dream. We do a few turns of the room and her talking gets a bit clearer.

'I didn't do anything, I didn't do anything,' she's saying, but she's slurring and it's quiet. She's saying it again and again. I don't say anything to her still, and I'm trying not to boak because the stench coming off her is really bad, like rotten vegetables or something. Then I realize that she's crying and it's truly pitiful.

She's so old and pathetic, how can anyone think she has any power?

But what do I know, I'm just a lad, as my mother says. I need to trust that the minister and the baillie know what they're doing. They must do because this is the seventh witch they've discovered this year.

She's dropping down to the floor again and I can't drag her anywhere, so I let her go. I'll let her stay there for a bit. I keep my eyes on the cell door. I've seen the other men giving her a kick to wake her up, but I can't do that because she's just an old wifey.

'Come on,' I say and hold the cup up to her mouth for some water. She takes a wee bit, but she's so weak some of it just dribbles out her mouth. I hear someone arriving at the door. It must be Thomas in time to change the shift. Thomas is a brutal man. I've seen the way he treats his animals.

Maybe this way the wifie'll finally confess and this whole sorry matter will be at an end.

9
HOW TO GATHER EVIDENCE AGAINST A WITCH

We know what witches are, how to round them up and prick them. But how do you prove their guilt in a court of law? How do you gather all the evidence together that you need in order to prosecute a witch? We know from *Daemonologie* that God protects those who hold witches to account, so we need not worry about the Devil interfering in our task, but what is needed for a trial?

For Claire, a student of the law, this is an endlessly fascinating subject. Let us try and take all the superstition out of it (impossible, but even so . . .) and dig deep into the legal system to expose the gears and levers that led to the terrible, unjust deaths of thousands of people, mostly women.

In 1833, a century or so after the last witch trials, a man called Robert Pitcairn Esq, a Writer to the Signet,† decided to research and preserve details of trials held during the reign of King James VI in a book called *Ancient Criminal Trials in Scotland*. His work gives us an excellent insight into the machinery of the trials on a very practical and legal basis.

To say that, a hundred or so years down the lines from these events, there is a change in tone in the way he, and probably most others, thought of witchcraft by then, is very apparent from the outset of his writing on the subject:

> AMONG the circumstances which peculiarly characterize the earlier Criminal proceedings . . . none are more prominent than the unmitigated

† A lawyer who draws up documents requiring the King's Signet, or private seal.

> rigour with which the profession as well as the practice of Witchcraft, Sorcery, and Necromancy, were punished. The hecatombs of innocent victims, whose lives were sacrificed to satisfy the gloomy superstitions of Nations termed Christian and civilized, but who, in reality, were only emerging from a state of semi-barbarism, sufficiently attest the justice of this observation.

Times had certainly moved on. Pitcairn observed that, after the Reformation, the countries that had embraced the new religion were keen to outdo each other with their enthusiasm in '"rooting out from the land" every vestige of the professors of these "works of darkness"'. As evidence, he cites a memorandum which he described as a document that showed the 'proof of the nefarious wickedness which must have been perpetrated in Scotland' in the minutes of the Privy Council proceedings. Those of a sensitive constitution will wish to skip the next couple of paragraphs.

> 'December 1, 1608,—THE ERLE OF MAR declairit to the COUNSALL, that fum wemen wer tane in *Broichtoun*, as WITCHES; and being put to ane Affyfe, and convict, albeit thay perfeverit constant in thair denyell to the end, sit *thay wer BURNIT QUICK, eftir sic ane crewell maner, that sum of theme deit in despair, renunceand and blasphemeand; and otheris, HALF BRUNT, brak out of the fyre, and wes caft in QUICK in it agane, quhill thay* wer brunt to be deid.'

In rough translation: a number of women were tried by Baron Baillie at Broughton and, despite maintaining their innocence, they were convicted. Some were strangled before being burned and some were set alight while conscious.† While dying, many of them renounced their baptisms and blasphemed. Horrifically, some of them broke out of the fire, but were pushed back in to meet their deaths.

It's hard to get your head around this level of barbarity.

† We don't know why they weren't all strangled first. Perhaps the sheer numbers?

From the research Pitcairn conducted, he was able to conclude that only a very small number of the thousands of witchcraft trials were tried before the High Court of Justiciary, which was and is the place where the most serious criminal cases are tried in Scotland. Rather, the vast majority of trials were tried before the Lords of Regalities, the Baron Baillies or the Royal Commissioners. These courts are not in existence today, although the phrase 'Baillie Court' is still sometimes used to describe the Justice of the Peace (JP) Courts in Scotland. These JP Courts sit to deal with the most minor criminal cases in Scotland, presided over by lay magistrates. It's very strange to think that a crime that resulted in execution if convicted would be dealt with in anything but the highest court in the land, but this was indeed the case.

What starts a witchcraft accusation, and prompts consideration of a commission, is of course a claim that someone is a witch. This will either come from someone who claims to have been affected by witchcraft or it will be from a woman who, having confessed to acts of witchcraft, is further prevailed upon to name others as witches. Accusation statements from those who bring the complaint against the witch are essential. They begin by identifying the person accused, either by their description in writing or by pointing to them in the dock in the court room and giving evidence about what they had done. There are few recordings of the accusations themselves, but most can be ascertained by reading the confessions.

Unlike the modern trial process, an accused did not have the right to give evidence on their own behalf, although in some rare cases it is noted. In any event, for the vast majority of the accused, because they were women, they were not considered competent witnesses in their own right.

Once an accusation was obtained, the next step was a commission. Pitcairn recorded that his research on the commissions took him to the work of Baron Hume. Hume wrote *Commentaries on the Law of Scotland* – the classical exposition of criminal law. His work is still quoted today by advocates presenting cases and by the court in giving its decisions. Hume's work states that 'no fewer than fourteen Commissions' for trials of witches were granted, for different quarters of the country, in one sitting, on 7 November 1661. The commissions were a legal document that conferred power to commissioners for both examination and trial. They were granted by the Privy Council, the body in Scotland akin to the modern Cabinet in Government, assisting the King with his decision-making.

The requirement to obtain a commission from the Privy Council was an attempt to keep some form of control over the wildly enthusiastic prosecution of witches. To obtain a commission, a request would have to be made to the Privy Council complete with some evidential basis for requesting it. The test set by the Privy Council to obtain a warrant was not a high threshold to cross, but you still needed to produce at least a modicum of evidence. However, what might have been more off-putting, especially for those in the Highlands of Scotland, would be the time and effort required to have to go to Edinburgh and present the argument to obtain the commission in the first place. One of the reasons it may be that Scotland's witchcraft trials were more prevalent in the central belt was that it was just more convenient to get a commission if you lived locally. A horse and rider would cost a local jurisdiction time and money, which no doubt could have been spent elsewhere. Witchcraft trials were an expensive business.

Pitcairn explains that the part of the document in which the name of the accused was written also had a space for other names to be added if other people were later accused. Further, the jurisdiction of the commission – in other words, in what districts the Privy Council granted power for the commission to take place – was broad. This meant that the granting of a commission gave wide power to the commissioner. Pitcairn notes:

> As one unhappy creature was almost universally induced to accuse *several others* of the same crime for which he or she was to suffer, and as the evidence taken in one Trial was held to be conclusive in other cases, where the pannels were thus proved to be 'notour Witches,' it was competent for these Commissioners to try any number of persons, and to 'justify them to the death;' a practice which they were by no means slack of performing.

A feature of the fact that the Devil likes company is that where you find one witch, you find many, and when one witch confesses, she is pressed to name the rest, and so on. No wonder they left a big space to write in all the extra names that would end up being prosecuted, especially as once they had proved the existence of one witch, that 'proof' could be used in other trials.

So, assuming someone has been granted a commission to examine and try a suspected witch, the next step is the examination. There were two favoured forms of this: examining the mind of the accused and examining the body. We've already discussed the work of John Kincaid, the witch pricker extraordinaire, but how did his work become evidence that could be used in a trial? The answer is that he was required to sign a deposition, now referred to as an affidavit, setting out his expertise and then explaining what he had found. This official court document was used in lieu of John Kincaid having to attend court himself and was of great practical importance. A man who is so busy going round the country finding witches cannot be expected to return to every district he has worked in and give evidence. Time is money. That said, he clearly did give evidence in person where it was possible to do so. Who could resist attending a witchcraft trial to show off your great and godly skills? (With all due humility, of course.)

Pitcairn has preserved some documents so we can see exactly the evidence that was used – and we have to thank him for insisting on reproducing these confessions in his book, because he mentions that his editor was against the idea.[†] Here is one of the depositions, translated by us:

> Deposition of John Kincaid (Witch-finder) relative to the Devil's mark found on Patrick Watson and Menie Halliburton.
>
> At Dirleton, . . . of . . . [space left where the date would be inserted]. This day in the presence of Alexander Levington of Saltcoats, James

† As Pitcairn put it: 'The Editor has been induced, in compliance with the repeated desire of literary friends, contrary to his own private opinion, to annex to this work the CONFESSIONS of these unhappy women and a few other similar EXAMINATIONS.' If you are reading this, our editor has been similarly persuaded.

> Borthwick, chamberlain of Dirleton, John Stalker, baillie there, James Foirman, Drem, Mr James Acheson, in North Berwick, and William Daliell, notary, Patrick Watson of West Fenton and Menie Halliburton, his spouse, harboured and long suspected of witchcraft, of their own free will and uncompelled, hearing that I, John Kincaid, under subscribance, was in the town of Dirleton and had some skill and dexterity in trying of the Devil's mark, in the persons of such as were suspected to be witches, came to the Broadhall, in the Castle of Dirleton, and asked me, the said John Kincaid, to use my trial of them as I have done with others. Which, when I had done, I found the Devil's mark upon the backside of the said Patrick Watson, a little under the point of his left shoulder, and upon the left side of the said Menie Halliburton, on her neck a little above her left shoulder; whereof they were not sensible,[†] neither came forth from there any blood, after I had tried in exactly the same way as I had with any others. This I testify to be the truth, upon my credit[‡] and conscience. In witness whereof, I have subscribed this in their presence with my hand, day, and place aforesaid, before the witnesses above specified.

Such a document was used in place of Kincaid giving evidence at trial if necessity meant he was not able to attend, busy as he was accusing other people of witchery.

While witch prickers were very much believed in the 17th century, as time went on, their influence, as we have seen, began to wane. (Certainly, by Pitcairn's time, views had changed significantly, and he describes them as 'worthless impostors'.) The evidence of confessions, however, showed no such decline in favour.

A confession, being a statement against someone's self-interest, is powerful evidence against an accused witch. Why would anyone admit to being a witch, knowing it would mean almost certain death? In the present day, if a confession

† We think this means that these areas had no sensation.

‡ His credit perhaps means his credibility.

was extracted from someone by keeping them awake for days on end and constantly interrogating them, this would be deemed inadmissible in law. The legal system at the time had no such compunction.

While the Privy Council specifically outlawed torture as a way to extract a confession, it did not recognize sleep deprivation as a form of torture. Now we know it is one of the most insidious ways to create psychological distress, and likely to cause people to lose their minds. Such torture, said to have been designed by psychologists although it could equally have been designed by anyone studying Scottish history, was used by the US Government as an 'enhanced interrogation' technique at Guantanamo Bay. The irony of this technique was that studies showed that the 21st-century technique was equally as bad at getting reliable information as the 16th-century one. As was not appreciated in those days, but should have been at Guantanamo, any evidence extracted from someone in the throes of sleep deprivation is likely to be completely fantastical, given that the line between reality and fantasy would be lost.

Which brings us to arguably Pitcairn's most valuable contribution to historical knowledge of the witchcraft trials: the record of the confessions – four in total – of Isobel Gowdie. The confessions of Isobel Gowdie are incredibly detailed, fantastical and fascinating. Pitcairn calls them 'by far the most *unique* and wonderful, in the Records of this, and perhaps of any other country'.

Pitcairn records that on 13 April 1662 in the presence of the 'Minister of the Gospell at Aulderne' (modern-day Auldearn, a village in the Highlands) and the 'Shereffe deput of the shereffdom of Nairne' (the nearby town of Nairn) and nine other local men, the confession was (we translate) 'spoken from the mouth of Isobel Gowdie'. She is described as the spouse to John Gilbert, living in Lochloy, a small hamlet by the coast. The document is signed on that day, in the presence of the notar public and all the other aforementioned witnesses, stating that Isobel Gowdie, 'appearing penitent for her heinous acts of witchcraft, and that she had been over long in that service; without any compulsion, proceeded in her confession'. Quite why this confession required 11 people to hear is not known.

It was important that it was noted that there was no compulsion for her to confess, meaning that there was no torture, at least as it was understood at that time. (Though of course it's worth noting that the fact that it was recorded that the confession was given without compulsion does not mean that compulsion was not used.) This emphasis on saying that statements had been freely given makes it clear that those who had collected the confession knew that if it had been cajoled, threatened or extracted under torture people hearing the confession would be less likely to accept it as true. Why this was not also important to those extracting the confession is not wholly known, other than their desire to uncover witchery wherever it may arise.

The following first confession from Isobel Gowdie is the most detailed and lurid confession ever to have been recorded in Scotland. Again we will précis it into more modern language, but the original is available online so you can study it too.

> As I was going between the towns of Drumdewin and the Heads, I met with the Devil, and there covenanted, in a manner, with him. And I promised to meet him in the nighttime in the Kirk of Auldearn, which I did. And the first thing I did there that night was I denied my baptism and I did put one of my hands to the crown of my head and the other to the sole of my foot, and then renounced all betwixt my two hands over to the Devil. He was at the lectern, a black book in his hand. Margaret Brodie, of Auldearn, held me up to the Devil to be baptised by him, and he marked me in the shoulder and sucked out my blood at that mark, and spouted it into his hand, and sprinkling it on my head, he said, 'I baptise thee, Janet, in my own name.' And within a while, we all went away.
>
> The next time I met with him was at the new Wards of Inshock and he had carnal copulation with me. He was a meikle, black, hairy man, very cold. I found his nature cold within me as spring well-water.† Sometimes

† The description of him as 'black' did not relate to ethnicity, but refers to his hair and/or clothing. As for his 'nature' – her description of his semen inside her – it made sense that, if the Devil appeared in human form as compressed air, and therefore cold, then his semen would also be cold as spring well-water.

he had boots and sometimes he had shoes on his feet, but still his feet were forked and cloven. He was sometimes like a deer, or a roe deer.

John Taylor, his wife Janet Breadheid of Belmakeith, [illegible] Douglas and I myself, met in the Kirkyard of Nairn and we raised an unchristened child out of its grave; and at the end of Breadley's cornfield, just opposite the Mill of Nairn, we took the said child, added the nails of our fingers and toes, pieces of grain and leaves of colwart, all chopped small and mixed together, and we put a part of it among the dung heaps of Breadley's land, and thereby took away all the fruit of his corn, and we parted it amongst two of our covens.[†] When we take corn at Lammas,[‡] we take about two sheathes when the corn is full; or two heads of cabbage, and that gives us the fruit of the land or cabbage patch where they grew.[§] And we will be able to keep the yield till Christmas or Easter and then divide it amongst us. There are thirteen persons in my coven.

Pitcairn notes that the number 13 was known as 'the Devil's Dozen' in Scotland, although alas this designation appears to have fallen out of use in the 21st century.

Isobel continues: 'The last time that our coven met, we and another coven were dancing at the Hill of Earlseat [she also lists several other places], and after a time we went home to our howffs.'

She then explains that the coven also yoked some frogs to a plough using long grass that served as chains – although quite how that worked was left to the imagination – and they drew the plough like oxen. The Devil himself held the plough. The blade of the plough was formed of the horn of a half-castrated ram. They went twice about; and all of the coven went up and down with the plough, praying to the Devil for the fruit of that land, and that thistles and briars might grow there.

† Pitcairn suggests in his notes that 'coven' might come from 'convenire', to come together.

‡ Lammas is a harvest celebration on 1 August.

§ Stealing a symbolic amount of corn or cabbage allowed them to spirit away the whole crop.

Isobel continues:

> When we go to any house we take meat and drink, and fill up the barrels with our own piss, and we put brooms in our beds with our husbands till we return to them again. We were in the Earl of Moray's house in Dernway, going in through the windows, eating and drinking his best fare and taking some away with us. I had a little horse and would say, 'Horse and Hattock, in the Devil's name!' and then we would fly away wherever we wanted to go, as straws fly upon the highways. We fly like straws when we please, wild straws and corn-straws will be horses to us, and we put them between our feet and say, 'Horse and Hattock, in the Devil's name!' And when anyone sees these straws in a whirlwind, and does not bless themselves, we may shoot† them dead at our pleasure. Any that are shot by us, their soul will go to heaven but their body will remain with us and will fly like horses to us, as small as straws.

Unlike many other confessors, Isobel Gowdie spoke in some detail of the fairy world. She begins: 'I was in the Downie-Hills and got meat from the Queen of the Fairies, more than I could eat. The Queen is beautifully clothed in white linens, and in white and brown clothes, and the King of Fairies is a braw man, well-built and of broad face. There were elf-bulls rutting and frolicking up and down, and they gave me a fright.'

However, Pitcairn notes with obvious regret that he thinks that Isobel's 'gossiping' about the fairie world was cut short at this point, in favour of returning more strictly to her confessions, 'which were obviously drawn out of her, and listened to with the utmost complacency by her reverend inquisitors'.

Back on track again, Isobel goes on to discuss how she used witchcraft to steal milk from a cow:

† There was a belief that the Devil gave witches 'elfshots', which were fired at people using their thumbs rather than bows. There is some scholarly debate around whether these elfshots were actually prehistoric flint arrowheads or possibly the act of causing illness or pain in people or livestock by 'shooting' disease at the victim. Either way, it's a method used by witches to cause pain, illness and, as here, death.

> We pull the tow,[†] and twine and plait it in the wrong way in the Devil's name, and we draw this handmade tether in between the cow's hind hoof, and everything between the cow's front and hind feet is taken in the Devil's name, and this is how we take all the cow's milk. We even take sheep's milk too. The way to give back the milk again is to cut the tether. When we take away the strength of a person's ale and give it to another, we take a little quantity out of each barrel into a stowp in the Devil's name: and with our own hands we put it among the other person's ale, which gives them the strength and substance and good health of their neighbour's ale. To keep the ale from us, bless it well, and we have no power over it. We get all the power from the Devil and when we take it from him, we call him 'Our Lord'.

Isobel then returned to a discussion of the work of other members of her coven:

> John Taylor and his wife Janet Breadheid, Bessie Wilson in Auldearn, Margaret Wilson, wife of Donald Callam of Auldearn, and I made a picture of clay to destroy the Laird of Parkis's [Parks] male children. John Taylor brought the clay in the corner of his plaid and his wife broke it up very small, powdered like meal. We sifted it with a sieve and poured water in it, in the Devil's name, and kneaded it into a hasty-pudding, made of rye flour. From this we made a picture of the Laird's sons. It had all the parts and makeup of a child, such as head, eyes, nose, hands, feet, mouth and little lips. It wanted none of a child's features: and its hands were folded down by its sides. It was like a large roll or a flayed suckling pig.[‡] We laid it face first onto the fire till it shrivelled with the heat, with a clear fire around it, and till it was red like a coal. After that, we would roast it now and then; each alternate day a piece of it would be well roasted. The Laird

† This likely means they take hairs from the tail of the cow.

‡ If you are having difficulty imagining what this looks like, rest assured it was also a bit of a puzzle to Pitcairn who transcribed it!

of Parkis's healthy male children will suffer because of it, both those that are born and those already dead, if [the clay model] is not taken or broken. It was still being put in and taken out of the fire in the Devil's name. It was hung up on a knag. It is still in John Taylor's house, and it has a cradle of clay around it. Only John Taylor and his wife Janet Breadheid, Bessie and Margaret Wilson in Auldearn, and Margaret Brodie and I were involved in the making of it. But all the multitude of our witches in all the covens knew of it all, at our next meeting after we had made it. And all the witches that are yet untaken still have their own powers, as well as our powers which we had before we were taken.† But now I have no power at all.

Margaret Kylie in [illegible] is in one of the other covens. Meslie Hirdall, spouse to Alexander Ross in Loanhead, is one of them. Her skin is fiery. Isobel Nicoll in Lochley is one of my coven. Alexander Elder, in Earlseat, and his wife Janet Finlay are of my coven. Margaret Hasbein in Moynes is also one, as is Margaret Brodie in Auldearn, Bessie and Margaret Wilson there, and Jean Martin there, and Elspeth Nishie, spouse to John Mathow there. The previously mentioned Jean Martin is Maiden of our coven. John Young in Mebestowne is our Officer.

Pitcairn notes that each coven appears to have had an officer for the men, and a maiden for the women, 'but whether the province of these personages was to preside over them or to act as messengers, to call them together, does not seem so certain'.

Isobel goes on to describe one particular escapade at a neighbour's dye-house:

Elspeth Chisholme and Isobel More in Auldearn, Maggie Brodie [illegible] and I went into Alexander Cumming's dye-house in Auldearn. I went in in the likeness of a jackdaw and the previously mentioned Elspeth

† Here is an interesting idea, if we understand this correctly: that however many witches the authorities seize, their power is just transferred to the ones that are still at liberty.

> Chisholm went in the shape of a cat. Isobel More was a hare and Maggie Brodie was a cat and [illegible]. We took a thread of each colour of yarn that was in Alexander Cumming's dying-vat and tied three knots on each thread, in the Devil's name; and we put the threads in the vat, stirring it widdershins in the Devil's name, and in this manner we took all the healthy strength of the vat away, so that it could only dye black, the colour of the Devil, in whose name we took away the strength of the right colours that were in the vat!

The first confession having taken place on 13 April 1662, three more were to follow. The second confession was taken on 3 May and tells the tale of the 'Grand Meeting' of all the witch covens. Many spirits attended and are described in detail, along with nicknames, including such bizarre ones as 'Over the Dyke With It' and 'The Thief of Hell Wait Upon Herself' and the perhaps less complimentary 'Able and Stout'. Isobel explains that 'there would be many devils which wait upon the Master Devil, for he is bigger and more awful than the rest of the devils and they all revere him'. In the second confession there are also verses of poetry, one ending with the words: 'And I shall go in the Devil's name, and soon I will come home again.' Pitcairn's views on these pieces of poetry are that 'the preceding and following rhymes are probably unique, even in the history of trials for witchcraft, and show, in a very forcible manner, the criminality of the bigoted, though learned and well-intentioned, individuals who dragged forward such wretches to public trial and ignominious death.' This confession is also not complete, with the side of a document destroyed and the end, according to Pitcairn, 'torn off'.

Was Isobel an amazing poet who even under the incredible strain of being accused of witchcraft was able to create lines of poetry? Pitcairn's editor, who did not want copies of the confession to be included in the book in the first place, had a theory, as Pitcairn records:

> It has often been remarked by the Editor, in the course of the numerous witch trials which occur in this collection, that a great proportion of the

> charms, in use to be repeated by these unhappy women, were actually paraphrases of portions of the mass-book – and in some cases . . . there appears to have been used doggerel versions of the Creed, etc! Others were taken from ancient popular rhymes and songs.

The third confession of Isobel Gowdie was taken on 15 May 1662 and sets out the same story of meeting the Devil, having sex with him and renouncing her baptism as before. However, on this occasion she gives a much more detailed description of sex with the Devil, describing how he would have 'carnal dealings with all at every time he pleased'. The witches would never refuse him. He came to Isobel's house in the shape of a crow, or a deer, or any other shape and, on recognizing his voice, she would have sex with him. She also added, no doubt to the chagrin of the listening men: 'The youngest and swiftest women will have very great pleasure in their carnal copulation with him, yea much more than with their own husbands.' As if this wasn't enough, she followed it up with: 'They have an exceedingly great desire of it with him, as much as he can have to them and more, and never think shame of it. He is abler for us that way than any man can be.'[†] She described the Devil as 'very heavy like a malt-sack; a huge nature and very cold, like ice'.

In this third confession she describes various shape-shifting episodes and also admits murder: 'But that which troubles my conscience most, is the killing of several person with the arrows which I got from the Devil.'

Isobel's fourth confession took place on 27 May 1662. Again, we have a reprise of her first confession, which gives lie to the claim that these are Isobel's own words: clearly she would not keep repeating the same thing again and again. She also returns to her confession for murder using the arrows made by the Devil. She explained that one of her coven shot at a laird crossing a burn but missed him. Pitcairn notes that of course the laird was beyond the reach of their power

---

† If we were to guess about what parts of this confession were truly uttered by Isobel, it's probably this bit about the Devil being better at sex than men.

when he crossed the water, as it was believed that bad spirits can't chase you across water.[†]

If proof were needed that Isobel Gowdie did not confess 'without compulsion' and that her words were probably the result of her being repeatedly asked questions until the desired answer was obtained (or indeed whether her words were simply fabricated by her questioners), the confession of her coven mate Janet Breadheid, spouse of John Taylor provides it. There are startling similarities. It is exactly the same in describing where the Devil sat when she met him (at the lectern) and that he had a book in his hand; the baptism is word for word the same, and almost word for word is her description of the Devil having carnal connection with her – right down to the description of his 'nature' within her, as cold as spring well-water.

We can never be sure, of course, whether what we read are the words of the women themselves, words attributed to them by their interrogators, or a mixture of both. It's not surprising that many women, having been questioned for days on end and losing their mind with lack of sleep, made outlandish confessions. The strong similarities between the accounts were no doubt a result of the fact that those doing the interrogating knew what it was they wanted from the women: a confession required a meeting with the Devil, a renouncing of a baptism, and an act of witchcraft. Often, as we have seen, the confessions would include stories of 'carnal connections' with the Devil and of course the names of other witches in their coven. It wasn't only the interrogators who knew what was required; so did the women themselves. Some may have confessed through fear, some through resignation, some not at all. Call us suspicious, but we wonder whether these so-called unprompted confessions can really have been made by Isobel and Janet at all.

Reading these strange tales now, it's easy to lose sight of the visceral terror that lay behind the words. We tried to imagine the horror of the situation these poor

† The witches that chased Tam o' Shanter in Robert Burns's poem of the same name were thwarted when his horse Meg gets him across a small river – but alas for poor Meg, the witches managed to snatch her tail before it crossed the water.

women would have been in: a woman accused of witchcraft is likely to have been stripped, shaved and searched by men looking for the Devil's mark. She would be in custody in dire conditions, not knowing when her incarceration would end. She would have no lawyer to help her. She would be kept awake day and night being asked questions about when she met the Devil and what sex was like with him, and whether his semen was cold. She would be asked if she had renounced her baptism. She would be asked who was in her coven – was it her friend? Her neighbour? Her daughter? Her mother?

All the while she would be feeling her ability to tell between fact and fiction slip away from her, fearing what she might say if she lost her mind, knowing that if she confessed she would damn herself with her own words to a most brutal death, knowing she would be burned, never given a proper burial on consecrated ground – damned to spend eternity in hell, never seeing her loved ones in the Kingdom of God. We can only guess at how terrified she must have been to admit to the crimes that would consign her to such a fate.

For the interrogators, however, they have done their godly work: the witch has confessed by her very own words. What is to be done now?

So – gather together our case to prosecute a witch. We have an accuser, any physical objects that they may bring as proof,[†] the expert testimony of a witch pricker, and the confession.

Now we have everything we need for a witch trial.

† For example, a witch's charm found in the home of the person accusing the witch, placed there by her to work magic against the homeowner. These would be labelled and referred to as 'productions' for the court.

PORTRAIT OF THE ACCUSED

THE PAISLEY WITCHES

PAISLEY 1697

In 1696 in Paisley, a large town in the west central lowlands of Scotland near Glasgow, an 11-year-old girl from a well-to-do family called Christian Shaw witnessed a family servant, Catherine Campbell, stealing a glass of milk. When Catherine discovered Shaw had told on her to her mother, she supposedly cursed her, entreating the Devil to 'haul her soul through Hell'.

A few days later, Christian Shaw encountered an old woman, Agnes Naismith, who was feared as a witch locally. The next day, Shaw fell ill with symptoms eerily similar to those suffered by the Salem girls six years previously. Eventually, after she had suffered violent fits and shaking for eight weeks, Shaw's parents had her examined by a top local doctor called Matthew Brisbane, who was unable to explain her illness. There were then some days of relative health, but then Shaw again fell ill, suffering from violent fits and fugue states where 'she would become as stiff as a corpse and be senseless and motionless'.† On her return visit to the doctor, Shaw started bringing forth strange items from her mouth, including hair balls, chicken feathers, coal, gravel and straw. She supposedly also spoke to thin air, entreating Catherine to be friendly with her again. As no rational explanation could be offered for Shaw's behaviour, the doctor suggested its origin was demonic. Shaw's father pushed for arrests and although Shaw initially accused only Catherine and Agnes Naismith, as events spiralled, she ultimately accused 35 people.

Lord Blantyre chaired the commission and in the end seven people were summoned and charged with murder and tormenting various people: Margaret

† As described by Brian P Levack in his *New Perspectives on Witchcraft*, vol. 3.

Lang, brothers John and James Lindsay, John Reid, Catherine Campbell, Margaret Fulton and Agnes Naismith.

Dr Matthew Brisbane testified that no natural causes could explain the girl's condition and the minister, James Hutchison, sermonized to the court about witches' marks and cast doubt on the doctors that argued these marks on the accused's bodies could have innocent origins. In addition, the prosecutor threatened the jury, telling them that acquitting the defendants would essentially align them with the Devil, making them 'accessory to all the blasphemies, apostasies, murders, tortures, and seductions etc'. Somewhat unsurprisingly, all seven were found guilty.

The executions took place on the Gallow Green in Paisley on 10 June 1697, where the convicted were hanged then burned. By all accounts, the execution was particularly distressing. The original accused, Catherine Campbell, screamed, cursed and tried to wrench herself free as she was carried to the gallows. The two convicted brothers, James and John Lindsay, heartbreakingly clutched each other's hands as they were hanged. Margaret Fulton lost leave of her senses and was heard to talk about the land of the fairies as she faced her brutal death. Margaret Lang supposedly confessed to the accusations being true but insisted she had since reconciled with God. Finally, Agnes Naismith cursed everyone present and their descendants. For many years afterwards, every tragedy to befall the people of Paisley was blamed on Naismith's curse.

This was the last mass execution for witchcraft in western Europe.

There are elements of the Paisley witches story that seem almost filmic to modern eyes. For example, one of the convicted, John Reid, was found dead before they could execute him. He had a scarf wrapped around his neck that was secured by a stick to the fireplace, presumably like a garrotte, but he was still seated on a stool, and witnesses claimed that the mechanism wouldn't have been strong enough to support his weight in any case. In addition, his cell was locked, and his window secured with boards.

In another ghoulishly filmic touch, a contemporary statement about the executions insisted that not all the convicted were dead when they were set on fire. A local man, Mark Canavan, had his walking stick taken by executioners to push the flailing limbs back into the fire. Canavan refused to touch it after it had been in contact with witches.

Finally, sometime after the executions, a hole in Shaw's bedroom wall was discovered through which, it has been speculated, an accomplice had passed the items that she had regurgitated. Could Shaw have known about the Salem case and fancied some notoriety for herself? She wouldn't be the first or last young girl to cause a supernatural drama† in order to gain attention.

Christian Shaw went on to become a successful businesswoman in the textile industry and the last recorded mention of her was her marriage to a businessman called William Livingstone in 1737.

It has been speculated by modern-day psychiatrists that she may have been suffering from conversion disorder when she was originally cursed by Catherine. The theory being that the anxiety she felt at the curse during these heightened times was converted into her strange behaviour. But we will never know the truth.

In 2008, a memorial was placed in the ground at Maxwellton Cross in Paisley at the location where the witches' remains were said to be buried.‡ An inscription reads: 'Pain inflicted, Suffering Endured, Injustice Done.' Campaigners have fought for years to have the convicted people pardoned.

† See the case of the Fox sisters of upstate New York in 1848. They faked mysterious spiritual contact, which was instrumental in creating and popularizing the growing practice of Spiritualism.

‡ This was, of course, highly unusual.

10

HOW TO TRY A WITCH

One of the most difficult elements of investigating witchcraft trials is that the records are very poor. The records in relation to Isobel Gowdie's own personal history are even poorer. Save for the name of her husband, and the fact she hailed from Lochloy in the parish of Auldearn, we have very little information about her. From the Survey of Scottish Witchcraft we know that the grant of the commission from the Privy Council indicated that there was to be no torture of the accused witch. We know that a total of four confessions were given by Isobel in April or May, two post-dating the start of her trial, which began on 13 April 1662. We know she named 18 other people as witches, 15 of them women. We also know that no fewer than nine commissioners (church men) and 11 investigators (senior and important men of the parish) were involved in the process. But that is where the trail goes cold.

It is particularly aggravating that despite four detailed confessions, we do not know the outcome of the trial. Given that we know what evidence was against her, however, we feel it was very likely that she would have been convicted. Extrapolating from the records of the witch trials that we do have, we can see that approximately two-thirds of those accused of witchcraft were executed. We know that a few were 'banished' from the parish – although it is not clear why they avoided the usual witches' fate, as the official punishment was death. A small number were acquitted.

Given these numbers, and the amount of evidence against her, surely it's likely that Isobel was executed?

Claire, looking at it with her experience of being a modern-day KC, considers this. Isobel confessed, which is pretty strong evidence that came directly from her.

And she didn't just confess once; she gave four separate confessions over a period of about six weeks. We don't see anywhere that she renounced her confession. So that would certainly have been a very significant fact to be weighed up by a judge.

So exactly how did judges decide who was guilty of witchcraft and who wasn't?

The court rules were not as regulated then as they are in the 21st century and judges did not write down why they had come to their decisions. It wasn't until the Criminal Appeal (Scotland) Act was passed in 1927 that a court of appeal came into being in Scotland,[†] so up until that point judges were not obliged in criminal cases to set out their reasoning as to how they came to their decision, because there would be no higher court to check if they got it right. Given that there was no appellate process, and no one could challenge decisions, what would have been the point in setting out the thinking of the court?

But just because we don't have a record of it does not mean that the legal reasoning did not take place. And we can make an educated guess as to how that reasoning would have run. Although laws and procedural rules have changed a great deal since the 17th century, it's likely that the way a judge considered evidence and how he (it was always a 'he', of course) came to a conclusion was the same as now.

Firstly, the judge would consider the charge. So the judge would have considered that Isobel Gowdie was alleged to have committed acts of witchcraft that came to light after her local minister became concerned about allegations that were circulating in the village of Auldearn.

† The Appeal Court in Scotland was founded after a public outcry over the conviction of Oscar Slater, found guilty in 1909 of the murder of Marion Gilchrist. The campaign to have him pardoned was lengthy and its ultimate success was in part due to Sir Arthur Conan Doyle, author of the Sherlock Holmes novels, who became involved post-conviction. He wrote a book called *The Case of Oscar Slater*, in which he argued that the prosecution was flawed and the trial had not been fair. It was not till 1927 that public opinion was such that a Court of Appeal was instituted to hear his case. At the appeal it was accepted that his conviction had been a miscarriage of justice at trial, and his conviction and sentence were quashed.

The judge would then ask himself what was the evidence before him that might support such a charge. Evidence was then and is now separated into categories, such as physical, eyewitness and expert evidence.

In this case, he had the four confessions of Isobel Gowdie herself in both written and oral form. Before the judge came to the contents of the confessions themselves, he would have given consideration as to who had collected the statements and whether they could be trusted to have recorded everything correctly. In this case, the confessions were taken by the notar public, John Innes, who had been very careful to set out Isobel's words in great detail. In addition, they had been witnessed by ten other highly respected gentlemen.

In the same way that judges now look to check that evidence has been lawfully obtained, the judge then would also be thinking about whether the circumstances in which the statement was taken were fair. So he would definitely have taken note of the fact that the confessions highlight from the outset that the words spoken are directly from the mouth of Isobel Gowdie on each occasion, as witnessed by all those who signed the confessions, and that she had said these words of her own free will and had not been compelled or tortured to confess (while sadly not recognizing sleep deprivation as a form of torture).

Of course, from our modern-day perspective, we'll never know if this woman was talking from a state between consciousness and unconsciousness, whether she was hallucinating or suffering from a mental illness, or indeed if one of her accusers made the whole thing up. The judge may have been satisfied that everything was proper and above board, but the fact that the men recording the confessions felt they had to spell it out so deliberately and repeatedly only makes us more suspicious now.

Nevertheless, the judge would have weighed up her confession evidence by asking, 'Do I find this evidence both credible and reliable?' The test of credibility is asking whether you think you can believe the evidence given; reliability is whether or not that evidence can be depended upon. And, in this instance, it is likely he would have answered yes in both cases.

As to the content of each of these confessions: the fact that she had given evidence against her own best interest would have been an important factor for the judge to consider. After all, who in their right mind would confess to being a witch unless they were one? This reasoning is used to this day, and when an accused has confessed to a crime in Scotland, the jury is told that very little more is needed to convict them.

Isobel Gowdie claimed that she met with the Devil and that she willingly agreed to become his servant: in order to ensure her loyalty to him she renounced her own baptism and engaged in a perversion of the sacrament. She said the Devil sooked out the blood from her shoulder, leaving her with a visible mark there, and she also engaged in carnal relations with him. This is a full-house bingo card of 'confession essentials'. Doubtless the judge would have dealt with many witchcraft accusations and he would have been well acquainted with what the witches and Devil did together when they met up, so this confession would seem to be in line with the others. He may have thought that some of the details that Isobel supplied – for example, the Devil's 'cold' nature, his cloven feet – would not have been known by a God-fearing woman unless she had seen it with her own eyes. The 'Devil's mark' could have been witnessed by the eyes of the judge himself, providing independent corroboration to the confession.

If the judge accepted the evidence as both credible and reliable, he had to then carry out a further assessment. The terms of the Witchcraft Act 1563 made it clear that being a witch is itself not a crime: it is the act of using the knowledge of witchcraft, sorcery or necromancy to perform an act of witchcraft that is criminal. (The other crime of witchcraft being consulting a person to use witchcraft, sorcery or necromancy does not apply in this case.)

Sadly for Isobel, this would have been an easy matter for the judge to rule on. From the four confessions it is likely that a judge would have formed the view that there was overwhelming evidence – from Isobel's own mouth – that this was the case.

After assessing the evidence against her, it does therefore seem highly likely that Isobel Gowdie would have been convicted of witchcraft. Then, of course, the court would have to move to sentence.

As the Bible confirms, 'thou shalt not suffer a witch to live'. This was taken literally in Scotland and the only official punishment for acts of witchcraft was death. King James VI, in Book 3, Chapter 6 of *Daemonologie*, spoke of the sentence imposed in the following terms:

> PHILOMATHES: Then to make an ende of our conference, since I see it drawes late, what forme of punishment thinke ye merites these *Magicians* and Witches? For I see that ye account them to be all alike guiltie?
>
> EPISTEMON: They ought to be put to death according to the Law of God, the civill and imperial law, and municipall law of all Christian nations.
>
> PHI: But what kinde of death I pray you?
>
> EPI: It is commonly used by fire, but that is an indifferent thing to be used in every cuntrie, according to the Law or custome thereof.
>
> PHI: But ought no sexe, age nor ranck to be exempted?
>
> EPI: None at al (being so used by the lawful Magistrate) for it is the highest poynt of Idolatrie, wherein no exception is admitted by the law of God.
>
> PHI: Then bairnes may not be spared?
>
> EPI: Yea, not a haire the lesse of my conclusion.

Therefore, on the basis she was convicted, Isobel Gowdie was probably sentenced to death for her acts of witchcraft. She is likely to have been strangled on a funeral pyre and her body burned to make sure the Devil couldn't bring her back to cause more mayhem.

So, we can see that a confession extracted from a deliriously tired woman, together with a mark on her body, could find a woman convicted under the Witchcraft Act and executed by the state.

It didn't take much, clearly.

Nonetheless, it's important to remember it was a proper legal trial, with evidence being put forward and the judge assessing it and carrying out legal tests. Some people think that witchcraft trials were carried out by angry peasants waving pitchforks. Perhaps this is a more acceptable way for a modern person to think about it. No one wants to think that a judicial system can get it so wrong. But it did, with catastrophic consequences for those accused.

After conviction and sentencing, the legal part of the process was over. The most gruesome part – the practicalities of killing a witch – was yet to come.

PORTRAIT OF THE ACCUSED

JANET HORNE

DORNOCH 1727

Janet Horne was the last person to be executed for witchcraft in Great Britain and the fact that the stone marking her execution bears the incorrect date is symbolic of the wrong that was perpetrated against her. We don't even know her real name, as Janet (or Jenny) Horne was a kind of catch-all name for any women accused of witchcraft in Scotland at that time. Janet† lived with her daughter in Dornoch, in the Highlands, and in 1727 (some sources say 1722) the two women were arrested and put in jail. It seems some of the townsfolk believed that they were in league with the Devil, and, following a rushed and almost certainly illegal trial led by the sheriff-depute of Sutherland, Captain David Ross, it was ordered that the two be burned to death the following day.

Janet was accused of turning her daughter into a pony and it was said that she was shod by the Devil himself. Sadly, there's a much more rational and indeed pathetic explanation for the accusations: Janet was probably suffering from what we would think of as dementia today, and her daughter likely had a disability affecting her hands and feet. Contemporary witnesses of the execution described Janet being stripped, paraded through the town and covered in tar, and then laughing and warming her hands at 'the bonnie fire', as she called it, of the burning barrel that she was to be executed in. There's no record of what happened to her daughter, so we can but hope that she was spared.

Janet Horne was executed in 1727. Public sentiment was by this time turning against witch-hunts, and less than a decade later, the Scottish Witchcraft Act

† The witchcraft equivalent of Jane Doe: we'll keep calling her that as she can't be anonymous and, like it or not, that's how this poor woman is always referred to.

and the English Witchcraft Act were repealed. They were replaced by a new act of 1735, which made the law the same for the whole of Great Britain, making it a crime for anyone to claim they could practise witchcraft. In other words, instead of starting from a premise that witches were real, the law now worked on the assumption that no one had magical powers and anyone who claimed otherwise was a charlatan. The law also abolished the hunting and execution of witches.

With this new act – too late for Janet Horne, sadly – the age of the witch trials of the Early Modern period finally came to an end.

WITNESS TO THE EXECUTION

It starts early, sometimes even the night before. The men moved backwards and forwards, carrying the wood and stacking it in its great pile. Their friendly voices conceal the horror of their industry. They are like evil ants, mindlessly following the orders of the queen. Except, of course, in this case it's not a queen, but a king. Or more specifically, here in this village, the minister. Certainly, he views himself as king and acts accordingly.

And here in this house, his house and my house, he is most brutal without even raising a hand. I wish daily that it was he who would die rather than this recent seemingly ceaseless trail of filthy women. But it's as if he gains strength from their demise and every accusation and burning fortifies him and pushes him on.

What can I do but play my part? I too am an instrument of God, even if my husband is wilfully mistaken and has interpreted the word of God incorrectly. Naturally, I cannot express this traitorous thought. For then I fear I too would be accused of an alliance with the Devil. How else to explain a pious, devout wife (I play my part perfectly) turning against such a paragon of virtue. Why, only the Devil could intercede so foully.

Instead, I do what is expected of me. I attend the interminable services that gather all of the Lord's Day in a terrible drear. I smile benignly at the other wives of a similar station. I turn a patient countenance on all the women of the village, who wish to court my husband's good graces by appealing to his sinless, godly helpmate.

In accordance with this, I must welcome the local worthies: the laird, the baillie, the great and the good who gather here to congratulate themselves on their discovery and routing out of the evildoers in our midst. I must supervise the laying out of fine china for their brute hands of which I have heard whispers of great cruelty flowing easily in less domestic settings. I must ensure they have enough to eat and drink, though I know their quarry (usually harmless, if irritating, old biddies or nuisance gossips or women who have lost their way – hardly the Devil's marching army) is starved into submission … among other tactics I have overheard discussed. Yes, I have eavesdropped, but that's hardly a crime in these circumstances. Then I must ignore the bottles of whisky taken and ignore the pale, bilious state of the gentlemen the next day as we gather around the witch and see her hanged then destroyed.

You would not imagine that a person could bear to watch these violent entertainments, but watch we must, as to not see means to not understand the scrubbing away of the Devil's filth.

My husband is very clear on that.

I suspect it is to soothe a wee part of his soul that remains not quite smothered by his prideful self-righteousness. If he has company in the watching, we are all complicit in the act.

I feel a strong need to watch, but not for his purposes, either spoken or thought. Rather, I know I must witness these women's ends. And pray as hard as I can that my husband is wrong and that God Almighty will remove the poor souls to eternal peace elsewhere and that one day the minister and his ilk will be punished and will know the Almighty's burning wrath.

Until then I will watch, though it distresses me, and I will keep a peaceful countenance and I will pray, pray, pray.

11

HOW TO BURN A WITCH

The Howff, located in the heart of Dundee, is a place as familiar to us as it is alluring. In 1564, the land was granted to the burgh of Dundee as a burial ground by none other than Mary Queen of Scots and the graveyard now has a Category A listing due to its historical tombstones.[†] The final burial there was in 1878 and it's often quoted that 80,000 people are buried there, but, given the small size of the place, we'd be surprised if that were so. The reason we are such frequent visitors to the place is not solely due to Zoe being fascinated by the human bones that often break the surface or Claire enjoying a Goth moment, but because the burial site has become inextricably linked to a woman called Grissel Jaffray, who was burned as a witch in Dundee in 1669.

Very little is known about Grissel other than she was born in Aberdeen where she married James Butchart in 1615. In 1669, the couple were accused of witchcraft, Grissel specifically of being a spaewife, a woman who could foretell the future. Their accusers were three Dundee ministers: John Guthrie, William Rait and Harry Scrymgeour. As was often the case, when Grissel was tortured, she named several others as witches, though no records exist of their names or fates. At her trial in November that year, the Dundee local court found her guilty and she was strangled then burned. The local legend has it that upon returning to the city from the sea, her son saw the flames of his mother's pyre before he docked and he fled Dundee, never to return again.

No records exist to indicate where Grissel was executed, yet despite the scant

† Some of the more famous dead include James and Janet Keiller, who invented the famous Keiller marmalade, and James Chalmers, inventer of the adhesive postage stamp.

details, her story is woven into the fabric of Dundee's history and now, in a little cobbled lane that leads down to where the docks would have been, a blue plaque and a mosaic depicting flames and waves marks her tragic end.

There's no great fanfare about these markers and many people are surprised when their attention is drawn to them. As is often the case, if a story intrigues, but details are missing, people will fill in the gaps. This is where the link to the Howff comes in, as there is a stone post there – not a gravestone, but rather a slim marker that reaches about mid-height on an average woman – and this marker has become known as the Witch's Stone. We're not sure why people have become convinced this is Grissel's resting place as it was actually a marker for a meeting point for local businessmen; however, it has taken on symbolic relevance and is usually decorated on its top with shells, coins and little stones.

We have done various interviews at this spot with journalists from all around the world as it's the only place near our homes that has a witch connection (even though it's an imagined link) and it never fails to make us think about how an ordinary woman could very quickly find herself in a position she would find impossible to escape from with her life. We always take a moment to think about what it must have been like for Grissel (and all the other accused) to be publicly executed and then for the spectators to watch her remains being burned to ash.

As deeply unpleasant and upsetting as this aspect of the witch trials is, we must think about it and understand it as it was a key driver in the war against witches, and it helped to encourage people to keep a close eye on their neighbours and acquaintances and ultimately enforce public adherence to the laws of church and state.

Generally, in Scotland, witches were strangled first then their bodies were burned. Historians are not all in agreement about the methodology. Some say hanged, some say strangit, strangld or whirkened (an old Scots for strangled), although it is unlikely that this was done by hand, given how many women – sorry, witches – would have been executed in a day. Perhaps garrottes were used. Occasionally they were burned alive at the stake and sometimes bodies were burned in barrels filled with tar. That people did this legally and intentionally and as a spectator event is very hard to comprehend. However, these methods of dispatch were an integral part of how the public were educated and chastened about witchcraft and its consequences.

So, why burn a witch rather than bury them?

Put simply, it was to stop them from coming back. In the Early Modern period, there was a strongly held belief that the Devil was able to reanimate corpses and that, if given half the chance, he would 'revenir' the witches and have them carry on with their evildoing. People of the time (and remember, this was legal and led by the leaders of the church) truly thought that only by killing and then destroying the witch would they be protecting the community. So they completely obliterate the witch from the world, turning her to ash on the wind, leaving no trace that she had ever existed.

We are so familiar with the idea that witches were burned at the stake that the reality of it has little meaning for us. People talk sometimes quite glibly about this as it happened so long ago, and we like to distance ourselves from what it would look like to burn a human being's recently executed body at the stake. To that end, we spoke to world-renowned fire expert, Professor Niamh Nic Daeid, who we knew could explain what physically happened when witches were burned and therefore perhaps evoke some sense of what it was really like.

Niamh was an early supporter of our Witches of Scotland campaign and is someone to whom we never tire of talking. She is a professor of forensic science and the director of the Leverhulme Research Centre for Forensic Science. She is also a specialist in fire investigation, so the person you go to if you want to know anything about fire. In fact, Niamh was called as an expert witness in the Grenfell Inquiry.

We're always delighted to speak to Niamh, and Zoe was especially excited to discuss issues of forensic science. Niamh is originally from Ireland and has the uncanny ability to speak about horrendous and distressing subjects in a way that is both fascinating and informative, all in a soft, warm accent. She never lets you feel as if you're asking stupid or weird questions, even when they patently are.

So, how would burning a witch's body work in reality?

Niamh explains, 'If you think of the body as a solid fuel, you heat up that fuel and you cause the materials within it to thermally decompose and produce gases. That's the first thing. The fuel that burns isn't the solid, it's the gaseous products that come off the fuel.'

Therefore, if the person being executed is standing up, tied to a stake with lit wood beneath them, the body itself will act as further fuel. Then as the body heats up, it begins to thermally decompose and release gases that in turn keep the fire going.

Niamh continues: 'If the person is clothed, then the clothing may be the first thing to start to thermally decompose – the molecules of the material literally just starting to break apart. Because the fire is imparting lots of energy and lots of heat, the heat causes the molecules to break apart from each other and they produce the gas. It's a process called pyrolysis.'

The amount of thermal decomposition depends on both the fuel (the body) and on temperature. In a modern crematorium, the deceased is laid flat and the temperature is between around 1,000 and 1,300 degrees Centigrade. When a corpse is in those very controlled circumstances, it takes about an hour and a half to burn, after which it is allowed to cool for about an hour and then moved to a cremulator to reduce the ashes to a fine powder.

By contrast, during the witch burnings, there was clearly a much less scientific approach.

The main issue was that if you tie someone to a stake then, by definition, the body is upright. What this created was a situation where the flame was flickering rather than consistently static. These variable conditions meant that the temperature would most likely be less consistent than that within the furnace at a crematorium.

'That means it's going to take a longer period of time for that person to burn to ash and bone,' says Niamh.

This long burning time was something of a headache for Early Modern executioners. In order to speed up the process, they sometimes placed the accused inside tar-filled barrels. Despite this seeming like a good idea to them, we know that it was in fact less efficient. Getting tar ignited is not as easy as you might

Witch-burning engraving, 1555

think[†] and, once lit, the flames will only reach that matter that is above the tar's surface line.

'If you're in a tank submerged in tar up to your neck or waist, it's only the surface of the tar in the barrel that burns,' Niamh explains. 'The material beneath the surface is still cool. It could be much more prolonged, albeit in the immediate environment of where that surface tar is burning, the temperature would get very hot. It could again take a considerable amount of time for the body to burn down completely.'

As terrible as the visual image is of a burning body, it would not be the only sense that was shocked. The smell of burning flesh or, as we now know, the oils from the burning flesh would have been all-pervading for the town or village where the execution was taking place. There would be no escaping the carnage as the putrid, sweet smell would twist around the town and even into the houses of the inhabitants.

Throughout the long hours burning at the stake, the body would likely have moved and changed position. The tendons and ligaments, especially in the arms, legs and hands would have contracted and possibly pulled up into what is known as the 'pugilistic stance' by pathologists, in which the corpse takes on a posture as if they're raising their fists to fight. This is a physical reaction to the fire and doesn't mean that the person was actually fighting or even alive, but it must have made for a terrible sight and quite probably added to ideas about the power of witches.

For those of us who have hand-scattered ashes, we know that the cremains, as they're known in the business, are dusty ash but with slightly bigger bits of bone in it. Under the less regulated conditions of the witch trials, the resulting remains would have been much more irregular. In contemporary crematoriums, remains are gone over with a little hammer to reduce bigger bone fragments into more dust-like matter. It turns out that bones can withstand quite a lot and, under the

† Claire: 'I've literally never given it a moment's thought, but Zoe clearly has.'

circumstances we're describing, there would have been several reasonably big pieces left.

We've read some accounts saying that the ashes were just left to blow away, but it sounds as if those running the execution would have had to get involved with the remains as they weren't small enough or fine enough to be left to nature.

'Let me show you something,' says Niamh, getting up and going to her bookshelf, which is naturally stuffed with academic texts. She brings back a book and, flicking through, finds an image of different bits of bone that have survived a person being cremated. Niamh indicates a chunk of bone that is the joint at the top of a leg. This photo backs up the theory that there would definitely have been quite large fragments left over and those pieces may only become ashes (as we think of them) if someone had intervened and smashed them up.

Bones become brittle and change colour from white to grey to silvery as they are exposed to higher temperatures. But again, this all takes time and this only occurs in very high temperatures – it is much more difficult for them to break down to ash with the body upright, tied to a stake over a fire.

Peculiarly, in the Scalloway Museum in Shetland, we have been told that there is a collection of ashes, taken from the place where the guilty were burned. Though no scientific testing has been done on these ashes, many believe they are actually 'witches' ashes'. It is possible, but even if they're not, we're sure the sight of them in the museum sharpens the mind while contemplating the trials. The power of the human imagination is strong and, indeed, necessary, for acknowledging the full obscenity of what occurred.

It is incredibly hard to imagine living in a time where the whole community was compelled to watch the execution and burning of someone who you had lived alongside and had possibly known your whole life. As they stood and watched, we wondered what they would have actually seen.

'In terms of the way the individual will be positioned, they will start by standing upwards. As the body burns the soft tissues will burn first, exposing muscle and fat underneath, which will gradually disintegrate from heat exposure eventually revealing bone that will begin to also degrade.'

There may be a point where the body might disarticulate and collapse into pieces. If the head and the limbs came off, those organizing the execution could find themselves in the position of having to move body parts back into the fire. As mentioned earlier, there are contemporary reports during the Paisley witch trials of a bystander's walking cane being used for exactly this task.

The skin would blacken[†] just as chicken on a barbecue would cook.[‡] Because women have a higher fat content than men, there's a possibility that women might have burned faster. However, Niamh says it would not be enough to make any great difference to the time taken for the body to burn to bone and ash. There are also some differences to take into account regarding how humans burn based on body mass, in that it may take people who are larger a longer time to burn depending on circumstances, which makes an awful lot of sense.

Another variable to be considered is what materials the person was wearing. If someone was wearing a more protective layer such as leather or wool, it could certainly prolong the process. Natural fabrics also hold their shape better compared to modern, artificial materials.

'If you set fire to a wool jumper, it holds its shape for some time. The clothing that they wore would provide some level of a barrier that would slow things down. Their hair would catch on fire and hair changes colour when it's burned.'

Although it was rarer for witches to be burned alive, it did happen sometimes. And while the horror of this is almost impossible to contemplate, thankfully the victim wouldn't have actually had the long, drawn-out death that you might suppose – they were more likely to die of shock, smoke inhalation or heart failure, none of which would take very long.

There are some stories that well-meaning people would put gunpowder in the witch's clothing, to speed the process up and help the person to die quickly.

† As we're talking about the centuries-old Scottish witch trials, we're talking about white skin in this scenario.

‡ Sorry.

However, Niamh thinks it is unlikely that this would make much difference as, unless gunpowder was put into a closed, confined container, it would just cause a quick, localized effect perhaps similar to that of a sparkler, but it wouldn't move the process along in any meaningful way.

Some contemporary reports recorded that when a witch's corpse was burned, it would let out a gasp. Of course, we know now that noises such as that weren't a supernatural event, but surely back then it would have been seen as more proof that the guilty person was non-human.

But of course they were human; they were real people. When we visit the Howff, we always think about how many locations across Scotland where we go about our normal, daily lives are on the same ground where these horrific scenes took place just a few hundred years ago.

We must make the connection with these innocent people who were subjected to the most awful punishment. Think of someone like Grissel Jaffray, who was plucked from her normal life and made the most awful example of, in a city where thousands of people go about their own normal lives, never realizing that perhaps they are passing over the very spot where Grissel's strangled body was burned beyond recognition in order to keep the Devil at bay. It almost doesn't bear thinking about, and yet we must.

PORTRAIT OF THE ACCUSED

KATHERINE MACKINNON

SKYE 1747

In 1747, Katherine MacKinnon went begging at the door of a man called Rudy or Ruaridh† Mac Iain McDonald in the village of Camuscross on the south end of Skye. It was a fatal mistake and the elderly woman died a horrible death at McDonald's hands. Seven years later, he was accused of her 'barbarous and cruel' murder in Inverness in August 1754.

Recently uncovered archives have revealed the sad case of Katherine – the first and only recorded incidence of a witch accusation on the Isle of Skye in the Inner Hebrides. Ironically, Skye's oral history is rich with tales of witches. For example, according to legend, the imposing, jagged Cuillin Hills on Skye were believed to have been formed by witches. Unlike most of the rest of Scotland, Skye didn't suffer from the same appetite for accusing and executing witches. It had an easier relationship with the supernatural, possibly because it is a Gaelic-speaking area (as mentioned earlier, Ireland and other Gaelic areas had a stronger acceptance of the Otherworld).

One of the great tragedies about Katherine's murder is that it came more than ten years after the Witchcraft Act was repealed. It was also perpetrated by a man known locally for being difficult and cruel. He had previously been accused of various violent acts, including an assault on a family member. But as a tacksman of Clan MacDonald of Armadale, he was a powerful local figure.

McDonald alleged that the destitute Katherine had poisoned some of his men

† He is referred to as both names in the archives. The records were discovered by Skye archivist Catherine MacPhee, whose interest was piqued when she came across a little pencil mark at the side of the original 18th-century papers describing the case, saying, 'as a witch'.

and was intent on causing 'mischief' when she arrived at his house. He tied her hands behind her back and then held her feet over the fire in an attempt to force her to confess that she was a witch. Katherine's feet were badly damaged and, after escaping from McDonald's property and finding her way to a neighbouring house in Duisdale Beag, she succumbed to her injuries nearly two weeks later.

The events took place at a time of great social unrest following the Battle of Culloden in 1746, and McDonald was clearly in the thick of the rebellion. During McDonald's subsequent trial for Katherine's murder, he was also accused of treasonous behaviour, carrying arms and wearing the Highland dress that had been outlawed by the English government in an effort to quell rebellion.

McDonald denied the accusations made against him, calling them 'false and malicious'. He was acquitted of the murder. Perhaps poor Katherine was simply in the wrong place at the wrong time and McDonald used the accusation of witchcraft as a way to legitimize his apparent desire to inflict pain on those who crossed him. Sadly, McDonald will not have been the only person to use the fear of witches as cover for murderous leanings.

LILIAS ADIE'S BURIAL

She goes in the box. It is not a coffin, just a big box that Thomas McLean knocked together and brought to the tollbooth. We wrapped her tight in the shroud, tight as we could. Not that six turns of linen would make much of an obstacle to the Devil if he were so minded to bring her back.

She was tall and fairly sturdy. Manlike. She was an odd one in life, not a bad wifey, but quiet-like. She kept her own counsel. But I know people would go to her if they needed to borrow a bit of money between pays and she was reasonable too. Would take pity if you didn't have the money for an extra couple of days.

I had need of her services once, years back when we first had wee Jeannie, God rest her soul. Wee thing was never well. We saw a charmer for a cure for this scratchy cough the bairn had, which wouldn't clear. We had nothing then and we were desperate. Margaret crying so much because of the wean coughing and not eating or settling. It was pitiful, the two of them, and eventually I went to Lilias, and I asked her for a loan and saw the charmer. For all the good that did. Poor Jeannie never lived to her first year. Lilias was kind about it and gave me a coin back when I repaid her, told me to buy something nice for Margaret.

But that was years ago, and things have been tougher since. Work is hard. The weather is hard. Life is hard. Things have gotten meaner and more bitter. Especially since the new minister came. Now we know it is all down to the Devil getting in and about our business: niggling away at the animals; the crops; the bairns. No one keeps well. Nothing grows well. There are mysterious ailments and deaths.

But Reverend Logan is keeping us safe, and God willing, we'll see better days soon. Torryburn is a good, God-fearing community, and we don't deserve this ill treatment from the Devil.

Once she was accused, you could see the difference in Lilias. She told tales of such horror and sin. From an old woman, an old woman who never even married! That she would lie with the Devil! And now for us to be in this position where we must ensure that the Devil cannot get to her corpse and make her his puppet.

Still. It's a terrible thing. A terrible thing.

Once we got her in the box, we sealed it up and took it down to the shoreline. Reverend Logan had arranged to have a big slab of stone brought down to put over the box to make sure no one could get in or out. We had a job of it, moving the box out to the sands and digging it in, out on the water line. Not easy, but we managed.

Burials are never pleasant, but this was different. Not sad, but queer. None of us spoke all the while. We hardly even looked at each other. I think, really, we were all nervous. Six of the biggest men of the village and all of us scared half to death. We just wanted it done. Moving the stone was a struggle, but as soon as it was on top, we all brightened and went up to the shoreline. A great relief had washed over us. We all felt that something bad had been put away from us and we needed to make absolutely sure that the Devil wouldn't be bringing her back to cause more trouble.

It's hard to square the thought of old Lilias as the Devil's witch. But that's how he gets into villages, the Reverend says. It's through seemingly harmless old women. Maybe not having a husband is what causes it? They don't have a master in the house, so the Devil steps in.

Reverend Logan says that isn't the end, though, and that we must remain vigilant.

I hope he's wrong and that now Lilias has been taken care of, everything will settle back to how it used to be.

12

HOW TO BURY A WITCH

The witch had been troublesome enough in life, but she was even more bother in death and had left the Reverend Allan Logan with quite the problem: he had to find a way to dispose of her corpse in such a way as to make sure she stayed dead.

The Reverend Logan was the first Presbyterian minister at Torryburn, ordained in 1695, just a few years earlier. He was a youthful and energetic minister, determined to make his mark on the small village kirk. He had written a number of well-received books on church discipline and it was important he put into practice what he had preached. He was a man whose hard work and dedication to the Lord had seen him gain a good reputation in the church, where he was considered an intellectual. It hadn't hurt his public standing that he had married into a local landed minor aristocratic family.

Today, he would get rid of this troublesome witch, once and for all.

With its kirk sessions and parish elders, the Church of Scotland today retains the same structure as it did when it was first formed, although now women are allowed to sit as elders too. It is probably difficult to imagine in a 21st-century setting how central the reverend was to every part of his parishioners' lives at the beginning of the 1700s. Think 18th-century religious helicopter parenting and you would be getting close: it was the minister's job to guard the morals of the parish, to rigorously apply the word of God, and to institute and ensure the continuance of all things God and godly in his parish. There was no part of the lives of the people of Torryburn that he did not have the right to enter into and opine upon. Drinking, fornicating, swearing, stealing, lying – their business was his business because, ultimately, it was God's business.

For his local flock in Torryburn, a small fishing village in Fife that probably consisted of two hundred or so souls, life was not easy. The weather was usually cold and wet. It's probable that when the men worked at sea, or tried to mine sea coal from the shore, the woman of the village worked in the salt-panning industry. Although that might conjure up ladies sitting by the water's edge genteelly sifting the sea salt, the reality was that during the evaporation process to extract the salt, the blood of cattle was added to the heated water in order to gather up any impurities, which could then be skimmed off. The village would no doubt have regularly been covered in a haze of foul-smelling, boiling blood. Food was in short supply; medical treatments for any ailments were rudimentary. It is hardly surprising that villagers wanted to find some ways to brighten up their somewhat dismal lives – and it was here, monitoring their behaviour, that the Reverend Allan Logan had to be the most vigilant. In order to keep God's laws he had to remind the locals, frequently, that the sins of the flesh and drinking were the gateway behaviours to the Devil himself. To the modern eye it may seem that God was not much fun and insistently cracked down on what small amount of pleasure could be had in such difficult times, but Reverend Logan would have been assured he was helping to save their immortal souls.

As with most men of his time, Reverend Logan was, in 1704, wholly seized of the unshakable, genuine belief that the Devil was alive and a very real threat to his flock. To allow infractions of God's law in the village was to invite Satan himself to visit. The Devil's business was to tempt away the vulnerable, to make them his witches and to use them to bring misery on the good, law-abiding folk – stealing from the devout, ruining their food, afflicting them with terrible ailments, even killing them. The Reverend Logan was not going to let this happen to his parishioners, not on his watch.

From the start of his career in Torryburn, he had been scrupulous enough to ensure that, aside from those who drank a little too much, and the odd adulterous allegation, God's laws were properly observed. As a result, Satan had not infiltrated the parish. Sadly, that state of affairs was to end quite suddenly on

30 July 1704. That we know so much about the allegations that arose, and what happened in the following months, is down in large part to the Reverend Logan himself, as he was a man of punctilious kirk session minute-keeping. His notes reveal that he was very much concerned on this particular summer's day because he had just heard an allegation of witchcraft.

What fear he must have felt at that moment, knowing that despite his very best efforts Satan had managed to get a cloven-hoofed foothold in his hamlet. It is clear that he treated the matter with the utmost seriousness as he immediately convened an emergency sitting of the kirk. After discussion with the elders, it was agreed that in order to properly deal with an accusation of this sort, a public court hearing would need to take place. Witnesses would be called to appear and evidence would be taken from them so that the Reverend could assess the seriousness of the situation.

Imagine the stir such a hearing would have caused in a small hamlet where nothing much of *any* sort took place, where the only entertainment that didn't wholly fall foul of God's rules was gossip – and presumably gossip about a witch in the parish would be the very sort of gossip God would want to encourage, to warn everyone that the Devil was in town.

The first witness to be called to give evidence was a woman who lived about half a mile outside Torryburn, Jean Bissett of the parish. It was she who was the initial source of the witchcraft accusation. She said that she had left her house with her child on the previous Tuesday morning, and she was part of a group of six or so women and two men, socializing, moving from house to house, chatting with neighbours and friends. The Reverend's fears that drink had been taken were confirmed when she admitted that ale had been drunk by all. The evidence of Jean Bissett as part of this idle, drinking group can hardly have impressed Logan, but equally, if the Devil were to get anyone over to his side, the idle drinkers of the parish would be the very sort that were vulnerable to temptation.

Jean explained that she and her group of friends had visited three or four houses during the course of the day and that by about 9pm she had fallen into a deep sleep. She woke from this sleep disorientated. Her friends who were with her, also called to give evidence, described her as ranting, havering, talking nonsense.

Of this Jean was certain, though – an old woman in the parish called Lilias Adie had used witchcraft and put a spell on her. She also said that Janet White, another local woman, was involved in bewitching her. According to the eyewitnesses at the party, Jean said about Lilias, 'She's done for me, her and the Devil.' She also said to those that were still sober enough to listen: 'I think, and Janet White as well, she's put the spell on me.'

Janet White was a woman known to Jean, as Jean had borrowed money for ale from her and was yet to pay her back. From what can be gleaned from the evidence of others, the party continued on for a good few hours thereafter, with no one paying much attention to Jean. At around midnight she left the party, her child still in tow, and returned home. It was said she was acting out of sorts – jumping and skipping and suchlike. The next day a friend of Jean's travelled to her house at Craigmill to see how she was and found her very ill. She was feverish, had a headache and felt awful. This sickness lasted for a whole day.

What's happening here, then?

Well . . . The more doubting among us might think that far from suffering the effects of a satanic spell, was it possible that Jean was merely horribly hungover and looking for someone to blame? In this small village in the 18th century, it would certainly be frowned on for women to be seen careering around the village late at night, drunk and not taking care of her maternal duties. The gossips would have been in overdrive about this wild, ungodly woman – unless of course none of this was Jean's fault, unless Jean had been the victim of a terrible witch or two. It was coincidence, surely, that she owed one of them money, and a well-timed allegation would delay, if not disappear, an outstanding debt.

The minutes record that at the hearing there was at least one strong voice of dissention from the view that witchcraft was the cause of Jean's illness, perhaps from an unlikely source – that of Jean's own husband, John Tanahay. He seemed to take her allegations of witchcraft as the nonsense ramblings of a woman who had had too much to drink. He provided a damning character assessment of his wife to the kirk session, opining to them that she was far too given to keeping bad company and, yes, she drank too much. The records show he stated, 'Gie her to me and I'll ding the Devil out of her.' Perhaps it was because of these observations, or perhaps it was that the Reverend Logan found out that Janet White was a creditor of Jean Bissett, but he was satisfied enough to conclude that the allegation of witchcraft was without merit and the matter could be neatly brought to an end. Neither of the accused women were brought before the minister and his elders to answer the allegation.

And perhaps the history of witchcraft in Torryburn would have ended there, and the investigation into witchcraft accusations against Lilias Adie and Janet White would have been no more than a short, forgotten entry in the kirk session minutes, but for what happened next – the effect of which was to make one of the accused, Lilias Adie, into the most famous woman accused of witchcraft in Scotland – if not, at one time, the world.

Four weeks later, on 30 August, there was another accusation.

This time, a villager called Jean Neilson accused Lilias Adie of putting a spell on her and making her ill. Unfortunately for present purposes, the minutes do not record any further detail about the allegations. What might have happened, purely conjecture of course, is the tendency for gossip to congeal into rumour and then to solidify to fact. Although the Reverend Logan may have been persuaded that the allegations of Jean Bissett were nonsense, the parishioners may have revelled in the excitement of a witchcraft allegation in the parish and weighed for themselves whether or not there was a fellow villager in the Devil's employ.

Unfortunately for Lilias, she may have been more vulnerable to a witchcraft accusation than others. From what we can glean from the kirk session minutes, Lilias was an old woman, at least 60 years old and possibly as old as 80. At a time when life expectancy was much lower than it is now, even the lower estimate was still a considerable age. The minutes don't disclose any family – no husband, son or daughter to speak up for her or to try and protect her from the allegations. For reasons that will become clear, we also know a lot about what Lilias looked like. She was not a physically conventional woman. She was very tall – probably over six foot – and we know she had a smaller than normal head with an oddly shaped skull and significantly protruding front teeth. In short: a vulnerable old woman, without family support, who even looked physically different to the rest of the villagers – if the Devil was to choose a woman to do his evil work, who better than this old crone?

The Reverend Logan was once again quick to act. The minutes tell us that he immediately instructed his assistant, Baillie Williamson, to take Lilias into custody. Although not explicitly stated, we can be pretty sure that Lilias was taken to the strong room in the parish church, to await interrogation the next day. The church that can be seen in Torryburn now is a 19th-century replacement of that original 17th-century church standing on the same site. The Reverend Allan Logan's house remains in place, though, as does a nod to his legacy in the form of Logan Road.

The minutes record that the next day Lilias was interrogated by the Reverend. She was kept in poor conditions, no doubt, but there was little time for her to have been tortured, and there is no evidence to suggest she had been kept awake overnight to deprive her of sleep. Yet when asked if she was a witch, she responded in the most emphatic terms that, yes, she indeed was. She described the Devil and what they did, stating in detail about how he caused her to renounce her baptism, that 'the devil lay with her carnally; and that his skin was cold and his colour black and pale, he had a hat on his head, and his feet was cloven like the feet of a stirk'. She went on to talk of several meetings, of dancing in the moonlight (and in no moonlight) and revelry 'whereof none are now living but herself'. She confirmed she had been a witch for many years, but due to her infirmity in old age she wasn't able to do as much of the Devil's work as she used to, and explained that she had been a witch since what she described as the second burnings of witches, so it's likely that she remembered the trial of a woman, among others, named Anderson in 1666 and the trials before that in 1640.

Over the next month, Lilias was kept in terrible conditions, treated badly, probably kept awake for days on end, and her health no doubt further suffered. It is likely that the delay in obtaining a trial date was because the local court could not consider a case without a warrant from the Privy Council in Edinburgh.

On 29 September, she was interrogated again, and pressed to give up further information about the Devil – in particular, who else in the village had been converted to Satan. Lilias duly accused two local women, Agnes Curry and Elspeth Williamson. Immediately they too were hauled up in front of the kirk session and interrogated. The minutes record that Lilias remained emphatic in her confession, saying that, although her eyes were dimming, her words were as true as she could see the sun in the firmament.

Then, on 30 September, three months after she was first taken into custody, the minutes fall completely silent. Lilias, a very elderly, infirm, vulnerable, self-confessed witch – in a turn of events that was deeply worrying for the Reverend – had died in custody before she could be brought to trial.

So what do you do if you've proven a woman is a witch, but she dies before you have a chance to mete out her punishment in accordance with the law and the appropriate witch-destroying practices of the day? This state of affairs left the Reverend with a very real problem. Lilias's death did not end the agency of the Devil. Logan knew as well as anyone else that unless very significant steps were taken to stop the Devil, he could reanimate Lilias's body to wreak her satanic revenge on the villagers, the elders and himself. It would be highly likely that the Reverend would have heard talk of these 'revenants' who return from the dead and terrorize the community. He could not take the risk that Lilias could cause even greater harm to the community dead than she had in life.

This problem was unique to Lilias's circumstances. While she had confessed to witchcraft, she had not been convicted in a court of law. In the ordinary course of events, the disposal of the body of a witch was done by burning because it was well known that the Devil could not reanimate ashes. But could he burn the body of someone who had not had a lawful trial? And could he deny her a Christian burial? This was a terrible dilemma for a man of God, not only legally and morally, but also in terms of the limitations of his authority.

After some considerable thought the Reverend came up with what he thought was a fool-proof plan, and the evidence that he took this very seriously can be seen in the amount of money and effort it took to put his scheme into place.

It was of course completely out of the question to bury Lilias's body on consecrated church ground. Instead, the Reverend took the decision to bury Lilias in the Torryburn foreshore, where for most of the day, her wooden coffin would be covered in water. This would effectively trap her soul as the undead couldn't cross water, and the Devil wasn't able to do his work either crossing or under water. However, this was not enough on its own: with the changing tides Lilias's grave would not have remained underwater all day. The Reverend therefore decided upon an expensive but wholly necessary solution. He hired a local stonemason to provide a vast sandstone slab, six feet by three feet, and probably about half a tonne in weight, to place over her coffin to keep her remains firmly below the water line. Installing the block above her watery grave would be difficult and expensive but worth it in every sense to ensure that the good folk of Torryburn could sleep safe at night, knowing that the Devil's revenant envoy was not afoot.

And there lay Lilias Adie in her watery resting place on the Torryburn shore, trapped for ever more.

Or so the villagers thought.

It was on this foreshore some three hundred years later we stood nearby speaking to Douglas Speirs,[†] a local archaeologist. Doug, as he asked us to call him, arrived resplendent in tweed, just as a gentleman archaeologist should dress.

Some years before our meeting, Doug had been contacted by witchcraft expert turned broadcaster Louise Yeoman (whom we met in Chapter 4) who had asked him if he was aware of the story of Lilias Adie, and of the unusual gravesite.

---

† Doug Speirs (Dug Spears) is about as good a name for an archaeologist as you can get. Having met us in Culross in Fife for the opening of the Witches Walk memorial, and talked to us about Lilias, Doug was kind enough to speak to us again at length on our podcast. His words quoted here are an amalgam of these meetings.

She said that there were numerous historical references to Lilias being buried in the Torryburn foreshore. Doug didn't know the story but listening to Louise he became fascinated by Lilias's case and, more importantly for present purposes, obsessed with finding her grave.

Doug took a scientific route to the search. 'I immediately made an excuse to go and look for it. My colleague Steven Liscoe searched the Torryburn foreshore for the grave. Torryburn Bay is a big area, and the geology is very distinctive because it is whinstone, a hard blue stone, and what we were looking for was very different – a huge doorstop-shaped block of sandstone. For three long days we walked up and down looking but found nothing. We were looking at the intertidal space – not quite land, not quite sea. On the last day, heading back into shore we saw a large, rectangular-looking block, covered in seaweed. It was only about two metres from the edge of land – we had been searching far out in the bay – but we quickly scraped off the seaweed and there it was: a three-foot-by-six-foot, large, rectangular, sandstone block. It was probably about quarter of a tonne, with a dimple in the middle, showing it had been lifted from a quarry. It was completely alien to the rocks of the bay. We had found the site of Lilias's grave.'

Meanwhile and separately, Louise was carrying out her own, somewhat more haphazard investigations. When did *she* discover the grave?

'Well, I never like to use the word "discovery" because my point would be if you went and asked the right people in that community, they'd always kent about it,' says Louise when we spoke to her on a Zoom call. 'In a way, it was knowledge that was always there and people in the community would have known it. What I basically did was jump up and down about it!'

In truth, Louise did more than that; she put on her wellies and waded out into the sea, to the spot where Lilias's intertidal grave can be found.

Louise laughs her lovely, hearty laugh and says, 'I was recording with A L Kennedy and the fantastic Scottish historian Dr Martha McGill, and I was the mug who put on her wellies. There's always silty mud there. The thing is, my background is as a historian and manuscript curator. Show me a 16th-century document and I'll have a good go at reading it. I know about documents. I know nothing about stones! I was just armed with all this local history and was thinking it ought to be around here. I'll just have to wade out and have a look at it. I saw this grey, rectangular stone. One of the local histories had described it as being like a giant doorstep. That's got to be it!'

Now we stood staring at the large, grey sandstone slab, only a couple of metres from where we stood on the pavement at the foreshore. The sea water lapped around it. The land all around the slab was sludgy and grey. The sort of mud that you could easily lose a wellington boot to.

Doug explained that a horse and cart or a 'yanker' – a wheeled cart employed to move big stones – would have been used to hump the heavy stone to its destination. It would have been far from an easy job.

We fell to talking about Lilias herself. We know that the accusation against her was made-up nonsense, but we wondered why on earth she confessed.

'I don't think she did confess,' says Doug, who has looked into the case in a great deal of depth. 'On 30 June she has spent one night in custody and she's interrogated for the first time. The minute records that Lilias is being exhorted to declare the truth and nothing but the truth. She is alleged to have replied, "Be this as true as the sun is in the firmament." This declaration that everything she is going to say is true immediately makes me think that these minutes have been faked. Who speaks like that when they're panicking and frightened and in custody? It's recorded that she admitted she was in compact with the Devil, and that she had been so since before the second burning of the witches in this place. She further declared that the first time she met with the Devil was at a small local river between Torryburn and Newmills, in the harvest time before the sunset. He caused her to renounce her baptism by putting one hand on the crown of her head and the other on the soles of feet and declaring that all was the Devil's betwixt the crown of her head and the soles of her feet. Then the Devil lay with her carnally and his skin was cold, his colour was black and pale,[†] and he had a hat on his head.'

† As in, black hair/clothing, pale skin.

So, as Doug explains, 'on the very first day, at 9am, after being taken into custody, Lilias is interrogated and apparently those are her first words, or certainly that's what the minister in the kirk session recorded. And of course, what we see is there's a very clear black and white confession of evildoings with the Devil. With almost no prompting, Lilias confessed that she was a witch. She renounced Christian baptism; she had had sex with the Devil; she had willingly entered into an evil satanic baptism.'

As we have seen with other confessions – this is all very familiar from Isobel Gowdie's case, for example – it's conveniently all there. 'And of course,' Doug continues, 'she knew, and anybody would have known fine well at this point, that when you confess to witchcraft, it's certain death. So, it seems very suspicious that somebody would sit and make such a self-condemning confession on the first morning.'

Our interpretation is that, rather than the confession being faked, that Lilias might have just confessed due to the fear of torture, as she would have known what to say to make sure she wouldn't be tortured in the future. Or she could have just caved in from the psychological pressure. It's surprising, but Claire finds in her work that people confess regularly to things that they haven't done, even when no pressure is being put on them. There are all sorts of procedural safeguards against this in modern criminal law, such as having a lawyer present or giving a 'right to remain silent' caution. But of course no such safeguards existed then and we know people regularly confessed to things that just were not true. We wondered why Doug was so sure that the whole confession was fabricated by Reverend Logan and not just Lilias trying to avoid torture?

'Ah, well, firstly, as I said, she makes a cast-iron confession of guilt. She makes a very clear declaration she is telling the truth. She goes into detail about renouncing her baptism. Today we're not terribly worried about that, but back then baptism was a fundamentally important prerequisite of entry into heaven, so this was really, really, important. You couldn't get a bigger deal than confessing to having renounced your baptism. Not only that, but then it's said that she immediately confesses to taking part in a satanic baptism. And, of course, then to add to all of this, and to rubbish her character as a woman and as a person, she gives details of sealing that compact by having sex – fornication in a field with the Devil! I mean, goodness! In a single statement, she manages to absolutely condemn herself. Beyond any question. Are these really the words of an elderly woman in a tiny little backwater parish in 1704? I would say what we're seeing here is complete fabrication of the minutes. What makes me utterly convinced that she did not say any of this, what is most compelling, is that if we study the kirk records of witchcraft in Fife, we find that in 1649 Margaret Martin in Inverkeithing confessed in exactly the same way about the satanic baptism. Is it likely that 55 years before these events, somebody would have used almost exactly the same words? This is a word-for-word copy. Now we can conclude one of two things. Either the Devil is real, and he was operating in West Fife from the 17th century, having sex with women and forcing them to renounce their baptism. Or we have an institution, in this case the church, which basically has a preconceived idea and is forcing it on those that it considered guilty.'

We have seen similar examples of word-for-word translations in the case of Isobel Gowdie and Janet Breadheid.[†] But for Doug, the copied confession is not the only issue. As he explains: 'If I needed to make the case any more clearly that this was a fixed record, when we really drill down into the minutes, we actually find that there are many entries in the minutes that describe events that don't happen until a week or a few days after the date of the minutes. So clearly these minutes should have been written up *immediately after* the event. But the fact that they include certain references to events that didn't happen for another two weeks gives us some kind of idea that these minutes weren't written up at the time as things were being said, or even the next day or that night. They could have been written up to two to three weeks afterwards in some cases. So, this is clearly an account of what the court wanted recorded and probably not an accurate account of what actually happened. So, for example, in the minutes it says that 20 June is a Tuesday. But when you actually consult the historical calendars, you find out

† There are also much more recent examples. In the 1980s 'Ice Cream Wars' case, which concerned gang turf wars in Glasgow, convictions for murder were quashed on appeal when the court decided it was not likely that a number of police officers could remember one of the accused's statements 'word for word'.

that that was a Friday. Now is it likely that they wouldn't know what day of the week it was in 1704?'

Could these minutes have been a retrospective back-covering exercise? Did the Reverend panic because Lilias had died in custody? Did he want to make it clear that what had happened was that a terrible old witch had got her comeuppance, so he over-egged it a bit, used a bit of artistic licence and copied the confession from previous minutes?

After a long, reflective pause, Doug answers, 'My view of things is that there are pages and pages and pages in the Torryburn kirk session minutes from mid-June 1704 to 3 September 1704 about this case and then suddenly nothing was mentioned after that for four weeks. Remember, the suspected witch Lilias has been incarcerated and interrogated. She has spilled the beans on another three women at least. They are then brought in and interrogated, and they start pointing the finger too. Other women and witches are being discovered everywhere. So, from nowhere, a single accusation has snowballed into this. A localized parish witch-hunt within a month has gone from one witch to witches absolutely everywhere. And then, suddenly overnight, the case closes and there's no further record or mention of anything or any charges or cases against anyone ever again. Now, how do we account for this? Well, my view – and it's only a personal view, not substantiated – I think two things happened. I think one is that the Reverend Allan Logan and his elders and baillie got carried away and they've treated Lilias so badly that she's died in custody. And when the kirk session and the minister have approached the civil authorities and asked for a mandate for a legal commission to try the remaining witches, the civil authorities have denied the warrant and effectively said, "Stop being so silly and stop torturing your poor old residents like this with trumped-up, ridiculous charges." So, knowing that they couldn't get a proper legal trial as they wouldn't be granted a warrant, they've just been told to pretty much drop the case. I think that's probably what's happened. Secondly, I think we have to appreciate the death was essentially an illegal killing, in the sense that there wasn't a legal mandate for it. While there were powers for the church to investigate this case and to take confessions and so on, there was no legal basis to actually bring about a death without due and proper authority.'

Doug means, of course, that there had been no trial; that her death before trial, possibly as a result of the way in which she had been kept or what she had to endure, was as a result of an as-yet-unsubstantiated allegation. It was not a good look for the authorities.

So after her death in custody, the minutes make no further reference to witches, witchcraft or compacts with the Devil. What happened to Agnes Curry and Elspeth Williamson, who had been accused by Lilias?

'There is just no further mention of it, like it never happened. It supports my theory that after Lilias's death everyone wanted to just forget about it. There's one last piece of information the minutes reveal, which seals the deal as far as I'm concerned that the Reverend Allan Logan was up to no good in relation to Lilias's "confession". In 1715, the Reverend left Torryburn Parish as the minister there, and he got moved up the road to Culross. There is a record of him writing back to his former parish, and guess what he was asking for? Of all the things, he wanted the minutes of Lilias Adie's case. Why did he want these minutes all these many years later? My feeling is he wanted to rewrite history and to get rid of that record for some reason. Again, we don't have enough evidence to be sure of this, but why else would he want those minutes? Thankfully, for whatever reason, he didn't get them, which is why we know Lilias's story today.'

We watched the sea coming in, now almost covering the huge slab of stone under which Lilias's casket lay. So this is where Lilas Adie lies to this day?

'Oh no,' said Doug. 'Lilias did indeed revenant, although it wasn't the Devil who brought her back.'

PART THREE:
A THING OF THE PAST?

13
HOW TO LOSE A WITCH

'Her grave was robbed,' said Doug Speirs.

'By witches?'

'Nope, by locals.'

The water lapped around our feet as we continued to look at Lilias's grave, being swallowed up the incoming tide.

'So, wait, are you meaning to tell us the same poor woman who died in custody and was locked in a box and buried at sea in an effort to stop her coming back was then in fact brought back by the folk who had put her there?'

'Not quite,' said Doug.

The mastermind of this criminal act wasn't born until 1797, some 62 years after the revocation of the Scottish Witchcraft Act. Joseph Neil Paton was, as was not uncommon of men of his time, deeply religious. The son of a Unitarian, he joined the Presbyterian Church as a youth, then turned Methodist, then Quaker, before finally settling into Swedenborgianism, a type of Restorationist Christianity. While the belief in witches had waned, the belief in God had not. However, more uncommonly, his religious fervour was such that he built his own chapel in the grounds of his land so he could deliver sermons from his very own pulpit.

It's not every man that could afford to build his own chapel but Joseph Neil Paton had done very well in business. His trade was weaving, which was a common business of the time, but he combined this with a natural gift as an artist to create intricate and delicate designs in damask. His cloth was so admired that after his death in 1874 the Victoria and Albert Museum bought over seven hundred of his designs. He was married to folklorist Catherine MacDairmid, who hailed from the Highlands. They lived in Dunfermline, a town a couple of miles inland from the Firth of Forth, in a grand family home. His interest in all things religious went much further than sermons, however; in fact it was his hobbies of phrenology and the collection of witchcraft artefacts that led him to Lilias.

Phrenology was the brainchild of a man called Franz Joseph Gall, an 18th-century German doctor who believed that he could tell the mental traits and character of a person through the study of their skull. The theory was that different areas of the brain were shaped according to character trait, and that by examining the skull you could ascertain the character of a person. Later 'scientists' in this field, Johann Spurzheim and George Combe, went on to create the well-known picture of a human skull split up into different areas, which many would later associate with this wholly discredited field of study. It would appear that the misplaced confidence of delusional men is not a new phenomenon.

No doubt living in Dunfermline, only five miles from Torryburn, with a wife who collected folk tales, Paton was well aware of the story of Lilias Adie and her revenant grave. As intersections go, a witch's skull would be the apex of twin obsessions with local tales of witchcraft and phrenology. And so, with the unfettered ambition of a typical Victorian collector, he decided he had to have it.

In order to turn his desire into reality, he contacted Robert Baxter Brimmer, grave robber for hire.

The crime of grave robbing, or to give it its official name 'violation of a sepulchre', was all the rage for criminals in the 18th and 19th centuries. Graves were sources of jewellery and artefacts that could be obtained for little work by those with a disregard for superstition and a strong stomach. In Scotland, stealing corpses to sell to anatomists was particularly common, as Edinburgh was a leading centre of anatomical study and Scottish law had strict controls about which corpses could be used for medical research. It was a simple case of supply and demand.† Violating sepulchres became such a frequent occurrence that

† The most infamous criminals associated with this period were William Burke and William Hare, who took this trend to its logical conclusion. In 1828 they committed a series of

steps were taken to deter those who sought to tomb-raid by erecting large iron 'mortsafe' cages, bolted above the grave. They could be rented for a time to allow bodies to decompose in dignified peace or they could be installed permanently. If that wasn't enough, many cemeteries had watchmen appointed to ensure that the graveyards stayed as quiet as, well, the grave. By the middle of the 19th century, the tide was turning against the 'resurrection men'.

For Robert Baxter Brimmer, a young man in his early twenties in 1852, the grave of Lilias Adie provided some interesting challenges. It would not be easy robbing a grave half-buried underwater, particularly in the dead of night. Added to that, this grave belonged to a witch, making this not so much an illegal endeavour – as the ground was not consecrated – but one that might threaten his mortal soul and those of the local villagers.

So, how do you go about finding a witch buried for a century? With surprising ease, as it happens. The local folklore was quite clear that under an enormous cut stone in the Torryburn Bay lay the box that held the witch's mortal remains. As we have seen with the 21st-century efforts to locate the slab, it is still visible at low tide. In the 19th century it would presumably have been even easier to find, as less time had elapsed since it had first been laid there.

In any event, once he and his accomplices had located the incongruous slab, they set to work to gain entry. They knew they had to work quickly before the tide returned or the locals woke, but moving a six-foot-by-three-foot stone in ordinary circumstances is challenging enough; adding to that the boggy mud in which they stood complicated matters enormously. It was only dogged determination and the promise of Paton's purse that enabled Brimmer and co to achieve their grisly endeavour. Once they had revealed the box, the men doubtless caught their

16 murders in order to sell the corpses to an anatomy lecturer for dissection, for which crimes Burke was hanged (Hare was later released as he had given evidence against his former partner). Contrary to popular belief, it appears they did not actually rob any graves themselves.

breath before breaking open the lid sealed a century before. Inside, among the sludgy silt, was the disarrayed mortal remains of the now revenant witch, Lilias Adie.

Working quickly, the grave robbers exhumed their bony treasure. They carried away the skull, ribs and a femur. Brimmer, no doubt realizing the interest in such a curio, also took some wood from the box before sealing up the lid again and replacing the stone slab above it, where it lies to this day.

In his collector's zeal, Paton had ordered a number of grave robberies across Fife but this particular assignment held more than the usual promise of phrenological interest. So what did Paton do with his haul? Given his interest in phrenology and religion, it would seem extremely likely that he carefully studied poor Lilias's skull, to see what knowledge he could glean from it. Could he tell her to be evil from her skull? Had the Devil left his mark not only on her body and soul but in her brain itself? By the time these investigations were taking place few people believed in witchcraft any more, but we think it reasonable to assume that Paton's strong religious beliefs may have led to him taking a more traditional approach to his study than most.

Phrenology was the process of dividing the brain into 27 parts, each denoting some human sentiment. The difficulty was – and perhaps here was the clue that this was not a legitimate science – hardly anyone could agree on what each of these 27 parts signified. It provided an opportunity for anyone with confidence, fingertips and a measuring tape to feel a human skull and proclaim knowledge of that person's character. That findings promoted gender and racial stereotyping are, we are sure, not a coincidence. You might be unsurprised to learn that phrenologists believed that the majority of women's skulls revealed that they were good at childcare but that their brains were underdeveloped when it came to science, art and pretty much everything else.

History records that the highheidyins who visited Paton in Dunfermline would be treated to a display of Lilias's skull, which was kept in Paton's private collection until his death in 1874. Paton left a detailed will, and from that it can be gleaned that Lilias's skull is likely to have gone to his first-born son, Joseph Noel Paton.

Joseph Noel Paton (1821–1901) was a gifted and famous Scottish artist and his art depicts many images of witches, demons and fairies. He received a knighthood in later life, and some of his works can now be seen in the National Gallery of Scotland.

'You can see his father's artefacts in his paintings,' explained Doug. 'Swords and such. I have a theory that you can even see Lilias's skull in a couple of them. If you look at the painting *Luther at Erfurt* [1861], there is a skull in the background. I think there is a reasonable chance it's the skull of Lilias Adie.'

Sure enough, Paton Junior had painted a tortured Martin Luther, former disillusioned Catholic priest and founder of Protestantism, poring over his texts at the University of Erfurt – and there, lurking on the corner of his desk, was a skull. Could this be Lilias? And if it was there in 1861, where is she now?

In 1884, Paton Junior passed on Lilias's skull to a Dr William Dow of the Fife Medical Association. Dr Dow in that same year conducted a detailed examination of the skull and wrote a paper on it, as well as giving lectures on it. After keeping it for several years he gave her skull to the University of St Andrews' collection of anatomical artefacts. It was still being held there in 1901 as a member of the Dunfermline press photographed it for an article on Lilias's case.

But Doug has some bad news for us. 'In 2014 when I discovered her grave, the first thing I did was to contact the university to ask to see her skull. To my surprise, they couldn't find it!'

Doug thereafter undertook a painstaking search for any mention of her skull in documentary evidence that was available from that time. Almost miraculously he found a small item in a local newspaper from Falkirk in 1938, which had a throwaway reference to the Empire Exhibition in Glasgow, where readers were informed they could view the skull of a real witch, Lilias Adie.

The Empire Exhibition of 1938, a show intended to showcase Scotland on an international stage, was based on the Great Exhibition of 1851 in London.

Little did the planners realize the success of their exhibition would outstrip all the others; in total it received an amazing 12,800,000 visitors – every single one of whom had the opportunity to view Lilias's skull.

Sadly, from this point in 1938 the trail runs cold, and to date there have been no further mentions or sightings of Lilias's skull.

And where did the rest of Lilias's remains go? Are there still bones under the huge slab? As robbers are not the best at completing inventories, we can't be sure how much of Lilias's remains remain in Torryburn, but Doug thinks there are probably some bones still there.

But what about her femur and the pieces of wood taken from the box she was put in?

'For that,' said Doug, 'you'll need to go to Dunfermline.'

Robert Baxter Brimmer, erstwhile grave robber, had moved on since his early days as a tomb raider for hire. He had left the shores of Torryburn far behind and had long since emigrated to Ontario, Canada, where he had become a successful man of business.[†] His youthful high jinks in Torryburn were long gone but not forgotten.

On 11 November 1871, an incredibly successful fellow Dumfries émigré visited Ontario, and this presented Robert Baxter Brimmer with an unusual problem: what gift would you give the man who literally has everything? His fellow Scot, Andrew Carnegie, was one of the richest men in the world – if not *the* richest – an industrialist who made his money from the steel industry. And then it came to Brimmer. He had the perfect, most unique, quite unforgettable gift – a memento from the old country.

We made the trip to Dunfermline on a dreich Tuesday afternoon to meet Jennifer Jones, the co-manager of the Andrew Carnegie Birthplace Museum.

† Alas, details of his business are not known.

Dawn: Luther at Erfurt, Sir Joseph Noel Paton, 1861

The museum is made up of two buildings. One building is a small cottage which has a plaque on the wall that boasts of, you guessed it, being the birthplace of the 'philanthropist and businessman'. The other, a larger, more ornate building with a big hall, tells the incredible story of Carnegie's life and is filled with historical artefacts gathered by him and his wife.

As much as we wanted to stay in that hall and find out what the connection was between Carnegie and Big Bird from *Sesame Street,* whom we saw nesting in one of the glass boxes along with puppet pals Bert and Ernie,[†] we dutifully followed Jennifer to an office above the main hall. There, on the desk, lay an unassuming long, wooden walking cane.

Jennifer carefully picked up the cane and handed it to us to examine. As we looked closely, we saw there was very faded, carved handwriting that ran down the length of the stick. To the untrained eye what was written couldn't be deciphered but helpfully Jennifer showed us a typed museum label, which read:

> *A walking stick with a grisly history which reminds us that dark deeds were carried out only a few centuries ago, often in ignorance, against women who were deemed to be witches. Written in ink on the straight, wooden cane is the following inscription:*
>
> 'This is made from part of the coffin of Lillian Eadie, who was burned for a witch[‡] and buried within the sea mouth of Torryburn, Fifeshire, Scotland, and dug up by James Bonner[§] and others about 1860. The skull and some of the bones and parts of the coffin are now either in the British

---

† In 1911, Carnegie established the Carnegie Corporation of New York, to provide grants to deserving causes. One such grant was given to fund a groundbreaking TV show to help the education of children – *Sesame Street*!

‡ As can be seen, the inscription is not entirely accurate in respect of her name or the manner of death.

§ Presumably an accomplice of Brimmer's.

Museum, London, or Saint Andrews, sent there by Mr Paton, father of Sir Noel Paton.'

Presented to Mr Carnegie by R B Brimmer, Toronto, 11th November 1871.

It was the very wood from the box that Lilias Adie was buried in.

Knowing about history is one thing. Seeing and touching history is a very different proposition. The power of a historical artefact is hugely important. It is not a coincidence that, in war, enemy invaders not only target vital utilities but also take care to destroy places of historical importance and treasures of history.

To think that this nondescript piece of wood had been part of the box that once held the body of a woman accused of witchcraft, had travelled to Canada as the loot of a tomb raider, and had been gifted to the world's richest man before making it back home to Fife and into our hands, was quite extraordinary – a tangible connection to the past that left us feeling humbled and amazed.

In 2017, Lilias Adie's connection to the present took another extraordinary step when forensic artist Dr Christopher Rynn worked with the University of Dundee's Leverhulme Research Centre and reconstructed her face from the photographs and measurements that had been taken of her skull before it was lost.

If you want to look into the eyes of a woman from Torryburn who lived as a woman and died as a witch, then Dr Rynn's reconstruction is remarkable. The face of Lilias Adie shows a kindly woman, with a half-smile, a little bemused at the fame she never, ever could have imagined she would achieve in her lifetime.

So we remember Lilias as a poor, old, probably ostracized and lonely woman who was accused of something of which she was not guilty, of being imprisoned and harassed by the very society that ought to have protected her, and then even in death further exploited for the entertainment purposes of wealthy men. Her death is only one example of the thousands of women and men who were also accused without foundation, terrified, tortured and executed.

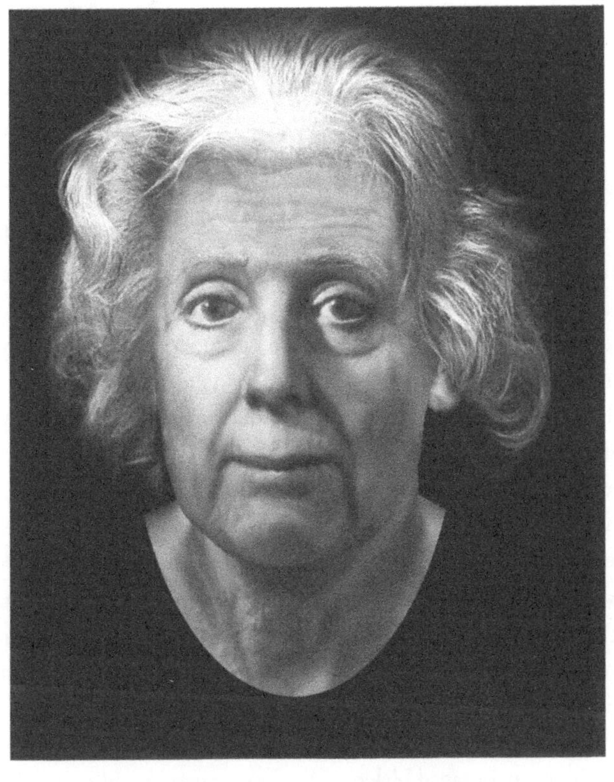

Reconstruction of Lilias Adie's face by forensic scientist Dr Christopher Rynn, 2017

PORTRAIT OF THE ACCUSED

HELEN DUNCAN

LONDON 1944

Victoria Helen MacFarlane was born in the autumn of 1897 in Callander, Perthshire. She was one of eight children. Despite coming from a typical Presbyterian background, Helen (as she was known) was given to bouts of high drama and terrifying her friends with tales of the supernatural. She believed she could prophesy the future: she told people about dangers they should avoid and claimed she had psychic abilities. It was at primary school that she was given the nickname 'Hellish Nell', which still clings to her name now.

When she left school, Helen moved to Dundee, a much bigger town, where she gained work first in a munitions factory, then as a nurse in Dundee Royal Infirmary. On 27 May 1916, she married a cabinet maker named Henry Duncan, who had been invalided out from the war. The couple had 12 children but, sadly, only six survived. As well as bringing up the children, Helen had to take up part-time, arduous work in a bleach factory to make ends meet, as her husband's ill health made full-time work impossible.

Helen and Henry both said that they'd had visions of each other before they met and Henry encouraged Helen to develop her psychic abilities, as he came from a family who purported to have the gift of second sight. She started to hold séances for both the wider public and in more intimate, private settings, and steadily gained a tremendous reputation for her readings. Séances would take place in various locations, including Spiritualist churches and people's homes; she would commune with the dead, often reassuring the bereaved that there was life after death and that loved ones were watching from beyond the grave.

By the mid-1920s, in the wake of the devastating losses of the First World War, Helen had developed her skills and reputation for her sittings to such an extent that she was in demand all over Great Britain and was becoming well known in Spiritualist circles. When so many families had recently suffered losses, many saw Spiritualism as a way of keeping in touch with their dead sons and husbands, or at the very least to be reassured that they were in a better place.

At a Spiritualist sitting, the attendees sat in a very dark room in a semicircle, gathered around a 'cabinet' to which the medium was led. The medium would be searched to make sure they weren't hiding any tricks or gadgets, then they would get into the cabinet. In Helen's case, Henry usually sat at the back of the room during the sitting. Then the medium entered a trance and usually a spirit would speak through them and deliver messages and also speak to other spirits who had come to talk to the sitters. Helen had a spirit guide called Albert Stuart who, although he had originally come from Dundee, had emigrated to and died in Australia. His voice came out of Helen's mouth and supposedly he spoke in a less Scottish accent than the one Helen usually spoke in. He'd then introduce the other spirits who would arrive during the sitting. The curtains on the cabinet would be opened and 'ectoplasm' – so-called 'spiritual energy' – would make an appearance, usually streaming from Helen's nose and mouth. Sitters often thought the ectoplasm (actually white cloth) resembled their deceased loved ones.

During her career, Helen's work was frequently investigated, during which, among other measures, she was sewn into a special tamper-proof suit and samples of various types of ectoplasm were examined. Ultimately the researchers found that Helen's mediumship used some fraudulent practices but was genuine too. Confusing. There were clearly some very obviously fraudulent aspects to Helen's séances – such as her use of cheesecloth as ectoplasm – but there were also aspects that couldn't be so easily explained away.

In 1931, the great psychic researcher and sceptic Harry Price[†] weighed in when he had Helen do five sittings to gather evidence. The ectoplasm was photographed,

† Price (1881–1948) was a British psychic researcher who found fame debunking various fake mediums, although he did endorse those he believed to be genuine. He covered several famous cases, including that of the Borley Rectory ('the most haunted house in England'), the Battersea Poltergeist and Gef the talking mongoose, along with many others.

scientifically examined and subsequently exposed as being cheesecloth, and Price also discovered that Helen had used various tricks, including using a cut-out picture of a child's face to simulate a head appearing and safety pins to shape the ectoplasm. A former maid of the Duncans also alleged that she had been given the task of cleaning the filthy and foul-smelling used muslins.

Helen was first convicted in 1933 of fraudulent mediumship and fined £10. Despite this, her reputation grew, and she was in great demand for sittings. At the height of the Second World War, in November 1941, Helen held a séance in Portsmouth where her performance included her 'seeing' a sailor who had died in the sinking of the HMS *Barham* a short while previously, a tragedy in which 862 crewmen had died. The only problem was there was a strict hush-hush policy on the ship's destruction for reasons of national security. No one was supposed to know. Having said that, with that number of sailors dying, of course their families were informed and naturally hundreds of people *did* in fact know about the sinking. Despite this, the powers-that-be kept an eye on her.

In 1944, two naval men, Lieutenant Worth and Surgeon-Lieutenant Fowler, saw Helen at a sitting organized by a local couple, Mr and Mrs Homer. The two men were suspicious about some of the details, not least Helen's claim to be in contact with a woman who wasn't yet dead, and some of the sounds emanating from Helen. They reported her to the police. Worth attended a second sitting (this time with a plain-clothes policeman) at which a white-shrouded vision appeared – rather pathetically, this turned out to be Helen covered in a sheet, which she was caught attempting to hide when she was apprehended. Helen, the Homers and a lady called Mrs Brown were all arrested.

Normally in England, this sort of fraudulent mediumship was dealt with under the 1824 Vagrancy Act, but as the authorities wished to deal harshly with Helen (perhaps to make an example of her), she was also later charged, rather sensationally, under the Witchcraft Act of 1735. The prime minister Winston Churchill was unimpressed with what he viewed as the 'obsolete tomfoolery' of the charge, but the case ran, and after a seven-day trial, she was found guilty and sentenced to nine months in prison.

Helen Duncan died in 1956 following a police raid that her supporters blamed for her early death. She was the last person to be convicted under a Witchcraft Act in the UK.[†] There have been various recent campaigns to pardon her. All have failed.

The 1735 Witchcraft Act was repealed in 1951.

† The legal systems of England and Scotland are different and have different laws, although confusingly sometimes the statutes passed have the same names: in this case, we are talking about the 1735 Witchcraft Act that was in place in both Scotland and England.

14

HOW TO ACCUSE A MODERN-DAY WITCH PART I

The very last witch trial in England[†] was towards the end of the Second World War in 1944, a full 217 years from Janet Horne's execution in Scotland in 1727. Unlike the traditional witchcraft accusations, this story is markedly different, not least because we can much more easily identify with the people of this period. However, some key points remain the same. A woman causes anxiety and falls out of favour during a difficult time for the country. The woman must be made an example of and suitably punished.

When Helen Duncan was brought to trial, the judge addressed the court and said very clearly, especially to the assembled journalists who were hungry for lurid headlines: 'Though we are using the Witchcraft Act, Mrs Duncan is not on trial for witchcraft. This is not a witch trial – this is an accusation of fraud.'

Yet, inevitably, by choosing to prosecute using the Witchcraft Act 1735, the authorities had ensured that the trial had all those connotations firmly embedded. In Scotland, when the Witchcraft Acts of 1563 and 1649 were repealed, and the Witchcraft Act 1735 was put in place, the crime of witchcraft as defined by the earlier acts was firmly rejected in favour of the crime of 'pretended witchcraft' – so ironically the charge was that she was *not* a witch, but was pretending to have powers that she did not have.

Of course, despite this legal distinction, the public saw the whole circus as a salacious witch trial and it firmly grabbed everyone's imagination for several weeks during the seemingly interminable war.

† Technically speaking, it was a 'pretended' witch trial as the crime of witchcraft changed to that of 'pretended witchcraft' to reflect the fact that witchcraft did not exist.

We spoke to historian Malcolm Gaskill who has written various books on witch trials and a standalone book on Helen Duncan. Malcolm is emeritus professor at the University of East Anglia. We love speaking to Malcolm and, in fact, the first couple of times we chatted over Zoom, we almost forgot we were all in different locations and indeed why we had to meet online rather than in person.† Malcolm is not only very knowledgeable, but also great fun.

The first thing we wanted to clarify was why on earth did the Crown charge Helen Duncan with such an antiquated crime? Malcolm told us that the Spiritualists who were defending one of their own in the case had asked the exact same question. It turns out that the Crown also charged her with another crime 'in the alternative', which is a perfectly acceptable thing to do in law. A person may be charged with more than one crime if the Crown thinks that one charge isn't quite guaranteed, or that the evidence may be stronger in favour of one charge over another. In the case of Helen Duncan, she was originally accused of the much more straightforward crime of fraud under the Vagrancy Act,‡ which includes the crimes of 'pretending or professing to tell fortunes, or using any subtle craft, means, or device, by palmistry or otherwise, to deceive and impose on any of his Majesty's subjects', as well as being charged under the common law of public mischief, and it seems the witchcraft charge was tacked on as well because the Crown wanted to make an example of behaviour, which was not considered good for the war effort. Her colleagues Ernest and Elizabeth Homer, who ran the psychic centre in Portsmouth, and her agent Frances Brown were also charged. The conspiracy element of the charge related to the four appellants who 'conspired together and with other persons unknown to pretend to exercise or use any kind of conjuration, to wit, that through the agency of the said Helen Duncan spirits of deceased persons should appear to be present in fact in such place as the said Helen Duncan then was in, and that the said spirits were communicating with living persons then and there present'.

† Thanks, Covid.

‡ Section 4 of the Vagrancy Act 1824 has the raffish title of 'Persons committing certain offences to be deemed rogues and vagabonds'.

'Helen is charged under Section 4 of the 1824 Vagrancy Act, which is mainly for exactly this kind of fraud,' says Malcolm. 'It was introduced after the Napoleonic Wars, particularly to stop returning soldiers fleecing people by becoming palmists.'

After the Napoleonic Wars of 1803–15, many soldiers were coming back injured and unable to earn an 'honest' living, and were therefore forced to turn to various means to survive. Fast forward around 120 years and the law was still in use in England and Wales, but now it was used more for Spiritualists and mediums who were taking advantage of distressed people who had lost loved ones in the two world wars.

As Malcolm points out, it has always been the case that poverty and witchcraft are often closely intertwined. As we've seen time and again, it is generally people with less power who are viewed with suspicion and who may on some occasions have to make money with charming, or who may fall out with neighbours due to the kind of issues that can surround poverty, such as alcohol problems or anti-social behaviour.

In the 1940s, someone charged with the Vagrancy Act for this kind of fraud would have usually just received a fine for fraudulent crimes, as other Spiritualists had done in the past. But in Helen's case the authorities also charged her under Section 4 of the 1735 Witchcraft Act, which covers anyone who 'pretend[s] to exercise or use any kind of Witchcraft, Sorcery, Inchantment, or Conjuration, or undertake[s] to tell Fortunes'. When the case came to trial, the vagrancy charges were dropped and the Crown only proceeded on the charge under the Witchcraft Act. The authorities were keen to stamp out the trend of Spiritualism – which they considered fraudulent – by any means necessary.

However, as Helen was a high-profile medium, the Spiritualist National Union (SNU) decided that they were going to use her case essentially as a show trial, to try to prove that Spiritualism was real. Yes, you read that right: perhaps surprisingly to a modern reader, Spiritualists had their own union, as well as dozens of Spiritualist organizations, clubs, associations and publications across Britain. The movement was enjoying a huge wave of popularity and it had

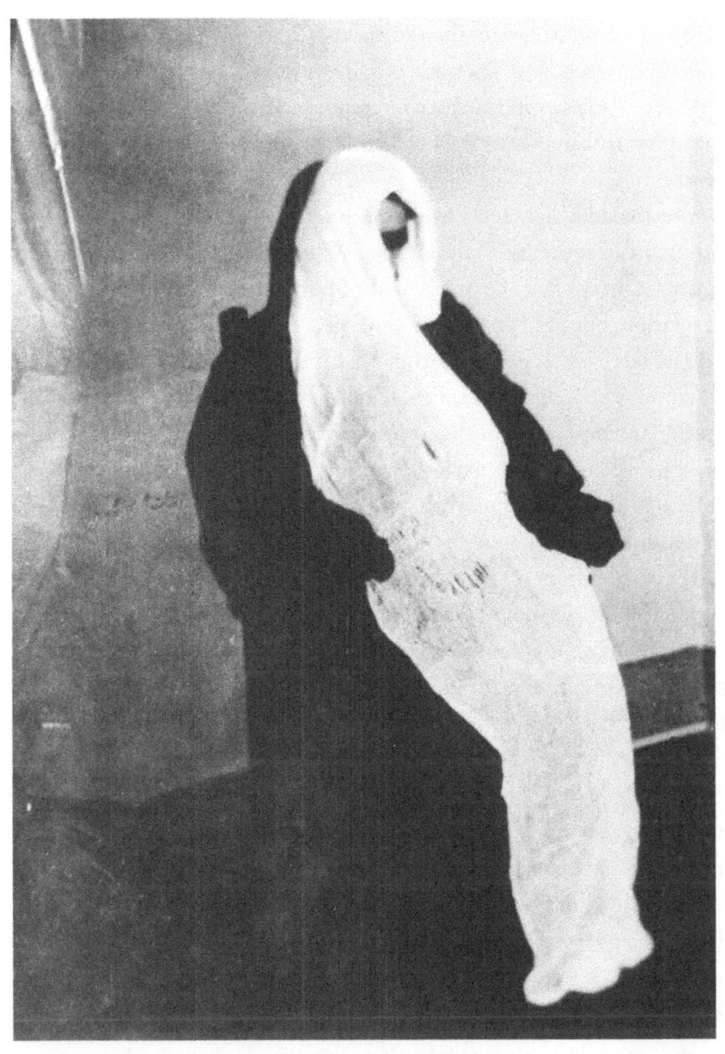

Contemporary photograph of Helen Duncan with muslin 'ectoplasm', published in the *Daily Mirror*, 9 October 1933

many influential people onboard. As a result, there was a great deal of money available to strike a blow for the legitimacy of Spiritualism in the public arena.

Malcolm elaborates: 'The world of Spiritualism a hundred years ago is not the world of old ladies in Spiritualist churches in back streets in small towns. This is a very powerful, important part of British religious and social culture between the wars.'

It's no wonder that there was a strong resurgence of a desire to communicate with the dead at the end of the war years. The psychological damage wrought on the country after the losses of the First World War were bad enough in isolation, but to have another conflict with such high casualties a mere 21 years later – a single generation – is almost impossible to comprehend. When we're talking about spiritual beliefs, we always need to factor in the emotional temperature of the country. Britain in 1944 was reeling from its losses, so of course it was ripe for something to cling onto psychologically and spiritually. One could argue that Spiritualism is a fairly logical response in the circumstances.

'It's respectable. It's not a crank movement,' says Malcolm. 'All these Spiritualist organizations have a relationship with psychical research, which is another respectable enterprise that's going on in Britain and Western Europe at this time. They're often in tension with each other, but psychical research has some very respectable scientists, who have money to spend on trying to prove the reality of mediums contacting the spirit world.'

With Helen's trial, the SNU saw a golden opportunity to bolster their reputation and reach the masses. They engaged Charles Loseby KC – a Spiritualist himself – and were convinced they would win the case.

Meanwhile, the Crown engaged John Maude KC. He was also an MI5 officer[†], whose specialist area was shipping security during the war and, as

† A KC, or King's Counsel, is a special type of top lawyer. Claire is a KC, but not an MI5 officer. Although doubtless that is what John Maude KC would have said at the time, too. 'I'm not,' says Claire.

such, he was a worthy opponent for Loseby. The stage was set for a very public showdown.†

Perhaps it all might have quietly gone away if Helen had just accepted the charge of fraud. However, with Helen denying the charges, the case took on circus-like dimensions and it's clear how diverting it would all have been to the public amidst the horror and tedium of the war. Malcolm thinks that Helen's part in the process was fairly passive, but that the SNU were determined they were going to use her case to make people understand what Spiritualists did. At the same time, the state was utilizing the proceedings to force people to comply with wartime rules: the powers-that-be were alarmed by her revelation of classified information regarding the HMS *Barham* sinking, and they wanted to make sure there were no repeat incidents.

It is easy to feel a great deal of sympathy for Helen Duncan. Helen had found a fairly lucrative manner to look after her large family in very difficult circumstances. The money became better over her career, commanding over £100 a week for readings in Portsmouth, and it was something that she was very good at. She seemed to genuinely believe she was in touch with the dead and was also performing an important service to the living. Malcolm thinks that she may have turned to fraudulent methods simply because she was under a great deal of pressure to provide results.

'The standard line about Helen Duncan is that she was the greatest medium that ever lived,' explains Malcolm. 'However, that comes with huge pressure. She had to deliver so much love to her followers that one human being couldn't possibly have so much love and so much energy to reach out to the spirit world.'

It has been proven that she sometimes faked results and messages, and also the physical manifestations of her communication. However, Helen and her

† Interestingly, while Maude was prosecuting Duncan in one courtroom, he was also defending a man in a murder trial in another, with the assistance of junior counsel. He won both cases.

supporters saw this as just part of the process and, in point of fact, it is very difficult to legally disprove that Helen was speaking to the dead.

It is an accepted point of law, as Claire knows so well, that in criminal trials the Crown must prove their case *beyond reasonable doubt.* In contrast, the defence merely has to raise a reasonable doubt, because the accused does not have to prove their innocence and it's impossible to prove a negative.

'In the Helen Duncan case,' says Malcolm, 'the crucial thing about using the Witchcraft Act was that you only had to prove that somebody had attempted to conjure spirits. So actually, they moved it away from fraud, and moved it to attempting to conjure spirits, which of course was Helen Duncan's job. Charles Loseby KC got it completely wrong because he got 40-odd witnesses to prove that Helen Duncan had genuinely conjured the spirits. Therefore, she wasn't a fraud. But that's exactly what the Witchcraft Act of 1735 required. Every time one of his defence witnesses came up, the prosecution didn't really have to do anything.'

The defence was seeking to prove that there had been no fraudulent behaviour or deceit because Helen could, as a matter of fact, speak to the dead. But now, in law, there was an underlying assumption that this was not possible. In essence, both the Vagrancy Act and the Witchcraft Act concerned crimes of deceit – of pretending someone could speak to the dead in séances or tell fortunes when they could not. So there was no way Helen could win her case with this argument.

Ultimately, the Witchcraft Act was repealed in 1951 and replaced with the Fraudulent Mediums Act. But that was too late for Helen, unfortunately, and she was convicted and given nine months' imprisonment.

The sentence illustrated perhaps the most important difference between the Witchcraft Act and the Vagrancy Act – an individual could not be jailed under the latter act, whereas a sentence of up to 12 months' imprisonment could be imposed under the Witchcraft Act. It was certainly preferable to the former sentence of execution, but still a devastating outcome for anyone who wasn't a hardened criminal.

The public response was mixed. Naturally, many were fascinated by the case. At the same time, a great deal of people felt sympathy towards Helen and many wrote to the Home Office arguing that we were fighting Germany to ensure Great Britain kept her freedom and this case was, in fact, state control.

After she was convicted, Helen appealed against both the conviction and sentence under various grounds, most of which were dealt with in short order. The ground of appeal which they took most time over was the submission by Loseby KC that Helen could not have been guilty of the conspiracy to use conjuration because she did not attempt to summon the Devil or evil spirits, rather the spirits of the dead. He relied upon a definition of the law in a very early legal dictionary called *The Interpreter*, published in 1607 by John Cowell, which states: 'It is especially used for such as have personal conference with the Devil or evil spirit.'

The appeal court disagreed, for two reasons. First, the statute says 'any kind of. . . conjuration', which must mean that there is more than one kind. In addition, the court's opinion was that the crime of witchcraft had been abolished because people no longer believed in it. The statute therefore doesn't specify that the crime of pretending to converse with spirits refers only to evil ones; it means any type of spirit, precisely because neither were believed in. The court explained: 'Such a distinction would raise an issue of fact incapable of determination and based on no intelligible principle of law or religion.'

In relation to sentence, the appeal court's opinion was stark: 'On the footing of the verdict of the jury, nine months' imprisonment was, in our opinion, in no way excessive.'

Ultimately, the case and conviction achieved what the state had set out to do, which was to silence Helen and remove her from the public eye in order that the powers-that-be could draw a line under proceedings and focus on more important matters. We now know that preparations were underway for D-Day and, of course, it is undeniable that the state did have a responsibility to control people from talking about shipping.

But to learn of someone being sentenced under the Witchcraft Act in 1944 still has the power to make the mind boggle. Helen said she would not conduct séances thereafter, but some years after her release police raided a house in Nottingham where she was performing again. She fell seriously ill shortly thereafter, and it was said by Spiritualist supporters that the arrival of the police to the séance had caused the ectoplasm to snap back into her body – like an otherworldly elastic band – and caused this illness. This time round she evaded the earthly reach of the law, but she died shortly afterwards on 6 December 1956.

While on the face of it, Helen Duncan's story is very different to the witch trials of the 16th–18th centuries, we can draw some comparisons. Helen's case was about the state asserting dominance against a person who, despite her fame, was vulnerable. Helen, like many of the accused during the witch trials period, was used as a figure to control the populace at a time of social anxiety and fear. And finally, of course – and it does need stating very clearly, despite being obvious – as with many of the original accused, Helen was a woman.

MODERN-DAY PASTOR

The guitars are still propped up against the back of the tent from when the praise band finished the last hymn. Everyone in the tent is hot and flustered, and there are rings of sweat visible under the pastor's arms. His tie is a little undone as if he's loosened it during a bout of hard work. His voice is raised and energized. He paces backwards and forwards on the podium set up at the front of the tent.

'Now, we've got the first and last names of six witches that are in our church. And you know what's strange? Three of you are in this room, right now!'†

He taps the mic firmly three times on the lectern. People murmur and sounds of shock ripple through the tent.

'Three of you in the room, right now! You better look in my eyeballs. We ain't afraid of you, you stinking witch. You Devil-worshipping satanist witch. We cast you out here in the name of Jesus Christ.'

He points out into the congregation.

'We break your spells; we break your curses. We got your first names; we got your last names. We even got an address for one of you.'

People turn to each other, shocked and delighted.

'You so much as cough wrong and I'll expose you in front of everybody in this tent. You stinking witch! You were sent to this church to destroy us. You were sent to this church to lure us in! You were sent to this church to cast spells!'

---

† The pastor's words in this section are quoted directly from a real-life sermon delivered by Pastor Greg Locke in Tennessee on 13 February 2022. Source: www.youtube.com/watch?v=Rzn8QBXtqV0. Our publisher has asked us to clarify that Locke has since contacted the publication *Religion News Service* (religionnews.com) to say that his words had been taken out of context and the video was edited. He also stated that two of the alleged witches were men and were 'ALL sent here on assignment to disrupt'.

He's still pacing back and forth, and the crowd is shouting sounds of approval.

'Listen, some of you been sick because you befriended that witch . . . Two of you are in my wife's Ladies Bible study and you know who you are and we're gonna ask you to GET OUT or I'll expose you in front of everybody.'

He's shouting by this point and people are starting to get to their feet.

'We got all six of their names.' Now he whispers menacingly into the microphone: 'ALL six of them . . . Two of 'em had already been confirmed . . . First and last names!'

He crouches down behind the lectern, peeking over it.

'This chick is new to our church and don't know none of you! . . . So you got a choice. You can leave with your spells all by yourself. Or I'll show up next Sunday with a stage full of brooms and I'll give you one and I'll fly your tail up out of this place in the name of Jesus. But we ain't playing your spell casting witchcraft nonsense sage-burning games.'

He pauses, takes a long draft of 7 Up.

'Everybody OK?'

There are shouts of 'Yes Jesus!' from the crowd.

He grins at them.

'The witches are like, "Nope!"'

He leans out to the crowd, rocking his head like a little dolly behind the mic. 'And your little dog too! You're out, witch!'

The crowd goes wild, and I think, God help that little hippy that's sitting shivering up the back of the tent. She's only joined us to try and make some friends, but I guess we'll not see her again after today.

Shame, she brings those good chocolate chip cookies to Bible study.

15

HOW TO ACCUSE A MODERN-DAY WITCH PART II

RESOLUTION ADOPTED BY THE HUMAN RIGHTS COUNCIL ON 12 JULY 2021

Elimination of harmful practices related to accusations of witchcraft and ritual attacks...

Expressing its concern that harmful practices related to witchcraft accusations and ritual attacks have resulted in various forms of violence, including killings, mutilation, burning, coercion in trafficking of persons, torture and other cruel, inhuman or degrading treatment and stigmatization, particularly for persons in vulnerable situations, including women, children, persons with disabilities, older persons and persons with albinism, and that these forms of violence are often committed with impunity...

- *Urges* States to condemn harmful practices related to accusations of witchcraft and ritual attacks that result in human rights violations;
- *Also urges* States to take all measures necessary to ensure the elimination of harmful practices amounting to human rights violations related to accusations of witchcraft and ritual attacks, and to ensure accountability and the effective protection of all persons, particularly persons in vulnerable situations;
- *Calls upon* States to ensure that no one within their jurisdiction is deprived of the right to life, liberty or security of person because of religion or belief, and that no one is subjected to torture or other cruel,

inhuman or degrading treatment or punishment, or arbitrary arrest or detention on that account, and to bring to justice all perpetrators of violations and abuses of these rights in compliance with applicable international law;

- *Invites* States, in collaboration with relevant regional and international organizations, to promote bilateral, regional and international initiatives to support the protection of all persons vulnerable to harmful practices amounting to human rights violations related to accusations of witchcraft and ritual attacks, while noting that, in providing protection, attention to local context is critical.

Quite aside from the horrors of thousands of people being persecuted as witches between the 16th and 18th centuries in Scotland, we push on with our campaign because, quite unbelievably, it is still going on.

Accusations of witchcraft and their attendant human rights abuses are so endemic in some parts of the world that not only have some governments been debating adding laws against practising witchcraft back on to their statutes, but the United Nations has also made a resolution against people being accused of witchcraft. The extract above is taken from it. Some people† say to us, 'Leave the past behind, we've moved on', or words to that effect, but we know from fellow campaigners who are kept incredibly busy in their own countries that, sadly, this is absolutely not an issue of the past.

As of 2025, there are several countries where witchcraft accusations are still rife. These include but are not limited to: Nigeria, Malawi, Ghana, China, Papua New Guinea and India. Figures are imprecise due to stigma and secrecy, but researchers are confident that accusations are in the hundreds. As with the Scottish experience, the accused are often (though not always) older, isolated women and consequences can range from banishments (such as the witch camps of Ghana, set up for women who have been excluded from their community due to witchcraft accusations), to physical punishments, to – and we cannot believe we are writing this in the 21st century – executions.

† It has to be said, almost exclusively white, middle-aged men.

Billboard advertising a Nigerian 'anti-witch' event, 2024

Leo Igwe heads up an organization called Advocacy for Alleged Witches (AfAW), which works across various African countries, but largely Nigeria and Malawi. Coming from a humanist background, Leo is primarily interested in developing critical thinking in communities and is a good-humoured and very engaging speaker. Although based in Nigeria, he travels a lot to educate and advocate.

Leo tells us that his work is focused on two main fronts. Firstly, his team are on the ground intervening in as many cases of accusation as they can get to – 15 last year, though they were called to more cases than their resources could stretch to.

Secondly, they also target schools to help develop resources to encourage critical thinking skills. The aim is to help young people to question socially held beliefs to make them less vulnerable to indoctrination and radicalization.

So why has the belief in witchcraft continued to hold sway in certain parts of Africa?

The reasons for these accusations are largely down to what Leo terms 'gaps': 'Gaps in law enforcement, political gaps, legislative gaps, humanitarian and social welfare gaps, human rights gaps,' he says. 'What we are trying to do is to draw attention to these gaps because over the years they have been ignored and witch accusations have been taken as cultural to Africans, which is a misrepresentation of the situation.'

As was the case in Scotland, a lot of the drivers are down to poverty and prevailing philosophies. But what complicates the matter in African countries is a misconception that witchcraft accusations are just part and parcel of African culture. Leo is very clear that the European concept of 'witchcraft' (i.e. one that involves communion with the Devil) is not African, but rather an idea that Western anthropologists forced upon a culture they did not understand. In many parts of Africa there is a long-established belief in supernatural causes for misfortune. What that means is that if something goes wrong, such as someone dies in an accident or has a disappointment in business, some people will assume an occult cause is to blame. Leo shakes his head. 'The Western anthropologists came and subsumed that into the level of witchcraft.'

Within many African societies, says Leo, so-called witch doctors were originally viewed simply as healers. These were the people you would go to if you had a problem that you thought had a supernatural source. It wasn't until the Europeans came along that the connotations of the words changed.

'Back when this happened, we didn't speak English,' says Leo. 'Some people who speak English and who tell us what English words mean, came and told us, "*This* thing is healing and *this* thing is witchcraft. This is a witch doctor." Now, because of colonization, because of Englishization, because of westernization, we have adopted those words.'

Leo says that there are many different types of healers in African society. 'We use the word "healers" here because I don't know what to call them. Some of them are healers, some of them are partially healing and partially doing occult practices, because many of them are not well trained.'

Often people have grown up saying they have inherited power, meaning that their families taught them their practices. Not unlike charmers of the witch-hunt period in Scotland, they work with both the physical (herbs) and metaphysical (spells and charms). These days, there are also many pastors or imams who use healing as part of their religious approach alongside the traditional practitioners.

'Africa has become a spiritual supermarket. So, if you call the traditional healer a witch doctor, then the Christian pastor is a witch doctor. The Muslim imam is also a witch doctor. So, when they say a witch doctor, they always have this idea of an old African man, sitting with tattered clothes, half naked, working with herbs. But it is a misrepresentation.'

The year 2024 started badly in Malawi. Leo was contacted by an advocate there about a case with an elderly woman who had been accused of being a witch and was then buried up to her neck. The police arrived just as the woman's accusers were about to close the grave up, killing the woman. Thankfully, they arrived just in time and the woman survived.

This is a particularly startling image and Leo has had people accusing him of giving Africa a bad name, but he is adamant that people understand the reality of this sort of event in order to stop it from happening again.

While this woman in Malawi was lucky and she survived, not all stories end so well. In other parts of Africa, Leo's organization has encountered serious situations in which people were killed. A similar case occurred recently in Benue State in central Nigeria where a person was also buried alive. By the time Advocacy for Alleged Witches became involved, it was too late. Afterwards, the family would not speak about the death.

Leo often finds that a circle of silence surrounds such cases, either because of shame or fear. But Leo know that it is only by highlighting what is happening that his organization can put pressure on the accusers or local law enforcers to stop events from developing further. Leo's team gets the story in the media, emails the government and shares it on social media. All these pressure tactics often force accusers to step back.

In another case that Leo was involved in, a woman was accused of witchcraft by her own brothers. Initially they had planned to throw her in the river to drown her, but they decided instead they would banish her from the community by using a traditional masquerade as a form of enforcement. Her sons also turned on her and literally chased her out of the community. Leo's team used publicity tactics to force the government to intervene and a reconciliation was arranged between the community and the woman who was accused. Sadly, though, the after-effects of the accusation meant that the woman wasn't allowed back where she had been living and her catering business was ruined as no one would buy from her – either because they believed she was a witch or didn't want to be associated with someone who had been accused. AfAW raised money to get her a flat and to start again.

Leo's organization makes sure the accused are safe, helps fund them to get away and, if the case makes it to court, they will arrange a lawyer and help with the police. Sometimes once the police are involved, the situation settles – but not always. In those cases, Leo's organization tries to educate the communities and agencies involved. They also work with the community and local police so they can develop what Leo terms 'early warning systems', such as signalling if a local person's (possibly untimely) death may lead to an accusation of witchcraft, to head off possible future problems.

Bringing cases out into the open is key. In this they are aided by growing access to the internet and social media, which means that word gets out quicker and it's harder to hide what's happening. Leo has been told that in one community the killing of alleged witches had been occurring for years and that it had been hidden due to the location. The community had been killing accused people and throwing their bodies into the river or the bush. But once the word got out, Leo's group was able to intervene.

As was the case during the witch trials in Scotland, most of the accused are women and are generally elderly. Leo says that in Nigeria the state doesn't offer much in the way of protection for the vulnerable, and (just as it was in 16th–18th-century Scotland) those with children are less likely to be accused as they have the support and strength of a family. The location of the accusations is often rural, and this is part of the problem for Leo as the phone and internet networks are less reliable.

While we've been speaking to Leo via Zoom from Nigeria, he has been walking about in his garden. The evening has deepened into nighttime and Leo points out to us that the electricity has gone off and he is in almost complete darkness. This is common in Nigeria, and one of the main struggles his group has is lack of consistent power and communication.

'One woman told us that it took about 24 hours for her to know that they had killed her mother in the village because there was no phone network,' he says. 'Sometimes that is part of the challenge.'

Overall, Leo feels there is still a long way to go. 'Until we have a critical mass of advocates, I don't think I can say that things are really getting better. We have made some progress, but that progress is just a scratch on the surface.'

A lot of this is down to the worsening of poverty in Nigeria. The Nigerian currency has devalued, which has caused economic and social issues. The country is experiencing a brain drain where educated people such as doctors are leaving to find better prospects in places like the UK, America and mainland Europe. This then leaves a gap in health care, particularly in rural areas, where healers and so-called prophets (or 'charlatans', as Leo terms them) step in to offer their services. Unfortunately, as long as this health care vacuum continues, there will be a demand for healers, diviners and prophets, and people will look for non-scientific explanations for their misfortunes. This is all frighteningly similar to the conditions in Scotland all those centuries ago. Times change, but people rarely do.

However, Leo remains optimistic. He says he constantly references what happened in Scotland to show that things can change. 'I don't see any reason we can't beat this battle,' he says. 'The challenges are there, but I think that the world is more interconnected than it was three hundred years ago, and we can use that to end the vestiges of witch-hunts and barbaric practices. As long as we're alive, somehow problems will lead to solutions.'

Charlotte Baker, who is a Professor of French and Critical Disability Studies at Lancaster University, initially started off working on albinism in sub-Saharan Africa for her doctoral project in 2006. Albinism† is a rare genetic condition where people have little or no melanin, often resulting in the person having very pale hair, skin and eyes. The condition often causes problems with the eyes such as rapid eye movements and poor vision, and it increases the chance of skin cancer. Most recent studies suggest there are around one in 18,000 people in North America with the condition, but the rate is as high as one in 3,000 in Southern Africa.

Alongside the obvious physical issues associated with the condition, people with albinism can face huge social issues. This is particularly prevalent in some parts of Africa where there is a complicated mythological narrative intertwined with the condition. In some places, people with albinism are seen as lucky; they may be viewed as valuable members of the community, and even be chiefs. However, more commonly, people with albinism are seen as being malevolent – neither black nor white, or even dead or alive. There is also the contradictory idea that their body parts are invaluable in spell-making and traditional medicine, and this has led to attacks and murders.

In the mid-2000s, when reports reached the media of people with albinism

† This is the preferred term over calling someone the old-fashioned 'albino'.

being attacked for their body parts, Charlotte decided she couldn't continue to solely focus on representation of people with albinism in academia and she created a network of people who could work on this issue. The network's focus is on educating and advocating.

The people involved are experts on all aspects of albinism, including the beliefs and the socio-cultural realities. But there are also medical experts such as ophthalmologists with expertise in visual impairments associated with albinism, oncologists who have experience with skin cancer, education professionals and policymakers. The network grew and became more visible.

'We started to work in all sorts of different ways to try and address the issues and to challenge some of the more harmful beliefs,' says Charlotte. She is calm and knowledgeable, and is clearly very determined to see justice done and to make sure that these horrendous situations are brought out into the light internationally. She began working with Ikponwosa Ero, who soon became the first independent expert on albinism at the United Nations. Through her collaboration with various advocates and non-governmental organizations, Charlotte also started working with Gary Foxcroft, who led the Witchcraft and Human Rights Information Network.

'One part of our work was to influence policy,' explains Charlotte. 'We wanted a change, not just a bottom-up change, which is very much needed, but a top-down change as well. We agreed in 2015 that the three of us would lead work with other stakeholders towards the UN resolution.[†] That resolution was passed in 2021.'

The network is now making sure the resolution is implemented and that change happens. Recent efforts have been focused on raising public awareness.

People with albinism fall under the same umbrella as those accused of witchcraft and the two areas are often bound together. People are targeted and accused because of their difference and vulnerability. With albinism, people are

† This is the same resolution from which we have included an excerpt at the beginning of the chapter.

very visibly different, and some communities try to explain that difference within their belief system and in relation to the spirit world. Even when people have had an explanation of the genes involved and the condition being passed down through generations, these communities cling on to the idea that the person's family has done something wrong or that they are suffering a curse. Sadly, this is still very much a current issue. Around 2006 or 2007, stories started coming out of Tanzania of accusations and attacks. Initially it seemed as if Tanzania was an unusually active area, but in reality all these stories were coming out because people were actually *reporting* them. In other areas, cases were being hushed up and hidden, and the scope of the issue has only become clearer through the work of activists and advocates.

A Canadian NGO called Under the Same Sun has been working hard to discover and collate records of attacks since 2007. Currently they have evidence of seven hundred attacks, including killings, mutilations and grave robberies, and researchers fear there are many more attacks that cannot be documented.

The idea of grave robbing is particularly chilling. This is done to find body parts such as limbs, teeth, and even hair of people with albinism. These items are believed to be very powerful and they are then sold on to people who want to use them in occult practices.

'A figure was put on a whole set of body parts by Amnesty, and it was just horrendous,' says Charlotte. 'Thousands and thousands of pounds for a whole set of body parts. The first independent expert argued that this was now an international trade.'

As a recessive genetic condition, albinism doesn't occur in every successive generation of a family, and that's something that causes problems when explaining it in communities: people don't remember it occurring in previous generations so assume it must be supernatural. Add to that its relative rareness and communities create a magical narrative to explain it.

When a woman gives birth to a baby with albinism it is a huge shock, which can lead to all sorts of accusations, says Charlotte. 'She can be accused of having slept with a white man. She can be accused of having been cursed herself, of having brought evil into the family.'

Superstition, hatred and crime around albinism is a live issue in 27 countries across sub-Saharan Africa. Charlotte says their research suggests that in some parts of Africa, and in a few other places in the world, some children with albinism are even being killed at birth.

'We would expect to see a certain number of people with albinism in any community based on the genetic data, but in some countries there just aren't the number of people with albinism that we'd expect to find. That suggests that something is going on, but it's incredibly difficult to provide any data or evidence.'

What the UN resolution is trying to do is stop harm from occurring to people. Following the successful adoption of the resolution, Charlotte and several colleagues created The International Network Against Witchcraft Accusations and Ritual Attacks. The language used is a deliberate choice and reflects the resolution's wording. But Charlotte is quick to state that people are still entitled to their beliefs. 'We've been really careful with the resolution and with the work we're doing on the back of it, not to challenge people's beliefs because everyone is entitled to believe what they may.'

Charlotte and her colleagues continue to make the issue visible and spoken about. It is important work, as the global statistics are quite shocking. Between 2010 and 2019, more than 20,000 occurrences of witchcraft-related harm were reported in various countries, not just on the African continent, but also in China and India where the research is only just beginning.

And if you think that false accusations of witchcraft are not an issue in Europe or America, you'd be mistaken. Charlotte is working with an organization called the National Working Group Against Spiritual and Ritual Abuse who began their efforts in 2011. The group was created by the UK government, initially looking at child abuse that occurred in relation to religion. It was a way to draw together various resources to share knowledge and create more robust safeguarding. Currently the group collaborates with around 70 organizations from the UK and internationally and it has a very practical focus to educate and share best practice between different agencies, such as social workers and the police.

The tragic case of Victoria Climbié is probably the most well-known example of faith-based child abuse. Eight-year-old Victoria was tortured and murdered in London in 2000 by family members after a catalogue of failings by professionals. Her murderers claimed to believe she was possessed. Several new child protection initiatives were introduced in response to her heartbreaking murder.

Charlotte says that there are still 'many, many children targeted' and that where she is based in the northwest of England, recent data shows the highest figures for faith-based child abuse are in that area.

'There's so much we still need to understand about this issue,' she says. 'Certain churches perpetuate beliefs around witchcraft. They wouldn't necessarily term it witchcraft, but perhaps they would call it ritual cleansing because they consider people to be cursed.'

These churches, much like in Scotland during the witch trials, think they are doing God's work, but we know that their actions lead to harm when vulnerable people cannot defend themselves.

And this final thought feels very circular to us. Although we're several hundred years away from the Scottish witch trials, the same things are clearly still happening all around the world. Vulnerable people are singled out and often hurt or, indeed, killed. It's so important that we understand what happened in our past here in Scotland to ensure that it doesn't happen again. This is why the work of activists and academics like Leo and Charlotte and their colleagues is so vitally important.

If we don't learn from our past, we are doomed to repeat it.

PORTRAIT OF THE ACCUSED

MISS B

NIGERIA 2023

In Benue State, Nigeria, on Saturday 15 April 2023, a junior secondary school pupil, known only as Miss B, was dragged out of her father's house to face a group of family members, who had gathered to question her following allegations of her being part of a coven.

Miss B's relative, Oga Job Okwori, demanded she attend a discussion with elders in the family. Having no choice in the matter, the girl and her father, Nathaniel Ijir Odege, arrived at the family house. Prior to their arrival, an elder relative called Abeni Oga told the others to build and light a big fire.

Miss B's elder brother Stephen states that a maid who was staying with their relative, Item Adaikwu, had been identified by Adaikwu's children as having chased them in their sleep whenever she suffered any punishments from their mother. The maid was interrogated and confessed she was part of a coven. During her interrogation, the maid identified Miss B as also being a member of the group.

When Miss B was questioned that night, she maintained her innocence. Angered by her resistance, the elders forced her to sit very close to the fire, which burned her. In intense pain, the child was forced to remain in place all through the night until 7am the next morning. Horrifyingly, Miss B's father was forced to witness this torture as the crowd threatened to attack him, too, due to his being accused of using witchcraft to murder a family member some months before. He was terrified that they would kill him if he gave the slightest provocation.

Eventually, Miss B couldn't endure the pain any more, and she confessed to witchcraft in order to make the torture end. Miss B and her father were able to leave.

Since the attack, the family and community have remained silent, despite the fact that Miss B's father and brother both reported the incident to the police. No arrests were made, even though the police were provided with a list of suspects.

Advocacy for Alleged Witches became involved when they heard the horrific story of what happened and they moved quickly to pay Miss B's medical bills. Miss B and her father were encouraged to leave the area and come to the city of Makurdi in central Nigeria, where AfAW initiated the prosecution. This can be a slow and difficult process, due to police reluctance and a culture of bribery and corruption.

Eventually, due to AfAW's pressure and perseverance, on 8 May the police in Oju arrested Abeni Oga, who allegedly engaged a group of enforcers to resist arrest. Abeni Oga was eventually charged in court on 15 May but not before AfAW had to pay sums of money to move the matter along.

At time of publication, the case was ongoing, and AfAW continues to support the girl and her family.

CONDEMNED WOMAN

To be led out of the cell where I have been held for weeks now like a dumb animal is almost more than I can bear. To be almost dragged past my old neighbours and people who I have known for years and for their faces to be twisted by hate, it's another fresh shock for me.

How is it possible that I can still feel shock? How is it still possible I can still feel anything?

I have felt more and more numb since the day I was taken from the church, and they cut my hair and they took my clothes. Nothing in my ordinary life had prepared me for such rough treatment.

But I could see it in their eyes that I was what they claimed I was. I had stopped being the woman that many of them had known for years. I had stopped being human to them. I tried to look into their eyes, to shame them into remembering who I am, who I was, to shame them to stop. But the only person with any shame was me. I was reduced to being like a talking animal, nothing to them but wickedness.

Not only could I see that they thought I was what they accused me of, but I could see they needed me to be the evil they had accused me of. Once they'd examined my body, despite my screams, then pleading, then sobbing, it was too late. They found their mark, just a birth mark, nothing more, and they lost what was left of their sense. They were like angry young boys carried away tormenting a cat until they had to kill it and find a way to blame the cat for her treachery.

I tried; I really did.

They kept me awake. Any time my head would drop heavily, I'd be nudged or kicked. I'd be pulled upright, my fingers bent back, my arms pinched, my toes trodden on. I tried to stay strong and say nothing.

I knew what they wanted.

Names. Names of other witches, really just names of other women, all as innocent as me. It was only when they began to talk of my sister and about bringing her in for questioning that I started to speak. But I was cunning. I just said the names of women who had already died. I'm sorry now that their names will be tainted, but I had no choice. Once they got their names, there was the court, and by that point I'd given up completely. I barely looked at anyone. I kept my head down. I tried to think about happier times, because it was as clear as day that I would be found guilty and that I would be killed.

I was so tired that I wanted it to be over, and now it is.

Now the crowd all look at me like I'm someone or something else. I can smell the fire; I can see the smoke as they lead me over to where this will all end.

I'm going to remain silent now, and I haven't spoken a word since I walked into the court. I don't search the crowd for anyone's face, in case they see me looking at my sister and she gets dragged in. Besides, I could not bear to see her face again and for her to see my brokenness and despair. I can only pray that, even though I will not be buried in the proper way, I will see her again someday. I pray she can remember how I was, and I pray she stays safe. I hope that Our Lord has more sense than these foolish men made in His image.

Rough hands turn my shoulders to face the rope, and I close my eyes and try not to think a single thing. I turn my mind into a fresh, white sheet, snapping on the line.

AFTERWORD

HOW TO FORGET A WITCH THEN REMEMBER HER

Why do we only remember Lilias Adie as 'Scotland's most famous witch'? The question that kept haunting us, as we explored this subject, was where are the graves of the others?

We saw that the townsfolk of Torryburn took great care to dispose of Lilias's body in a way she could not revenant – somewhat ironically providing the very best revenention that has ever been documented.† Lilias was very much the solitary exception – at least as far as is known – for a woman who confessed to witchcraft to have a grave. Everybody else was lost.

The fact is that with the burning of the accuseds' bodies and their deaths being recorded in the official documents in only the most basic of terms – in some cases not even noting the names of those executed but just recording that 'sundry witches' were burned – history quickly forgot them. Record-keeping was often very poor and there was no benefit to recording the details of a witch. They were not so much written out of history as never properly written into it. Although we have a note of thousands of those accused, there are rarely full records of what happened.

In stark contrast to Scotland, we've seen what happened in the USA after Salem. Their history is very different precisely because soon after their witches were killed there was an acknowledgement that they had suffered a terrible miscarriage of justice. Because of that acknowledgement, the history of those accused was written up, their property was preserved and now many thousands of folk claim direct descendancy from them. Given that 4,000 people were accused

† Not resurrection: that is a different matter, and Jesus is much more famous.

in Scotland, and at the time Scotland was a country of around 900,000, it is very likely that if you are Scottish and can trace your lineage back by a few centuries, you will likely be in some way related to an accused or, perhaps even more likely, an accuser. You could be reading this now, totally unaware that you are descended from an individual involved in the witchcraft trials.

So, seeing as there are no graves and few records, where are the memorials to all these women and men who were so cruelly and wrongly killed?

One of the things that started the whole Witches of Scotland campaign was Claire realizing that there were virtually no named monuments or memorials to the women of Scotland. Pretty much any little village or town you go to in Scotland has, quite rightly, memorials to those who died in the world wars. Naturally, these list men's names. However, you generally won't find Scotland's great and good women named and remembered in statue form. If you take a walk through Edinburgh, you will see various statues including David Livingstone and John Knox and a huge range of other gentlemen. Actually, that's not true, it's not a huge range. They're always white and they usually made money and secured power through subjugating other people. We know what we want from our heroes in Great Britain!

The one privately commissioned 'memorial' in Edinburgh, which marks the spot where hundreds of women and men were executed as witches, sits unassumingly in the corner of Edinburgh Castle esplanade. Doubtless many hundreds of thousands of people visit every year without having seen it. The memorial was commissioned by Sir Patrick Geddes (1854–1932), a town planner[†] who asked his friend John Duncan, an artist who specialized in folklore and mythological subjects, to draw up the plans. He designed a drinking fountain made of bronze with two heads facing out in opposite directions. It is often wrongly thought that the plaque depicts a young woman and an 'old crone' but in fact the characters are Greek deities Hygieia, the Greek goddess of good health, and her father Asclepius, the god of medicine. Around their faces is wrapped a snake. Foxgloves are also featured.

† This being only one of his many and varied skills and interests.

The inscription reads:

> This fountain, designed by John Duncan, R.S.A. is near the site on which many witches were burned at the stake. The wicked head and serene head signify that some used their exceptional knowledge for evil purposes while others were misunderstood and wished their kind nothing but good. The serpent has the dual significance of evil and of wisdom. The foxglove spray further emphasises the dual purpose of many common objects.

While we should not be too critical, given that Sir Patrick tried to remember those killed as witches, the rather obvious problem with the memorial is that it proceeds on the basis that those killed were indeed witches.

Otherwise, across Scotland there are hundreds of statues, but only a handful of them are of women.

As Dr Alison McCall, one of the admins on the Mapping Memorials to Women in Scotland (founded 2011) website, says, 'One of the reasons there are so many more statues of men is that the first statue of a woman appears to have been Queen Victoria in 1844. So the age of statues had waned before women got a look-in.' Hmmm . . . convenient. The patriarchy strikes again.

In fact, across the whole of Scotland, there are only 23 named female statues – seven Queen Victorias (two in Aberdeen; one young, one old); and then a small array of female worthies (several of whom aren't Scottish, including Florence Nightingale and Linda McCartney). There are also six statues that represent groups of women, including the Fisher Jessie statue in Peterhead (2001) and the herring girls in Stornoway (2003).

'If you look at the dates, it's interesting to see that there has been a growing commitment to statues of women since 1997,' says Alison. 'And of course, a statue to Elsie Inglis[†] is in the pipeline.'

† Elsie Inglis (1864–1917) was a doctor, surgeon, teacher and suffragist who founded the Scottish Women's Hospitals. Incidentally, following a call for artists to apply, the committee chose a male sculptor who hadn't entered the open call.

How we remember people (for good or for bad) is a growing conversation in the U K, not least the ongoing discussion about the statues of those who profited from the transatlantic slave trade and whether we should remove their monuments or keep them with supporting materials to teach the history. As Witches of Scotland, we're keen to remember history accurately and commemorate ordinary people alongside the war heroes and inventors and artists. We believe statues help us connect with stories as we see versions of ourselves in different times and places reflected back at us.

Memorialization is about connection. If we make that link between the past and ourselves, we are more likely to not repeat the more horrifying aspects of our history. Ultimately, we would like to see statues of women around Scotland that reflect what has made Scotland the country it is today. This, we feel, should include the darker parts of our history, and clearly that would include the witch trials.

One place that understands this is Salem in the United States. You could argue, in fact, that they have done this so successfully that Salem, with its far lower numbers of accused, is now seen as the main location of witch trials in the world.

Salem is steeped in history and there are many layers that make up the town's background and its current status as a tourist attraction. The witch trials are only a very small part of Salem's larger story. In among the accusations of witchcraft, there are also many tales of piracy and the industrial revolution, which had an enormous impact on the town.

Nonetheless, the witch trials themselves have been well commemorated. As well as the Salem Witch Museum, there is a memorial next to the cemetery, which was opened in 1992 (Arthur Miller had attended the announcement of the plans the previous year). While none of the accused are buried there, you can see the graves of some of the other people who were involved in the trials. In 2017, another memorial was placed at Proctor's Ledge where some of the hangings took place.

The memorial in downtown Salem has been designed as a space in which to sit and reflect quietly. It takes the form of a peaceful, grassy square surrounded by the last words of some of the victims inscribed into stone paving slabs on the ground. The words are cut off on either side, which represents how these people were silenced. Stone benches jut out on the perimeter with the name and the date of death of the 20 people who were executed, including Giles Corey, who was pressed to death. The Proctor's Ledge memorial consists of a stone arc embedded with the names of each of the 19 people who were hanged. A tree was planted there as well. There is also a further memorial at Hobart Street in Danvers, which used to be a part of Salem – it is located just over the street from the site of the Salem Village meetinghouse, where many of the accuseds' examinations took place.

'The Salem witch trials were very important but they're a tiny, tiny blip in the history of witchcraft,' says Rachel Christ-Doane, the director of education for the museum. 'It's really surprising how there's a lack of historical interpretation of these events; there's a lack of memorialization, really, across Europe. There are some places but it doesn't seem to be memorialized the way it should be, which is really fascinating, especially in an area like Scotland where so many people were executed. It was so much more violent than Salem. There should be memorials all over the place. The names should be recognized. This is something that's so relevant today. It's very much important for us to learn about now.'

In Vardø, Norway, the Steilneset Memorial is a stunning, provocative monument that marks the executions of 91 people for witchcraft in 1621. It opened in 2011 and was created by the architect Peter Zumthor and artist Louise Bourgeois. This was, in fact, Bourgeois's final work before her death in 2010, and we've always felt that as one of the 20th century's greatest artists – and one who is beloved by feminists – it was incredibly fitting that she took on this commission.

It's worth noting that, as in Salem, the Vardø trials were a great deal smaller than the Scottish trials. Around 100 people were accused, and 77 women and 14 men were sentenced to death by burning. Vardø is a town on an island off the north-eastern tip of Norway, in the district of Finnmark. The area experienced the highest rate of witchcraft accusations in any part of Norway, with the trials peaking around 1662–3.

The memorial is made up of two parts. Zumthor's installation is within a long wooden structure and consists of a long, narrow walkway that has 91 small windows representing the people executed. There are accompanying texts based on original sources at each window and each opening contains a single lightbulb. Bourgeois's work, *The Damned, The Possessed and The Beloved*, stands within a square room made of smoked glass where the walls don't quite reach the roof or floor. A metal chair has been placed in the centre and flames are projected through its seat. It is surrounded by seven oval mirrors mounted on poles, as if they are judges looking down on the condemned.

One of the issues we've faced in Scotland with creating a memorial to the accused and executed is the question of money. In Norway the money partly came from the Norwegian Public Roads Administration as a way of developing National Tourist Routes in Norway.

We spoke to Norwegian historian Liv Helene Willumsen about the part she played in the memorial (among other things, she wrote the exhibition text that is displayed there), the similarities between what happened in Norway and Scotland, and the importance and relevance of memorials in the 21st century.

'The Steilneset Memorial is based on three components: art, architecture and history,' says Liv. 'This place has a very painful history to tell, and the main idea was to lift this history into the public discourse and try to reflect on it, and also try to understand better what happened during the 17th century.'

Liv is very keenly aware of the connection between the witch trials of the 17th century and the violence still suffered by women today. She argues, and we would firmly agree, that the mechanisms which existed then to control and hurt women, still exist. Then, they believed that women were evil and weak, and that they were likely to be seduced by the Devil. Today we are much less likely in our secular, Western society to say that women are being seduced by the Devil, but we still see women being persecuted, marginalized, attacked and murdered.

There's a common denominator, of course, and as feminists, we would argue that it is the very existence of women that is problematic to some men. There has been a great deal written about this and, if you're reading this book, you are likely abundantly familiar with the fault lines between the sexes. However, the point Liv makes about the parallels between 17th-century witch trials and the experience

The Damned, The Possessed and The Beloved, Louise Bourgeois, 2010; installed as part of the Steilneset Memorial in Vardø

of women today is striking. Women are still too often seen as potentially dangerous so must be controlled.[†] When fearful men are running courts, states and governments, then dangerous precedents and laws are created and enforced. Especially if the religious men are in step with the political and legal men. There are numerous examples of this today, all over the world – see the battleground over women's reproductive rights in the US, Italy and Eastern Europe, for example. Other parts of the world face even graver problems: you only need look at the rolling back of women's and girls' rights in Afghanistan where the Taliban have stopped girls from accessing education as a means of social control, and have even banned women from speaking out loud in public places (this includes laughing and singing) and also holding conversations with other women. And before we get too comfortable about how superior we are in the 'West', look at the resurgence of so-called 'trad wives',[‡] who are endorsed by many politicians, religious leaders, and even some sporting icons. The fact that this 'movement' is being promulgated by the TikTok algorithm is particularly sinister.

In the 17th century, women were not seen as having the same worth or qualities as men. Women's weakness and susceptibility to falling into a pact with the Devil made them incredibly dangerous. This mindset was held by the male officials, and it shaped the laws and attitudes very clearly.

Liv believes this mechanism still exists in many countries today. It is very clear that, generally speaking, women just do not hold the same worth as men. In so-called 'progressive societies', how many times have you, as a woman, been in a meeting and felt your view less valued than that of your male colleague? How many women have parity to men in the workplace in terms of the distribution of senior roles and equal pay?

---

† It amazes us almost daily that women haven't taken to the streets and burned the world to the ground.

‡ This is an American movement where traditional wives are celebrated for being stay-at-home mothers presiding over big families. The concept centres around a notion of women in the days of America's expansion into the west. Picture lots of home-schooled blond kids drinking milk they've got from their own cow, presided over by a pretty, modest woman who does her husband's bidding. Mark our words, there will be an uprising of demented women in their late thirties in a few years' time. Or at least we fervently hope so.

The Burning, Rosie Andrews, 2023; an AI-generated artwork

'I have been working in this area since the 1970s, and I think it is very sad to say that I see the pendulum now is going in the wrong direction,' Liv says. 'It is not better today than it was 30, 40 years ago. It is worse, and I think this is very serious.'

This is the reason why Liv thinks it is so important to discuss the witch trials in modern society – so we can understand the past and also make the link between then and now. This connection is something that runs through the work of young Scottish artist Rosie Andrews, whose 2023 project, *The Burning*, reenacts the horrors of the witch trials through her clever use of AI. It creates a visceral feeling of us being able to witness the events around women being condemned to death, as if we were actually there. In addition, the uncanniness of the AI imagery brings to life the charges of being in league with the devil. They are incredibly creepy and evocative.

The biggest con of the early 21st century is that many women believe that we have reached parity. Yet the patriarchy is still trying to take away the rights that we do have, and women are still being attacked and murdered on a daily basis. In 2021, at least 147 women were murdered in the UK alone. Around 53 per cent of these women were killed by a current or ex-partner.[†] This may seem unrelated, but we need to be clear that the gendered aspect of the witch trials did not go away after the trials. The fear/hatred that is still seen in our society over three hundred years later is a straight line drawn from those days and attitudes. We must find a way to break this inheritance and put it firmly in the past, and we argue that understanding the drivers of the trials and the part that was played by embedded, often unconscious ideas about women, their worth and their 'danger' is an excellent method of confronting the past and changing the future.

This is a key aspect to Liv's work, too. 'I think the Steilneset Memorial has a very important part to play. As mature women, we must tell the younger

† These figures are taken from the horrendous, but much-needed, femicide census, which acts as 'a unique source of comprehensive information about women who have been killed in the UK and the men who have killed them': www.femicidecensus.org.

generation that it is not OK. We have not reached the goals that we had in the 1970s and you must not believe that we have come to the right solution and the right organizing of society and the right freedoms for women.'

Because a memorial exists in the real world as a physical, tangible symbol, it is a very effective tool to reach people's attention, especially the young. Liv and her colleagues have deliberately involved schools, especially young people between the ages of 12 and 15, because that is the perfect point to engage with ideas about sexism and abuse of power. Pupils visit from schools and take part in a teaching package that focuses on the story of one individual in particular. Through this the students are able to make a personal connection to what happened. If they can personalize it, they can make the connection and change can happen.

'In Steilneset, what was important to me was that all these persons should have a name,' Liv says. 'We do not have any images from the 16th and 17th century, but they should have a name.'

Visitors learn the individuals' names and stories, and make the connection between their very ordinary lives and their extraordinary deaths. Hopefully then they take that knowledge out into the world with them, engendering a change in attitudes that redirects society for the better.

The ambitious and striking Steilneset Memorial clearly shows the ambition and the possibilities of a 21st-century memorial that provokes thought and action.

Of course, it's impossible to remember things if you don't know about them in the first place. In Scotland, the best place to get a clear idea of who was accused and what happened to them is through the work of the Survey of Scottish Witchcraft – itself a staggering memorial of sorts, and the place where almost all the names of the accused are gathered. And, thanks to the ongoing work of citizen detectives, independent scholars and community campaigners, new names and stories are being uncovered all the time across Scotland.

In 1977, the historian Christina Larner created the Sourcebook of Scottish Witchcraft, which was later used as the foundation for the Survey of Scottish Witchcraft. The latter is an online database that features contemporary court documents covering the time period 1563–1736. The database went live in 2003 after two years of work by Professor Julian Goodare and Dr Louise Yeoman, working in conjunction with researchers Lauren Martin and Joyce Miller and the Department of Computing at the University of Edinburgh. We cannot overstate the importance of this work as it is accessed by anyone and everyone who is researching in this field. If you live in Scotland, we would strongly recommend looking up witches in your area.

When the project started in the 1990s, Julian Goodare and Louise Yeoman realized that there was no use made of church records in the existing Sourcebook of Scottish Witchcraft, and also that with the growing use of computers they could create something much broader and, crucially, searchable. In the course of their research they discovered that there were a great deal more accused than initially thought. But a great many records have disappeared or been damaged over time, so much of the detail is lost to us. There might be a name, a place, a date, a commission and maybe some names of the co-accused but then nothing about a trial or outcome. Julian suspects these people will have been executed but there's a great deal more to find out.

There has been even more work done in recent years. We spoke to Ewan McAndrew who is the Wikimedian in residence at the University of Edinburgh, facilitating Wikipedia entries related to the university's work and serving as a liaison between the university and the online encyclopaedia. Wikipedia is incredibly useful in this area of research, because it has been around since 2001 and is the largest open education resource in human history.

Ewan tells us that six years ago there were only three articles about Scottish witches. 'Now we have 49,' he says. He explains how the university got involved with the survey. 'The university wants to teach students how to work with open data, so they wanted to see if there was something we could do with data science students working with the Survey of Scottish Witchcraft to make it more explorable.'

Small short-term projects were developed with students to look at machine-readable data about the accused witches, then the team started to think about what else they could do using the survey.

'We noticed that there are lots of gaps in the database, obviously, because we're dealing with historical documents. One of the things we found was that there was often information about where the witches resided. For each of them, but not all of them, there was the name of a place which we could try and hunt down. We could assign coordinate locations, put it on a map and have the survey's information explorable in a completely different way.'

Anne-Marie Scott, who was Ewan's line manager at the time, suggested hiring an intern and geography student, Emma Carroll, to hunt down eight hundred place names using gazetteers, Gaelic resources, place name books and the Scottish archives. Research was required because a lot of these places don't exist any more.

'It was an enormous amount of detective work in six weeks,' says Ewan. 'Once they'd done all that, we could map the resource.'

A website was built and all the map visualizations were entered. They thought that was the end of it, but it turned out it was just the beginning. The public engaged massively, with huge interest from across the world. Another intern, Maggie Lin, discovered further trial details that were added to the website. In 2023, their third Witchfinder General intern,[†] Ruby Imrie, checked the data and made the site more searchable and interactive. Now you can look at where you live and see who was accused there and follow their story.

This is, of course, an evolving, highly useful and compelling way of remembering the accused. Although it's different to, say, a statue or a plaque, perhaps in the 21st century this is a fitting manner of remembering and exploring the past as it's so democratic and accessible.

That being said, we are still very keen to have a physical memorial somewhere in Scotland. There are already several plaques dotted across the country commemorating the trials – sometimes for groups of women, sometimes individuals. It is very moving to know that people have researched and fundraised in their local areas to discover and remember those accused. But we are calling for a national monument, hopefully of the scale and drama of Steilneset – something provocative and engaging. What we definitely do not

† Surely one of the best job titles ever.

want to see is a pretty girl gazing forlornly into the middle distance clutching her skirts against her legs.

We believe that what is needed is something that makes the connection between the staggering barbarity of the trials and the fact that these were real people, mostly real women, who were just like us; and also something that can connect with women's experiences today and help make real, significant change.

When we started this journey five years ago, we were initially focused on a campaign for a memorial and justice for the people involved in these historical outrages. However, it immediately became obvious to us that we had ignited a cultural conversation – because these issues are not actually in the past.

Just as in the days of the witch trials, as the global situation worsens, people are becoming more and more fearful. The current febrile political environment often veers dangerously to the right. Many of us anxiously contemplate the present and future realities of the climate crisis; struggle with the financial and social pressures of modern life; watch on in impotent horror at the seemingly constant worldwide conflicts – all while actively participating in the emotionally heightening petri dish that is social media.

We must take great care to guard against a new iteration of the witch trials.

We'd like to believe we're too sophisticated for that to happen again, but with recent diatribes about witches being abroad, we're not convinced it's outwith the realms of possibility.

In summer 2018, the US Supreme Court Justice Ruth Bader Ginsburg spoke to Margaret Atwood, author of *The Handmaid's Tale*.[†] When Atwood suggested that the '#me too' movement would spark a backlash against women,

† Atwood is on record as having said that in *The Handmaid's Tale* she only wrote things that had already happened to women somewhere at some point in history. 'I did not wish to be accused of dark, twisted inventions, or of misrepresenting the human potential for deplorable behaviour. The group-activated hangings, the tearing apart of human beings, the clothing specific to castes and classes, the forced childbearing and the appropriation of the results, the children stolen by regimes and placed for upbringing with high-ranking officials, the forbidding of literacy, the denial of property rights – all had precedents, and many of

RBG disagreed, also opining that the odds were not in favour of Roe v Wade (the landmark abortion ruling in the States) being overturned. It is telling that Atwood's response at that time was to say: 'I think there will be. We're already seeing it with Hillary Clinton . . . That's the first time we've seen this 17th-century talk of the female witch character.'

It's 2025. Roe v Wade was overturned, and the sniggered whispers of 'witch' and witchcraft have turned to mainstream discussions about 'demonic forces' in the US.† Red flags are waving like handmaids' gowns.

It is still the case that the weak and the helpless are attacked to protect the rich and powerful. Social media is used constantly to bully, harass and shut women down. Women are routinely sexually threatened if they stick their heads above the parapet. Domestic violence is just as prevalent now as it ever was. In the workplace we still don't have parity. At home we're still doing the lion's share of the domestic drudgery and childcare. Women were not safe then and we are not safe now.

So what of all this? What is the point of us setting out in such detail why and how women were characterized as witches, blamed for things wholly beyond their control, and ultimately brutally executed by the state?

The answer is that humans do not change quickly enough and, sadly, neither does history. When times are bad, we still look for people to blame. We demonize those people until they are no longer human and then do unspeakably inhumane things to them.

Accusations against the vulnerable in society do not happen out of the blue. Could they happen again now? If you do not think they can, we'd

---

these were to be found, not in other cultures and religions, but within Western society, and within the "Christian" tradition itself.'

† On 28 September 2024, US vice presidential candidate JD Vance spoke at an event hosted by an evangelical leader, Lance Wallnau, who had previously suggested that Vice President Kamala Harris used witchcraft. He said, about a Kamala Harris debate, 'She can look presidential. That's the seduction of what I would say is witchcraft. That's the manipulation of imagery that creates an impression contrary to the truth, but it seduces you into seeing it. So that spirit, that occult spirit, I believe is operating on her and through her.'

suggest you've not been studying history, or even given it the most casual of glances. Let's look at how it works.

First, when times are bad and people are scared, there are wild allegations of witchery, women who have devilish powers in league with Satan. This nonsense is believed by no one but the most tinfoil-hat-wearing of conspiracy theorists.

These witchcraft accusations are repeated until they become a background noise in society. The Church doesn't intervene to deny such allegations. Then, in time, support is found for the allegations. In the old days it would be a witness, a document – now it might be a video, a TikTok.

Are they real pieces of evidence or fraudulent? Made by AI? Few know. Few care.

Discussions take place on the basis that there is some proof of witchery. Now the accusations seem less crazy. You know someone who knows someone who was affected by a spell. After all, if we believe in God, should we not believe in the Devil and his witches?

The witchcraft allegations become mainstream, talked about on daytime TV, the pros and cons debated. 'Who are the witches? Join us after the break when we discuss who they are and how to spot them. Have you been affected? Call our viewer hotline on . . .'

A political party, realizing the popularity of witchcraft accusations, adopts what once was a wild allegation believed by no one as an issue that must be addressed.

It gains support; the party are voted in. Soon it's the law.

And it's coming for you. But you are not a witch! Surely this is madness and people can see that, right? Wrong. You are accused in a court of law. Evidence is gathered, the trial takes place and, after conviction, you are sentenced to execution.

So how do we stop this? How do we make sure that our society doesn't normalize accusing women as witches again?

We say this. Whether you take the lead from someone like Helen Mirren, who wished she'd said 'fuck off' more in her early career, or Julia Louis-Dreyfus who recently said, 'Listen to old women, motherfuckers', or indeed any number of non-famous women who get up every day and against the odds keep pushing back against the tide of misogyny, we urge you: embrace the title of 'quarrelsome dame' in your daily lives. Take up space, get involved in grassroots politics, educate people around you about what happened during the witch trials and draw the parallel with today. When you are met with resistance, call it out.

Do not let the patriarchy silence you.

We need to make sure we elect those who will actively protect our safety and the rights we have and promote real equality going forward. We need to hold our politicians and public bodies to account, and we need to join together with women all over the world to stop modern witch trials and show our strength in numbers.

So, we say, fuck 'being nice' to keep the peace or to keep other people happy; fuck having to keep quiet for fear of being labelled difficult (they'll do that anyway); fuck living, laughing, loving – try shouting, swearing, subverting.

Call out misogyny, challenge the norm, BE A QUARRELSOME DAME.

Claire and Zoe
Witches of Scotland

GLOSSARY OF SCOTS WORDS

Scots[†] is one of the three officially recognized languages in Scotland, the others being English and Scottish Gaelic. Most folk speak English, but with Scots words peppering the vocabulary. Some would say[‡] the best, most descriptive words are Scots, especially for types of rain and ways of calling someone an eejit. The pronunciation of Scots words varies a lot due to the different accents in Scotland. The spelling varies even more – many of the words and phrases have been passed down through speech rather than in writing, so sometimes it's just phonetic guesswork. What follows is our attempt to demystify the language for non-Scottish readers.

Ain: (your) own
Aw: all
Bachle: contemptuous term for a person
Baillie: magistrate
Bairns: children
Biding in: staying in
Birl: to spin around
Boak: be sick
Bowfin: smelling terrible
Braw: great or excellent
Burn: little stream

† Never 'Scotch' – that is a drink, not a language.
‡ Those 'some' being Scottish folk.

Canny: wise
Cantrip: spell
Caught bonny: caught out in the act
Connel: a candle
Couthy/couthie: a sound and friendly person or, if describing a place, a cosy, nice wee spot
Crabbit: grumpy
Cummer: troublesome, a close female friend and a godmother (go figure)
Dame: woman
Daur: dare
Deid: dead
Dreich: bleak, wet weather, a gloominess that pervades everything
Eejit: idiot
Folk: people
Hattock: fairy's hat, also a regional word for a stack of corn
Haver: to babble, to speak foolishly
Heid: head
Hen: a kindly term for a woman you are friends with
Highheidyins: literally, the 'high-head ones', or senior people
Hooley: party
Howff: graveyard, also used for home or shelter, or an enclosed space
Jackie: jackdaw
Ken/Kent: know/known
Kirns: churns (Old Scots)
Knag: wooden peg
Lang: long
Mair: more
Meikle: big or great
Merk: old silver coin, worth two-thirds of a Scottish pound
Midden: dirty person
Muckle: a lot, a big amount
Noo: now

Notar public: notary public, a lawyer commissioned to authenticate documents
Oot: out
Outwith: outside of (it's a mystery to all Scots why this isn't used everywhere, but ironically it is not used outwith Scotland)
Pannel: the accused (some KCs still use this in official documents – although debate rages as to whether it's spelled with one 'n' or two: no, we don't get out much, thanks for asking)
Pilliwinks: thumb screws
Scrieve: write
Scry: foretell
Shoogle: shake
Smeddum: a fine ash, a medicinal powder
Smirr: very soft rain
Smoored: choked or suffocated
Sneck: latch
Sooked: sucked
Stirk: young cow or bullock
Stowp: bucket or drinking vessel, also a basin for holy water
Tacksman: someone who held land and sublet it to other parties
Tak: take
Wan: one
Wean: child
Widdershins: anti-clockwise
Widdies: ropes made of flexible twigs
Willnae: will not
Wrang: wrong

SOURCES

General

Julian Goodare, Lauren Martin, Joyce Miller and Louise Yeoman, 'The Survey of Scottish Witchcraft', https://witches.hca.ed.ac.uk/ (archived January 2023)

National Records of Scotland: www.nrscotland.gov.uk

Scotland's People: www.scotlandspeople.gov.uk

National Library of Scotland: https://digital.nls.uk

Julian Goodare (ed.), *The Scottish Witch-Hunt in Context*, Manchester University Press, 2002

Lizanne Henderson, *Witchcraft and Folk Belief in the Age of Enlightenment: Scotland 1670–1740*, Palgrave Macmillan, 2016

Christina Larner, *Enemies of God: The Witch-Hunt in Scotland*, Blackwell, 1983

Stuart MacDonald, *The Witches of Fife: Witch-Hunting in a Scottish Shire, 1560–1710*, John Donald Publishers Ltd, 2014

Introduction

Statistics of accused: 'Witches of Scotland', The Royal Society of Edinburgh, www.rse.org.uk, 7 September 2023

Where Are the Women? A Guide to an Imagined Scotland, Historic Environment Scotland, 2021

Robert Pitcairn, *Ancient Criminal Trials in Scotland* (1833)

Julian Goodare, Lauren Martin, Joyce Miller and Louise Yeoman, 'The Survey of Scottish Witchcraft', https://witches.hca.ed.ac.uk/ (archived January 2023)

PART ONE: THE LAW OF THE LAND

Chapter 1: How to Believe in Magic

Diane Purkiss, 'Sounds of Silence: Fairies and Incest in Scottish Witchcraft Stories', in Stuart Clark (ed.), *Languages of Witchcraft*, Red Globe Press, 2000

Diane Purkiss, *Troublesome Things: A History of Fairies and Fairy Stories*, Allen Lane, 2000

'Any sufficiently advanced technology' quote: Arthur C Clarke, 'Hazards of Prophecy: The Failure of Imagination', *Profiles of the Future*, 1962

Tabitha Stanmore, *Cunning Folk: Life in the Era of Practical Magic*, Bodley Head, 2024

Julian Goodare and Martha McGill (eds), *The Supernatural in Early Modern Scotland*, Manchester University Press, 2020

Chapter 2: How to Start a Witch-Hunt

Historical background: 'The Scottish Reformation', The Scottish History Society, scottishhistorysociety.com

John Knox: 'The role of John Knox', Britannica, Britannica.com

James VI's sexuality: 'Filled with "a number of male lovelies": the surprising court of King James VI and I', BBC Scotland, 27 September 2017

1563 Witchcraft Act: '1563: Mary c.73: Anentis Witchcraft', 4 June 1563, The Statutes Project, statutes.org.uk

Chapter 3: Know Your Enemy Part I: *Newes from Scotland*

Newes from Scotland, Declaring the Damnable Life and Death of Doctor Fian, a Notable Sorcerer, William Wright, 1591. Facsimile of text: https://www.johngraycentre.org/wp-content/uploads/2021/11/Newes-From-Scotland.pdf

Confession of Agnes Sampson, 29 January 1590, Reference SP 52/47, The National Archives, Kew

Portrait of the Accused: Allison Balfour

'Orkney to get memorial for witch trial victims', *The Scotsman*, 14 August 2018

Chapter 4: Know Your Enemy Part II: *Daemonologie*

King James VI, *Daemonologie, in Forme of a Dialogue, Divided into three Bookes: By the High and Mightie Prince, James &c.*, Robert Waldegrave, 1597. Transcript of text: https://www.gutenberg.org/cache/epub/25929/pg25929-images.html

Definitions of philomathes and epistemon: Merriam-Webster Dictionary, merriam-webster.com

1603 Witchcraft Act: Nicole Hartland, 'Which Witch(craft Act) is Which?', UK Parliament Blog, archives.blog.parliament.uk, 28 October 2020

Chapter 5: How to Believe in a Witch

Author interview with Dr Louise Yeoman, 21 March 2022

Author interview with Professor Marion Gibson, 7 January 2022

Scottish literacy rates: 'The rise of literacy in Scotland', National Library of Scotland, https://www.nls.uk/collections/rise-of-literacy/

Portrait of the Accused: Margaret Aitken

Louise Yeoman, 'The woman who stood up to a witch-hunt', BBC News, 10 November 2019

PART TWO: BUILDING A CASE

Portrait of the Accused: Agnes Finnie

Mary Craig, *Agnes Finnie: The 'Witch' of the Potterrow Port*, Luath Press Ltd, 2023

Chapter 6: How to Accuse a Witch

Author interview with Judith Langlands-Scott, 14 July 2024

Brian P Levack, 'The Great Scottish Witch Hunt of 1661–2', *Journal of British Studies*, 10 January 2014

Quote from 1649 Scottish Witchcraft Act: J R Young, 'The Covenanters and the Scottish Parliament, 1639–51', in E Boran and C Gribben (eds), *Enforcing Reformation in Ireland and Scotland, 1550–1700*, Ashgate, 2006

English witchcraft laws and statistics: 'Witchcraft', UK Parliament, www.parliament.uk/about/living-heritage/transformingsociety/private-lives/religion/overview/witchcraft

Scottish economy in 16th century: C A Whatley, *Scottish Society, 1707–1830: Beyond Jacobitism, Towards Industrialisation*, Manchester University Press, 2000

Chapter 7: How to Prick a Witch

Devil's mark origins: Richard M Golden, *Encyclopedia of Witchcraft: The Western Tradition*, Library of Congress, vol. 4, 2006

'weaponized belief' quote: Adam Scovell, 'The terror of the old ways: 50 years of *Witchfinder General*', British Film Institute, bfi.org, 18 May 2018

Hopkins and Stearne: Malcolm Gaskill, *Witchfinders: A Seventeenth-Century English Tragedy*, Harvard University Press, 2007

Hopkins's Stowmarket fees: A G Hollingsworth, *History of Stowmarket*, Ipswich, 1844

Author interview with Mary Craig, 21 October 2022

Bierricht explanation: Dolly Stolze, 'The Bizarre Importance of Bleeding Bodies in Medieval Trials', Ancient Origins, ancient-origins.net, 11 February 2016

'John Kincaid, witch finder', engole.info, 12 August 2018

Mary Craig, 'John Kincaid the witch brodder', marywcraig.com, 18 April 2021

'Christian Caddell: Scotland's Female Witch Pricker', spookyscotland.net, 19 June 2018

Louise Yeoman, 'The woman who became a witch pricker', BBC Scotland, bbc.co.uk, 18 November 2012

Chronicles of the Frasers: The Wardlaw Manuscript, James Fraser, Forgotten Books, 2012

'There came then to Inverness' quote: 'The Patersons', The Douglas Archives, douglashistory.co.uk, 11 August 2021

'. . . by waking, hanging them up by the thombes' quote: L Henderson, 'Witch-hunting and Witch Belief in the *Gàidhealtachd*', in Julian Goodare, Lauren Martin and Joyce Miller (eds), *Witchcraft and Belief in Early Modern Scotland*, Palgrave Macmillan, 2008

Brian P Levack, *Witch-Hunting in Scotland: Law, Politics and Religion*, Routledge, 2007

Portrait of the Accused: Tituba

Stacy Schiff, 'Unraveling the Many Mysteries of Tituba, the Star Witness of the Salem Witch Trials', *Smithsonian Magazine*, November 2015

Chapter 8: How to Kill a Witch the American Way

Interviews with Rachel Christ-Doane, 19 March 2021 and 19 July 2024

Gretchen Adams, *The Specter of Salem: Remembering the Witch Trials in Nineteenth-Century America*, University of Chicago Press, 2010

Salem origins: 'History and Origins of the Salem Witch Trials', Peabody Essex Museum, pem.org

Diana DiZoglio quote: Maya Yang, 'Last Salem "witch" pardoned 329 years after she was wrongly convicted', *Guardian*, 27 May 2022

American elections: 'Witches cast "mass spell" against Donald Trump', BBC News, bbc.com, 25 February 2017

La Brujineta: Fernando Romero Nuñez, 'How 30,000 witches helped Argentina win the World Cup', *Buenos Aires Herald*, 25 December 2023

Chapter 9: How to Gather Evidence Against a Witch

Robert Pitcairn, *Ancient Criminal Trials in Scotland, Volume 3, Part 2*, The Bannatyne Club, 1833. Facsimile: www.google.co.uk/books/edition/_/9tdLAAAAYAAJ?hl=en&gbpv=1 (all quotes from Pitcairn cited in this chapter come from Appendix No. VII)

David Hume, *Commentaries on the Law of Scotland, Volumes 1 and 2*, Bell & Bradfute, 1797 (reprinted Gale ECCO, 2018)

'Hattock' definition: Dictionaries of the Scots Language, www.dsl.ac.uk

Portrait of the Accused: The Paisley Witches

'She would become as stiff as a corpse' quote: Brian P Levack, *New Perspectives on Witchcraft*, vol. 3, Routledge, 2001

Chapter 10: How to Try a Witch
Portrait of the Accused: Janet Horne

W N Neill, 'The Last Execution for Witchcraft in Scotland, 1722', *The Scottish Historical Review*, vol. 20, no. 79, April 1923

1735 Witchcraft Act: Nicole Hartland, 'Which Witch(craft Act) is Which?', UK Parliament Blog, archives.blog.parliament.uk, 28 October 2020

'Witchcraft', UK Parliament, https://www.parliament.uk/about/living-heritage/transformingsociety/private-lives/religion/overview/witchcraft/

Chapter 11: How to Burn a Witch

Author interview with Professor Niamh Nic Daeid, 22 April 2024

Portrait of the Accused: Katherine MacKinnon

'Dress Act 1746', 1 November 2023, Scottishhistory.org

Chapter 12: How to Bury a Witch

Author interview with Doug Speirs, 9 January 2021

Contemporary minutes of Kirk Session, 1704, https://www.gutenberg.org/files/41928/41928-h/41928-h.htm

PART THREE: A THING OF THE PAST?

Chapter 13: How to Lose a Witch

'Paton, Sir Joseph Noel', *Encyclopedia Britannica*, 1911

Paton's religious beliefs: Alfred Thomas Story, *The Life and Work of Sir J Noel Paton*, The Art Journal, 1895

'Forensic artist Dr Christopher Rynn reconstructs face of Scottish "witch"', University of Dundee, 31 October 2017: https://www.dundee.ac.uk/stories/forensic-artist-dr-christopher-rynn-reconstructs-face-scottish-witch

Portrait of the Accused: Helen Duncan

Harry Price: Paul G Adams, 'Harry Price: A Brief Survey of his Career in Psychical Research', www.harrypricewebsite.co.uk

Paul Tabori, *The Art of Folly*, 1961

Chapter 14: How to Accuse a Modern-Day Witch Part I

Malcolm Gaskill, *Hellish Nell: Last of Britain's Witches*, Fourth Estate, 2001

Author interviews with Professor Malcolm Gaskill, 25 March 2022 and 8 April 2024

Paul G Adams, 'Helen Duncan: Harry Price and the Regurgitating Medium', www.harrypricewebsite.co.uk/Seance/Duncan/duncan-intro

Charles Loseby, 'Papers on the trial of Helen Duncan 1944–1945', Society for Psychical Research archive, Cambridge University Library, archivesearch.lib.cam.ac.uk/repositories/2/archival_objects/632155

'Full text of the trial of Mrs Helen Duncan', https://archive.org/stream/trialofmrsduncan00duncuoft/trialofmrsduncan00duncuoft_djvu.txt

'1735: 9 George 2 c.5: The Witchcraft Act', The Statutes Project, statutes.org.uk

John Cowell, *The Interpreter*, 1607 (1658 edition), Oxford Text Archive, Bodleian Libraries, University of Oxford, https://ota.bodleian.ox.ac.uk/repository/xmlui/handle/20.500.12024/A34797

Chapter 15: How to Accuse a Modern-Day Witch Part II

UN Human Rights Council, 47th session, 'Resolution adopted by the Human Rights Council on 12 July 2021: Elimination of harmful practices related to accusations of witchcraft and ritual attacks', https://digitallibrary.un.org/record/3936009?ln=en&v=pdf, 16 July 2021

Author interview with Leo Igwe, 28 February 2024
Author interview with Professor Charlotte Baker, 1 May 2024

Portrait of the Accused: Miss B

Afterword: How to Forget a Witch Then Remember Her

Author interview with Dr Alison McCall, 1 April 2024

Rebecca Beatrice Brooks, 'Salem Witch Trials: Historical Sites & Locations', History of Massachusetts Blog, historyofmassachusetts.org, 26 October 2015

Author interview with Professor Liv Helene Willumsen, 16 April 2024

Liv Helene Willumsen, *Witches of the North: Scotland and Finnmark*, Brill, 2013

Author interview with Ewan McAndrew, 19 December 2023

Margaret Atwood and Ruth Bader Ginsburg: Jeffrey Rosin, '"They Will Not Allow Progress to Be Reversed": Ruth Bader Ginsburg and Margaret Atwood Discuss #MeToo', *Vanity Fair*, 1 November 2019

Margaret Atwood on *The Handmaid's Tale*: 'Margaret Atwood on How She Came to Write *The Handmaid's Tale*', lithub.com, 25 April 2018

Lance Wallnau quote: Mike Hixenbaugh and Alexandra Marquez, 'Vance to attend event with evangelist who said Harris used "witchcraft"', NBC News, 27 September 2024

PICTURE CREDITS

Alamy Stock Photo: Chronicle 41, 59, Science History Images 179, The Picture Art Collection 211, Trinity Mirror Mirrorpix 223; Courtesy Dr Christopher Rynn 215; Leo Igwe 233; Metropolitan Museum of Art: The Elisha Whittelsey Collection, The Elisha Whittelsey Fund, 1967 27; Rosie Andrew, www.rosieandrew.myportfolio.com / @r_o_s_i_eka 255; Shutterstock Creative: Maurizio Fabbroni. © The Easton Foundation/VAGA at ARS, NY and DACS, London 2025 253; TopFoto: Fortean 115; Wellcome Collection: The history of witches and wizards: giving a true account of all their tryals in England, Scotland, Swedeland, France, and New England; with their confession and condemnation/ Collected from Bishop Hall, Bishop Morton, Sir Matthew Hale, etc. By W.P. 15; Worldhistory.org/public domain 133.

ABOUT THE WITCHES OF SCOTLAND TARTAN

The Witches of Scotland Tartan was created by designer Clare Campbell in collaboration with The Witches of Scotland. The tartan will be woven to make products and create a 'living memorial' to those who suffered as a result of the Witchcraft Act 1563 to 1736 in Scotland.

The tartan's black and grey colours are intended to represent both the dark times of this period and the ashes of those who were burned. It also incorporates red and pink colours, symbolic of the legal tapes used to bind papers both during that time and now. The thread count of this design incorporates the years 1563 and 1736, represented as single entries, 1+5+6+3 = 15 and 1+7+3+6 = 17, shown in black and grey. These surround a white check of three threads that represent the core objectives of the organization: to ensure a pardon, an apology and memorials are achieved. The large black section of 173 threads is intended to represent the 173 years of darkness, and the red and pink sections are repeated three times, for the three prime objectives of the Witches of Scotland organization.

The Witches of Scotland Tartan has been used on the case of the *How to Kill a Witch* hardback edition and is available to view online at The Scottish Register of Tartans (www.tartanregister.gov.uk), reference: 14651.

ACKNOWLEDGEMENTS

Since we started the campaign in 2020, we have had the great fortune to speak to many wonderful experts in the fields of witch trials, Scottish history and human rights. Without these inspiring, illuminating and horrifying discussions, we couldn't have written this book. It bears repeating that we are not historians and any (and all!) mistakes contained here are entirely ours. We would strongly recommend that you dig further and read the tremendous books and research by Julian Goodare, Louise Yeoman, Malcolm Gaskill, Tabitha Stanmore, Marion Gibson, Martha McGill, Mary Craig, Mairi Kidd and Liv Helene Willumsen. We thank Sara Sheridan whose book *Where Are the Women?* inspired Claire to think about how we memorialize women in history.

We would encourage you to engage with and support the work done by Leo Igwe and Advocacy for Alleged Witches, and Charlotte Baker and her colleagues at TheInternational Network Against Witchcraft Accusations and Ritual Attacks. The issue of witch trials is not something of the past, but something that needs attention now in various locations around the world.

We would like to thank our skilled photographer Kathryn Rattray, Professor Niamh Nic Daeid, Douglas Speirs, the ever fascinating Catherine MacPhee, and the indomitable Judith Langlands-Scott for her ongoing support and spirit, Kyla McGilliard for all her hard work campaigning, and Sarah Cook and Andy Walker for their friendship and enthusiasm.

Although the Witches of Scotland is a team of two, we couldn't do the podcasts without the sound-engineering skills of David Mitchell (sorry we didn't stop at six episodes, David) and, more recently, Lola-Ray Venditozzi.

We want to thank Claire Campbell and all the staff at Prickly Thistle whose tireless work in producing our beautiful Witches of Scotland tartan ensures the campaign is known worldwide. We also want to thank Dr Yvonne Mitchell for all her tremendous work – we literally couldn't do it without you.

Our editor, Jake Lingwood, saw promise when we couldn't work out how to even start writing, and persevered when a lesser person would have given up with our idiosyncratic approach to writing a book. Thanks Jake.

The team at Octopus have been tremendous getting this book into the form you are now reading it and we thank them very sincerely for that.

Our agent, Jim Gill, is helping us navigate the world of publishing, for which we are truly thankful.

Claire would like to thank: 'my family – Pol, Redford, Crombie, Delia, Jim, Yvonne, David and all the friends who put up with my eccentricities, for their love and support, especially my ride or dies: Mel, Shanti, Jackie, Rosemary, Nicola, Caroline, Aamer and April who are always there for me, as are Kevin H, Kevin and Ross, Eddie J, Lesley H, Clare C, Stuart, David W, Sarah, Craig, Moira, Wendy, Kelly, Shelagh, Maggie, Garry Sturrock, Stuart Beveridge, Gordon Rosemary G, Fred, Chris and Claire D, Catherine S, Mary M, Emma A and Pete C: I love you all.'

Zoe would like to thank: 'my children – Luca Tavita, Lola-Ray and Rocco; my family – Natalie, Martin, Elspeth, my lovely late dad, David and auntie Sheena and the OG McLanders Bet/Granny Mum; all my great friends who listened patiently when I was not working and I should have been. I'd especially like to thank Emily for her weekly therapeutic coffee sessions; Jennie and Leonie for their intervention; Anna for getting me started in many ways; Jane Fulton, always ready with a clever joke and sardonic smile; also, Paula, Susan and Jill. Thanks, too, to Sheldon for the very welcome distraction.'

Zoe and Claire would both like to thank Mel and Drew, as it was Drew that helped Claire shape up the campaign in those very early days, and without you two getting married, Claire and Zoe may never have met!

Finally, we'd like to thank you Quarrelsome Dames and all our readers and listeners who have picked up this cause and are determined to right a historical wrong, and improve the present to boot.

INDEX

Page refs for illus. are in *italics*. 'n'= footnote

Y

Z

This monoray book was crafted and published by Jake Lingwood, Pauline Bache, Lindsay Davies, Mel Four, Jennifer Veall and Caroline Alberti.